ALSO BY MICHAEL T. KLARE

American Arms Supermarket

Light Weapons and Civil Conflict: Controlling the Tools of Violence

Low Intensity Warfare:
Counterinsurgency, Proinsurgency, and Antiterrorism in the Eighties

Peace and World Security Studies: A Curriculum Guide

Rogue States and Nuclear Outlaws:
America's Search for a New Foreign Policy

Supplying Repression: U.S. Support for Authoritarian Regimes Abroad

War Without End: America Planning for the Next Vietnams

World Security: Challenges for a New Century

RESOURCE WARS

RESOURCE WARS

THE NEW LANDSCAPE
OF GLOBAL CONFLICT

Michael T. Klare

METROPOLITAN BOOKS
Henry Holt and Company | New York

Metropolitan Books
Henry Holt and Company, LLC
Publishers since 1866
115 West 18th Street
New York, New York 10011

Metropolitan Books™ is an imprint of
Henry Holt and Company, LLC.

Printed in Canada by Fitzhenry & Whiteside Ltd.,
195 Allstate Parkway, Markham, Ontario L3R 4T8.

Table on page 146 copyright © Peter H. Gleick. Reprinted by permission.

Library of Congress Cataloging-in-Publication Data
Klare, Michael T., 1942–
Resource wars : the new landscape of global conflict / Michael T. Klare—1st ed.
    p.   cm.
Includes bibliographical references and index.
ISBN 0–8050-5575–4 (hc)
    1. United States—Military policy.   2. Security, International.
3. Natural resources.   4. World politics—1989–   I. Title.
UA23.K6267   2001
335'.033573—dc21   00–050001

Henry Holt books are available for special promotions and
premiums. For details contact: Director, Special Markets.

First edition 2001

Designed by Kelly S. Too

Maps by Glenn Ruga

Printed in the United States of America

1   3   5   7   9   10   8   6   4   2

To my partner, Andrea Ayvazian, and
my son, Sasha Klare-Ayvazian,
with immense love and gratitude for their
unfailing support during the
writing of this book

CONTENTS

RESOURCE WARS

Wealth, Resources, and Power:
The Changing Parameters of Global Security

On the morning of September 15, 1997, five hundred American paratroopers from the army's 82nd Airborne Division jumped into an arid battle zone near the Tien Shan mountains in southern Kazakhstan. Their assigned mission: to link up with friendly forces from Kazakhstan, Kyrgyzstan, and Uzbekistan and engage in simulated combat against "renegade forces" opposed to a regional peace agreement.[1] Heading the American contingent—and the first to make the jump— was General John Sheehan, a highly decorated marine officer and the commander in chief of the U.S. Atlantic Command. The parachute drop was undertaken, Sheehan told reporters at the scene, to reassure local leaders that the United States "is ready to stand beside them and participate" if American help is needed in a future regional crisis.[2]

General Sheehan's remarks were no doubt taken from the standard script provided to American officers for use on occasions of this sort. But nothing else about Operation CENTRAZBAT 97—as this exercise was known—can be described as ordinary. For one thing, the exercise began with the longest airborne operation in human history, entailing a flight of some 7,700 miles from Fort Bragg, North Carolina, to Shymkent in southern Kazakhstan. It also represented the first deployment of American combat troops in what had been the Central Asian republics of the Soviet Union. (Kazakhstan, until 1991, had been known as the Kazakh Soviet Socialist Republic.) Finally, it was the first instance of direct U.S. military cooperation with the newly independent states of the Caspian Sea region—states that are ruled, for the most part, by former functionaries in the Soviet imperial apparatus.

Why choose Kazakhstan, Uzbekistan, and Kyrgyzstan for such an ambitious undertaking? In justifying this elaborate operation, Pentagon officials maintained that their sole objective was to demonstrate American support for the continued stability of the former Soviet republics. "What we need here are independent, sovereign states that are able to defend themselves," explained Deputy Assistant Secretary of Defense Catherine Kelleher, the highest-ranking Pentagon official to attend the event.[3] Most observers understood, however, that much more was at stake: with new surveys indicating the presence of vast reserves of oil and natural gas in the Caspian region, U.S. officials have resolved to ensure that much of this energy eventually flows to the West.

According to the U.S. Department of Energy, the Caspian Sea basin (comprising Azerbaijan, Kazakhstan, Turkmenistan, and Uzbekistan, along with parts of Russia and Iran) harbors as much as 270 billion barrels of oil, or about one-fifth of the world's total proven reserves of petroleum. (Only the Persian Gulf, with 675 billion barrels in proven reserves, holds a larger supply.) The Department of Energy also estimates that the Caspian region houses some 665 trillion cubic feet of natural gas, representing one-eighth of the world's gas reserves.[4] Until 1992, these oil and gas deposits (except for those held by Iran) were the exclusive property of the Soviet state; with the breakup of the USSR, however, much of that supply came under the control of the new nations of the Caspian—all of which now seek to export their energy resources to the West.

For Western oil companies, the opening of the Caspian basin to foreign investment has proved an extraordinary bonanza. Virtually all of the giant energy firms have announced plans to team up with local enterprises in exploiting the Caspian's oil and gas supplies. For this reason the American government has focused enormous attention on the region and its economic development. Eager to promote the global expansion of U.S. trade and investment, the Commerce Department and other federal agencies have aided American companies in their efforts to establish joint ventures with Central Asian energy firms and to establish the necessary infrastructure and pipelines. Beyond this, however, American officials see a *strategic* interest in the development of Caspian energy supplies: because of the continuing risk of conflict in the Persian Gulf area, Washington hopes to convert the Caspian basin into an alternative source of energy that can satisfy Western needs if and when oil deliveries from the Gulf are blocked or suspended.

The strategic nature of American interest in the Caspian region was first articulated by the Department of State in an April 1997 report to Congress. As a major consumer of oil, the report indicated, the United States has a direct interest in "enhancing and diversifying" world energy supplies. Such diversification is important not only in economic terms—to provide an additional source of energy for American industries and transportation systems—but also as a security measure, to build a hedge against supply disruptions elsewhere. Accordingly, it has become U.S. policy "to promote rapid development of Caspian energy resources" in order to "reinforce Western energy security."[5]

The belief that Caspian Sea oil represents a strategic as well as an economic interest of the United States was expressed publicly for the first time by Deputy Secretary of State Strobe Talbott. In a speech at Johns Hopkins University on July 21, 1997, Talbott spoke of America's growing stake in the independence and stability of the Central Asian republics. "It would matter profoundly to the United States," he declared, if U.S. oil companies were denied access to "an area that sits on as much as 200 billion barrels of oil."[6]

Ten days later, on August 1, 1997, President Clinton elaborated on these themes during a meeting at the White House with Heydar Aliyev, the president of Azerbaijan. Aliyev—who had once served as a senior KGB official and member of the Soviet Politburo—was invited to Washington to discuss American involvement in the exploitation of Azerbaijan's vast energy reserves. After lengthy consideration of the practical issues involved, Clinton assured Aliyev of strong U.S. support for his plans to sell Azerbaijani oil to the West. "In a world of growing energy demand," Clinton explained, "our nation cannot afford to rely on any single region for our energy supplies." By working closely with Azerbaijan to tap the Caspian's resources, "we not only help Azerbaijan to prosper, we also help diversify our energy supply and strengthen our nation's security."[7]

American officials do not use such language idly. When a president suggests that the nation's security is at stake in a particular region or issue, it usually means that Washington is prepared to use military force to protect that interest. President Jimmy Carter made this explicit with respect to Persian Gulf oil in 1980, following the Soviet invasion of Afghanistan. "An attempt by any outside force to gain control of the Persian Gulf region will be regarded as an assault on the vital interests of the United States of America," he told a joint session of Congress, "[and] will be repelled by any means necessary, including military force."[8] (This was the original formulation of the "Carter Doctrine," later used to justify U.S. intervention in Kuwait.) Although President Clinton did not go this far in his 1997 remarks to Aliyev, he clearly laid the foundation for such a posture by associating the Caspian's energy potential with American national security.

Coming only six weeks after Aliyev's visit to Washington, Operation CENTRAZBAT 97 must be viewed against this backdrop. Having identified the Caspian's energy supplies as a security interest of the United States, the White House was now demonstrating—in the most conspicuous manner possible—that the United States possessed both the will and the capacity to defend that interest with military force if necessary. The fact that General Sheehan and Deputy Assistant Secretary Kelleher accompanied U.S. troops to Kazakhstan merely underscores the importance attached to this operation by senior government officials.

Since then, the Department of Defense has provided further indications of America's growing strategic interest in the Caspian Sea region. A second CENTRAZBAT exercise, held in September 1998, brought several hundred U.S. soldiers from Fort Drum, New York, to Tashkent in Uzbekistan, and then to a military training area in northern Kyrgyzstan.[9] In 1999, moreover, the Army Training and Doctrine Command devised an elaborate computer model of the Caspian basin for use in testing possible scenarios for U.S. intervention in the area.[10] American and Azerbaijani officials have also discussed establishing a permanent U.S. military base in Azerbaijan.[11]

THE TRANSFORMATION OF AMERICAN SECURITY POLICY

The extension of American military power into the Caspian Sea region is, by itself, a momentous geopolitical development. As shown by the CENTRAZBAT exercises, it will require Washington to build and sustain military relationships with the Central Asian republics, as well as to construct a globe-spanning logistical capability. In time, it could also involve the establishment of American military bases in an area that was once part of the Soviet Union. But these initiatives are significant not only in regard to U.S. involvement in Central Asia: they also signal a dramatic shift in the basic orientation of American military policy.

For over forty years, from the late 1940s until 1990, the overarching goal of U.S. strategy was to create and maintain a global system of alliances capable of containing and, if necessary, defeating the Soviet Union. All other considerations, including the pursuit of America's own national interests, were subordinated to the all-encompassing mission of "containment." Since the end of the Cold War, however, the requirement for far-flung alliances has appeared less urgent, while the need to promote America's own security interests has seemed more pressing. The maintenance of NATO and other alliance systems remains an important priority, but other objectives—

of a more self-interested, tangible character—have come to dominate the American strategic agenda.

Among these objectives, none has so profoundly influenced American military policy as the determination to ensure U.S. access to overseas supplies of vital resources. As the American economy grows and U.S. industries come to rely more on imported supplies of critical materials, the protection of global resource flows is becoming an increasingly prominent feature of American security policy. This is evident not only in the *geographic* dimensions of strategy—the growing emphasis on military operations in the Persian Gulf, the Caspian, and other energy-producing areas—but also in its *operational* aspects. Whereas weapons technology and alliance politics once dominated the discourse on military affairs, American strategy now focuses on oil-field protection, the defense of maritime trade routes, and other aspects of resource security.

This new focus can be seen, for instance, in the attention being paid to energy concerns by the U.S. intelligence community. "We have to recognize that our nation will not be secure if global energy supplies are not secure," John C. Gannon, the deputy director of the Central Intelligence Agency, observed in 1996. This is so, he indicated, because "we need a substantial quantity of imported oil to sustain our economy." Because much of this oil comes from the Persian Gulf countries, "the U.S. will need to keep close watch on events and remain engaged in the Persian Gulf to safeguard the flow of vital oil supplies."[12]

The protection of critical raw materials and transit routes has, of course, been a major theme in American security policy for a very long time. In the late 1800s, for example, the nation's leading naval strategist, Captain Alfred Thayer Mahan, won widespread support for his argument that growing U.S. participation in international trade required the establishment of a large and powerful navy.[13] Similar views were advanced by President Theodore Roosevelt in the early 1900s, and later by key figures in the administration of Franklin D. Roosevelt. Concern over the safety of resource supplies also influenced American strategy during World War II and the immediate postwar period. Only with the outbreak of the Cold War did U.S. strategists diminish their emphasis on resource issues, turning their attention instead to political and military developments in Europe and Asia.

With the end of the Cold War, resource issues reassumed their central role in U.S. military planning. One could argue, then, that the current stress on resource security represents little more than a return to the status quo ante—that is, to the strategic environment that prevailed during the first half of the twentieth century. To a certain extent, this appears to be true. For example, the navy's emphasis on the safety of America's "sea lines of communication"—the maritime trade routes that connect one part of the world to another—rests on arguments originally laid out by Captain Mahan in the late nineteenth century.[14] But the current focus on resource concerns represents more than just a return to the past; above all, it reflects the growing importance of industrial might and the economic dimensions of security.

At the heart of this shift in policy is a belief that the defining parameters of power and influence have changed since the Cold War's demise. Whereas, in the past, national power was thought to reside in the possession of a mighty arsenal and the maintenance of extended alliance systems, it is now associated with economic dynamism and the cultivation of technological innovation. To exercise leadership in the current epoch, states are expected to possess a vigorous domestic economy and to outperform other states in the development and export of high-tech goods. While a potent military establishment is still considered essential to national security, it must be balanced by a strong and vibrant economy. "*National security depends on successful engagement in the global economy,*" the Institute for National Security Studies observed in a recent Pentagon study.[15] (Emphasis in the original.)

This perspective was first articulated in a systematic fashion by then governor Bill Clinton, during the 1992 presidential campaign. "Our economic strength must become a central defining element of our national security policy," he told students at Georgetown University in December 1991. "We must organize to compete and win in the global economy."[16] In another campaign speech, Clinton promised to "elevate economics in foreign policy"—a process, he declared, that would require reconstructing the Department of State "so that economics is no longer a poor cousin to old-school diplomacy."[17]

This "econocentric" approach to national security became official American policy when the Clinton administration took office in early 1993. In his first appearance before the Senate Foreign Relations Committee, Secretary of State Warren Christopher declared that he and his associates would "not be bashful about linking our high diplomacy with our economic goals." Noting that the world had entered a period in which "economic competition is eclipsing ideological rivalry," he promised that the administration would "*advance America's economic security with the same energy and resourcefulness we devoted to waging the Cold War*" (emphasis added).[18]

Clinton made the expansion of international trade and investment the top foreign policy goal of his administration. To accomplish this, he negotiated new trading arrangements with Latin America and Asia, opened additional markets to the sale of U.S. goods, and loosened restraints on American exports of satellites, computers, and other high-tech products. He also promoted the overseas operations of U.S. companies and sought to stabilize international financial institutions. In defending these policies, Clinton never tired of expressing his belief that "our economic and security interests are inextricably linked."[19]

An outlook that views economic and security interests as "inextricably linked" will naturally tend to place high priority on the protection of vital resource supplies. Without a steady and reliable flow of essential materials, the American economy cannot expand and generate the products needed to ensure continued U.S. competitiveness in global markets. The uninterrupted flow of energy supplies is especially critical: as the world's leading consumer of oil and gas, the United States must retain access to overseas supplies or its entire economy will face collapse. As suggested by Clinton in 1999, "Prosperity at home depends on stability in key regions with which we trade or from which we import critical commodities, such as oil and natural gas."[20]

The perceived relationship between energy sufficiency and U.S. security also emerged as a significant issue during the 2000 presidential campaign. When oil products became scarce during the early fall, pushing up prices and generating talk of an economic recession, Vice President Albert Gore called for the release of millions of gallons from the nation's Strategic Petroleum Reserve (SPR)—a large cache of oil established in the 1970s to provide a hedge against future energy crises. (Citing a potential shortage of heating oil at the onset of winter, President Clinton did decide at that time to release thirty million gallons from the reserve.) Gore's opponent, Governor George W. Bush of Texas, opposed any removal from the SPR, claiming that such action would endanger national security by diminishing America's ability to withstand a greater crisis in the future. The two candidates later sparred over strategies for reducing U.S. reliance on imported petroleum—Gore favoring the development of alternative technologies, Bush the exploitation of oil reserves in wilderness areas of Alaska—but both agreed that protecting the nation's energy supply was a prime concern of national security.

For the American military establishment, this concern has particular resonance: while the military can do little to promote trade or enhance financial stability, it *can* play a key role in protecting resource supplies. Resources are tangible assets that can be exposed to risk by political turmoil and conflict abroad—and so, it is argued, they require physical protection. While diplomacy and economic sanctions can be effective in promoting other economic goals, only military power can ensure the continued flow of oil and other critical materials from (or through) distant areas in times of war and crisis. As their unique contribution to the nation's economic security, therefore, the armed forces have systematically bolstered their capacity to protect the international flow of essential materials.

The need to use the military to protect vital resource supplies is readily grasped by the American public—a not insignificant consideration at a time when traditional security justifications for military spending have lost much of their appeal. A revealing exchange in 1998 between Representative Tom Allen (D.-Maine) of the House National Security Committee and several senior officers illustrates the importance of public opinion. After listing all of the places where U.S. forces had recently served—Bosnia, Macedonia, Somalia, the Persian Gulf, and so on—Allen expressed doubt about his ability "to explain [all of this] to people back home." Just how, he asked, do these operations "reflect our national interest and our national security?" In response, several officers spoke in abstract terms of America's global responsibilities. But the most vigorous response was provided by General Anthony Zinni, then the commander in chief of U.S. forces in the Persian Gulf: "My region, the Middle East, is obviously valuable to us as a source of oil and natural gas," he said. Because instability in this region could jeopardize access to these resources, he continued, "the need to keep things stable in there . . . is critical to our own economy."[21]

To implement this new policy, the Department of Defense is deploying additional forces in the Persian Gulf and preparing for expanded operations in other resource-rich areas, including the Caspian region. The U.S. Navy is also expanding its presence in waters used for the transshipment of energy supplies. Resource concerns have decisively moved to center stage in international security affairs. As we proceed further into the twenty-first century, these issues are destined to play an increasingly significant role in the shaping of American military policy.

PARALLEL DEVELOPMENTS ELSEWHERE

The United States is not the only nation to have assigned greater strategic significance to economic and resource concerns in the post–Cold War era. Since 1990, almost every major government has done so. While the particular character of this restructuring has varied from country to country, the overall result of these efforts has been what might be termed the *economization* of international security affairs.

As in the United States, this process has often led to a heightened emphasis on the protection of critical resources and trade routes. Russia, for example, has placed fresh importance on the security of its vast oil and mineral supplies and its extensive offshore territories. In the military doctrine approved by President Vladimir Putin on April 21, 2000, it is noted that the functions of Russia's armed forces include "creation of the conditions for the security of economic activity and protection of the Russian Federation's national interests in the territorial seas, on the continental shelf, and in the exclusive [offshore] economic zone of the Russian Federation and on the high seas."[22] Moscow has also extended its reach into the Caspian area, often competing with Washington for influence among the newly independent states of Central Asia.

China and Japan have likewise modified their security policies in accordance with the new economic priorities. The Chinese have reduced their strength on the border with Russia (a site of periodic tension during the late Cold War period) while extending their reach into the South China Sea, a contested area thought to house vast reserves of petroleum and natural gas. In a guarded reference to China's extensive claims in this area, Prime Minister Li Peng declared in 1995 that the People's Liberation Army must strengthen its air and naval capabilities so as to "safeguard the sovereignty and territorial integrity of the motherland and our maritime rights and interests."[23] Similarly, in 1996 Tokyo adopted a new National Defense Program Outline that calls on Japanese forces to enhance their capacity to protect essential sea-lanes and other critical interests in the waters surrounding Japan.[24]

Other states have revised their national defense policies in a comparable fashion. With the superpowers no longer willing (or, in the case of Russia, able) to adjudicate regional disputes or protect the economic interests of their allies, many countries have felt compelled to buttress their own defense capabilities. In the South China Sea, for example, members of the Association of Southeast Asian Nations (ASEAN) have responded to growing Chinese power by expanding the reach and firepower of their air and naval forces—in some instances, obtaining oceangoing warships for the first time in their history.[25] A similar process is under way in the Persian Gulf and the Caspian Sea, with local powers seeking a wide range of modern weaponry.

A key factor in the evolution of these and many other states' security policies has been the adoption of the United Nations Convention on the Law of the Sea (UNCLOS), the international statute governing offshore resource development. Under this agreement, ratified by the U.N. General Assembly in 1994, nations that border on large bodies of water are able to claim an "exclusive economic zone" (EEZ) extending up to two hundred miles out to sea, within which they can claim unlimited rights to seabed development. This means that many coastal and island nations have suddenly acquired dominion over vast offshore tracts with substantial energy and mineral potential. In many cases, however, these tracts are divided up among several adjoining states, leading to often fractious disputes over the location of offshore boundaries. And because these disputes have sometimes turned violent, many of the states involved have bought new ships and planes or otherwise sought to enhance their offshore defense capabilities.

For many states, the protection of oil and gas deposits governs strategic planning. For others, however, it is not oil but *water* that is of greatest concern. Many of the nations of North Africa and the Middle East lack sufficient supplies of fresh water to satisfy the growing demands of their swelling populations, and so view any threat to existing supplies as a vital security matter. "The next war in our region will be over the waters of the Nile, not politics," observed Boutros Boutros-Ghali, then Egypt's minister of state for foreign affairs, in 1988.[26] Similar comments have been made regarding the waters of the Jordan River, the Tigris, the Euphrates, and other key systems that supply two or more countries. In these areas, conflict over water is a recurring and often violent phenomenon.

Competition over other resources, including minerals, gems, and timber, has also led to conflict in some areas. Such disorder has been especially prevalent in developing nations that rely on the exploitation of one or two key materials—diamonds in Angola and Sierra Leone, timber in Liberia, copper in Papua New Guinea—for most of their national income. In these cases, it is not uncommon for competing elites or power blocs to feud over control of valuable commodities, often producing prolonged and bloody civil wars. Indeed, researchers at the World Bank have found that states with significant "lootable resources"—diamonds, timber, copper, and so forth—are "four times more likely to experience war than a country without primary commodities."[27] Such states naturally place great emphasis on resource protection in their security policies.

THE PIVOTAL IMPORTANCE OF RESOURCES

Ever since the Cold War's end, political analysts of all persuasions have attempted to identify the central defining principle of the new international environment—what Thomas Friedman of *The New York Times* has termed "The One Big Thing."[28] Several authors have attempted to identify this "one big thing," most prominently: Samuel Huntington, who claims that global security dynamics will be governed by a "clash of civilizations"; Robert Kaplan, who vividly depicts a world overtaken by population excess and anarchy; and Friedman himself, who, in *The Lexus and the Olive Tree,* argues that economic "globalization" has become the world's dominant feature. Each of these explanations has something to contribute to our understanding of international dynamics, and each has entered into the global policy debate; none, however, provides a fully satisfactory analysis of current world affairs.

Huntington's thesis of a global clash of civilizations assumes that states will develop their security policies on the basis of loyalty to a particular religious or "civilizational" community—the Christian West, the Orthodox Slavic bloc, the Islamic world, and so on. "Conflict between civilizations," he explains, "will be the latest phase in the evolution of conflict in the modern world."[29] But while some recent developments, such as the fighting in Bosnia and Kosovo, appear to confirm this assertion, others do not. Especially noteworthy is the fervent pursuit of resource plenty in total disregard of any "civilizational" loyalties. In the Caspian area, for example, the United States has aligned with three Muslim states—Azerbaijan, Turkey, and

Turkmenistan—against two predominantly Christian ones, Armenia and Russia. A similar pattern can be seen in other areas where resource interests outweigh ethnic and religious affiliations.

Similarly, the outbreak of violence and anarchy in Africa, as predicted by Kaplan,[30] has failed to discourage the major energy firms from establishing lucrative oil operations in these areas, or from developing effective security arrangements with local elites and warlords. In 1999, for example, American oil companies announced major new exploration and production ventures in such troubled states as Angola, Chad, and Nigeria. Similarly, while Friedman's theory of globalization goes a long way toward explaining the current primacy of economic relations in international affairs, it assumes that most major resource disputes will be resolved through market mechanisms—thus ignoring the fact that governments have repeatedly gone to war over what they view as "vital national interests," including oil and water supplies.

Clearly, it is not possible to explain the dynamics of global security affairs without recognizing the pivotal importance of resource competition. For almost every country in the world, the pursuit or protection of essential materials has become a paramount feature in national security planning. As shown by Operation CENTRAZBAT, resource concerns also figure in the organization, deployment, and actual use of many of the world's military forces. While the competition for resources may not be "The One Big Thing" that lies at the heart of all international relations, it helps explain much of what is happening in the world today.

Why have resources become so important? As suggested earlier, the adoption of an econocentric security policy almost always leads to an increased emphasis on resource protection—at least for those states that depend on raw material imports for their industrial prowess. The almost complete disappearance of ideological conflicts in today's world has also contributed to the centrality of resource issues, in that the pursuit and protection of critical materials is viewed as one of the state's primary security functions. In addition, certain resources are worth an immense amount of money—the untapped oil of the Caspian Sea basin, for example, was estimated by the Department of State in 1997 to be worth some $4 trillion[31]—and so their possession is widely seen as something worth fighting over.

But these factors alone do not explain the current centrality of resource concerns: several features of resources themselves figure in this equation. These include the escalating worldwide demand for commodities of all types, the likely emergence of resource scarcities, and disputes over the ownership of valuable sources of critical materials.

INSATIABLE DEMAND

Global demand for many key materials is growing at an unsustainable rate. As the human population grows, societies require more of everything (food, water, energy, timber, minerals, fibers, and so on) to satisfy the basic material requirements of their individual members. Some nations may consume more than others—the United States alone consumes approximately 30 percent of all raw materials used by the human population in any given year[32]—but almost every society is increasing its utilization of basic materials.

The growing demand for resources is driven, to a considerable degree, by the dramatic increase in human numbers. During the past fifty years alone, the world population grew by over 3 billion people, jumping from 2.6 billion people in 1950 to just over 6 billion in 1999. The rise in population naturally entails an increased requirement for food, clothing, shelter, and the other basic necessities of life. This, alone, explains the growth in demand for many materials. But population increase accounts for only part of the explosion in demand; of equal importance is the spread of industrialization to more and more areas of the globe and the steady worldwide increase in personal wealth, producing an insatiable appetite for energy, private automobiles, building materials, household appliances, and other resource-intensive commodities.

Between 1950 and 1999, gross world product (GWP) soared by

583 percent, from approximately $6 trillion to $41 trillion (in constant 1998 dollars). Even when translated into per capita GWP, the increase has been substantial, jumping from $2,500 in 1950 to $6,750 in 1999.[33] While not all individuals have experienced the benefits of this impressive statistical gain—many millions, in fact, remained trapped in poverty—large numbers of people around the world can now afford items that were previously inaccessible to them. Private automobile ownership, for example, jumped from about 53 million cars in 1950 to an estimated 520 million in 1999.[34] The ownership of refrigerators, television sets, air conditioners, personal computers, and other such items has grown to a similar degree. Because the production and utilization of these products entails the consumption of vast amounts of energy, minerals, and other materials, the global requirement for many basic commodities has consistently exceeded the rate of population growth.[35]

The rising demand for energy and consumer goods has been sharply evident in Asia and the Pacific Rim, where the pace of industrialization and economic growth has been especially brisk. Particularly noteworthy in this regard is the tempo of growth in China: between 1990 and 1996 alone, the Chinese economy expanded by an extraordinary 93 percent. This, in turn, has produced an explosive demand for automobiles, home appliances, and other consumer products. In 1985, fewer than one urban Chinese household in five possessed a color television set; by 1998, the average home had more than one. In the same period, the percentage of such households possessing a refrigerator jumped from seven to seventy-three; similar increases were recorded for the ownership of VCRs, indoor showers, and air-conditioning units.[36] To produce and power all of these items, China has consumed vast quantities of oil, coal, timber, minerals, and other basic materials.

Most experts believe, moreover, that the Chinese economy will continue its rapid expansion in the decades ahead, further boosting its need for resources. According to the latest U.S. Department of Energy (DoE) predictions, energy consumption by China will rise by about 4.3 percent per year between 1997 and 2020—roughly four times the rate in Europe and the United States. This will entail an increase in oil consumption of 150 percent, an increase in coal consumption of 158 percent, and an increase in natural gas consumption of over 1,100 percent. A similar pattern is expected in other rapidly industrializing nations: according to the DoE, energy consumption in 1997–2020 will grow by about 3.7 percent per year in India, 3.4 percent in Brazil, and 3.0 percent in Mexico. These three countries plus China will require 151 quadrillion British thermal units (BTUs) of energy in 2020, three times the amount needed in 1990.[37]

It is sometimes argued that the rising demand for resources in the developing world will be offset by a declining demand in the older industrialized nations, as computers and other high-tech devices take over the tasks once performed by less efficient, resource-consuming systems. And, to some degree, this is true: the use of copper in electrical wiring, for example, has been substantially diminished through the introduction of fiber-optic cables, which are made from cheap and plentiful silicon. On the whole, however, the introduction of computers has been accompanied not by a decline in overall resource consumption but an increase. This is so because technological innovation in the advanced economies has generated a considerable increase in personal wealth, and this, in turn, has led to a huge increase in personal consumption. In the United States, for example, automobile owners are driving greater distances every year—from 1.5 trillion miles in 1982 to 2.5 trillion in 1995—in larger and less fuel-efficient vehicles; the average American home, moreover, has grown in size by one-third since the early 1970s.[38] As a result, net resource consumption in the United States has steadily risen over the past few decades, and a similar pattern is evident in Western Europe and other computer-rich areas.[39]

It is safe to conclude, therefore, that the global demand for basic resources will continue to grow in the decades ahead. Such growth will be driven, as before, by a combination of population increase and economic expansion. The human community is expanding by roughly 80 million people per year; at this rate, total world population will reach 6.8 billion people by 2010 and close to 8 billion by 2020.[40]

On top of this, global per capita income is expected to rise by about 2 percent per year over the next few decades, nearly twice the rate of population growth.[41] If this added wealth is used for the continuing procurement of cars, trucks, appliances, large homes, and other such amenities, the worldwide demand for most basic materials will be substantially greater in 2020 than it was in the 1990s.

THE LOOMING RISK OF SHORTAGES

Growing demand for basic materials is colliding with another key aspect of the global resource equation: the fact that the world supply of some substances is quite limited. While the earth is blessed with vast quantities of most vital materials—water, arable land, minerals, timber, and fossil fuels—there are practical limits to what can be extracted from the global environment. According to one recent study, the earth lost nearly one-third of its available natural wealth between 1970 and 1995 as a result of human activity, more than in any other period in history. This study, released by the World Wildlife Fund (WWF) in 1998, revealed a significant decline in the availability or quality of many critical resources, including forest cover, marine fisheries, freshwater systems, and fossil fuels. Although the WWF study did not cover all resources of concern, it did suggest that humanity could face significant shortages of many vital materials.[42]

When, or if, particular resources will reach the point of severe exhaustion is not something that can be predicted with any degree of certainty. Many minerals, for instance, are widely dispersed across the surface of the planet, and so new supplies are discovered all the time. Other resources, like timber, are theoretically "renewable," in the sense that new trees can be planted to replace those that have been cut down. Substitutes are also available (or can be developed) for many of the materials that are likely to experience future shortages. Nevertheless, it is evident that the world supply of certain key resources is being diminished at a rapid pace—in some cases, exceeding the world's capacity to exploit new sources or develop substitute materials.

Of the various materials that fall into this sensitive category, the most significant are oil and water. Both are critical for the functioning of modern industrial society, are being used in ever-increasing amounts, and most importantly are likely to be in insufficient supply to meet global requirements by the middle of the twenty-first century. At the beginning of 2000, the world's proven reserves of petroleum stood at 1,033 billion barrels, or sufficient oil to sustain global consumption (at the then-current rate of 73 million barrels per day) for another forty years.[43] If, however, oil consumption rises by 2 percent per year—as predicted by the U.S. Department of Energy—the existing supply will disappear in twenty-five to thirty years, not forty. Future oil discoveries will, of course, augment the global supply of oil, while the introduction of new technologies will permit the extraction of untapped supplies now considered too remote or too difficult to exploit (such as those in northern Siberia and the deep waters of the Atlantic Ocean). Even so, it is likely that the world will begin to experience significant shortages of conventional petroleum by the second or third decade of the twenty-first century.[44] (A more detailed assessment of the global petroleum supply appears in chapter 2.)

The global water equation is roughly similar. Although the earth possesses vast amounts of salt water, the global supply of fresh water is relatively limited: less than 3 percent of the planet's total water supply is fresh water, and much of this amount is locked up in the polar ice caps and glaciers. Of the amount that is readily available (approximately 12,000 cubic kilometers per year), half is already being appropriated for human use.[45] As in the case of oil, population growth and higher standards of living are constantly boosting the global demand for water. If this pattern persists, total human usage will approach 100 percent of the available supply by the mid-twenty-first century, producing severe shortages in some areas and intensified competition for access to important sources of supply. (A comprehensive assessment of the world's freshwater supply appears in chapter 6.)

Significant shortages of other vital materials can also be expected in the decades to come. The world's natural forest cover, for example,

is disappearing at the rate of about 0.5 percent per year—equivalent
to the loss of a forest the size of England and Wales—and many
individual tree species are at risk of disappearing altogether. Already,
approximately 70 percent of the world's tropical dry forest has been
obliterated, along with 60 percent of temperate forest and 45 percent
of tropical moist forest.[46] Some of these forests are being replaced
with tree plantations, but not at a rate fast enough to compensate for
the annual loss of forest cover.

The future availability of certain key commodities will also be
affected by changes in the global environment. The growing accumulation of carbon dioxide and other heat-trapping "greenhouse"
gases in the environment—itself a product of accelerated fossil fuel
consumption—is contributing to a gradual rise in average annual temperatures, producing drought in some regions and threatening the
survival of many plant and animal species. Climate change of this sort
could also reduce rainfall and/or increase evaporation rates in dry
inland areas, reducing the flow of water into vital river systems like
the Nile and the Indus. As suggested by Professor Thomas Homer-
Dixon of the University of Toronto, "environmental scarcities" of this
sort will further inflame the competition between groups and societies
over access to vital raw materials.[47]

As global consumption rises and environmental conditions dete-
riorate, the total available supply of many key materials will diminish and the price of whatever remains will rise. In many cases, this
will lead to the development of new sources of supply and/or the
introduction of substitute materials, thereby alleviating worldwide
shortages. Also, those societies with the means to do so will simply
pay higher prices for whatever they need or desire. But market
forces will not be able to solve every resource problem, nor avert
all future conflicts over scarce materials. Some commodities, such
as water, cannot be replaced by other substances, and many poor
societies cannot afford to pay higher prices for essential goods. In
these circumstances, conflict may arise between states over access to
vital sources of supply, and within states over the distribution of
the limited materials available. As prices rise, moreover, contending
groups and elites in resource-producing countries will have greater

incentive to seize and retain control of valuable mines, oil fields, and timber stands. The result, inevitably, will be increasing conflict over critical materials.

CONTESTED SOURCES OF SUPPLY

The risk of conflict over diminishing supplies of vital materials is all the more worrisome because of another key feature of the global resource equation: the fact that many key sources or deposits of these materials are shared by two or more nations, or lie in contested border areas or offshore economic zones. Normally, states prefer to rely on materials lying entirely within their borders for their requirements of essential materials; as these supplies become exhausted governments will naturally seek to maximize their access to contested and offshore deposits, thereby producing an increased risk of conflict with neighboring states. This situation is potentially disruptive even under the best of circumstances, when the states involved are relatively friendly with one another; when this sort of competition occurs against a backdrop of preexisting hostility, as is the case in many parts of Africa and the Middle East, disputes over contested supplies of vital materials could prove explosive.

Disorder can arise from several types of resource contests. Disputes may occur over the allocation of a particular source of supply that extends across international boundaries, such as a large river system or an underground oil basin. The Nile River, for example, carries water through nine countries, the Mekong River through five, and the Euphrates three. Because these rivers arise in one set of countries and travel through others before reaching their egress to the sea, the upstream countries in the system are always in a position to control the flow of water to the downstream states; when the upstream states actually use this power to increase their water allocations at the expense of those lying downstream, conflict can arise. (See chapters 6 and 7 for further discussion of this point.)

Similarly, when two states sit astride a large underground oil basin and one of the two extracts a disproportionate share of the total petroleum supply, this could diminish the oil revenues of the second state and lead to conflict. This was, in fact, one of the key irritants in the Iraq-Kuwait relationship in the late 1980s: Baghdad claimed that the Kuwaitis were extracting more than their rightful share of oil from the shared Rumaila field, thereby impeding its recovery from the Iran-Iraq war of 1980–88.[48] Conflict over shared oil supplies has also broken out between Saudi Arabia and Yemen, which share a poorly defined border in the Rub' al-Khaili (the "Empty Quarter").

A second type of conflict arises over contested claims to offshore areas that harbor significant energy or mineral resources. As noted earlier, the U.N. Convention on the Law of the Sea allows ocean-bordering states to claim an exclusive economic zone extending offshore for up to two hundred miles, within which they have the sole right to exploit marine life and undersea resource deposits. This system works smoothly enough in large, open bodies of water, but it generates enormous friction in situations where several states border on an inland sea (such as the Caspian) or a relatively confined body of water. In these circumstances, claims to maritime EEZs often overlap, producing disputes over the location of offshore boundaries. A prime example is the South China Sea, where a total of seven states—Brunei, China, Indonesia, Malaysia, the Philippines, Taiwan, and Vietnam—have laid claim to large areas of water. (For more on the South China Sea situation, see chapter 5.)

Finally, disputes can arise over access to bodies of water considered essential for the transportation of vital materials, such as the Persian Gulf and the Suez Canal. A very large proportion of the world's daily oil intake travels by ship from the Gulf to ports in Europe, the Americas, and Japan. In many cases, these ships must pass through narrow and circumscribed bodies of water, such as the Strait of Hormuz (at the mouth of the Persian Gulf), the Strait of Malacca (between Indonesia and Malaysia), or the Red Sea. Because the free passage of ships through these waters is considered essential for the uninterrupted flow of materials, major importing states have always resisted efforts by local powers to block or constrict them.[49] In 1986, for instance, the United States "reflagged" Kuwaiti ships with the American flag and escorted them through the Persian Gulf, then the site of naval clashes between Iran and Iraq. Concern over the safe transportation of vital materials can also extend to oil and gas pipelines, particularly those that travel through areas of recurring disorder.

THE EMERGING LANDSCAPE OF CONFLICT

Each of these three factors—the relentless expansion in worldwide demand, the emergence of significant resource shortages, and the proliferation of ownership contests—is likely to introduce new stresses into the international system. The first two will inevitably intensify competition between states over access to vital materials; the third will generate new sources of friction and conflict. Each factor, moreover, will reinforce the destabilizing tendencies of the others: as resource consumption grows, shortages will emerge more rapidly and governments will come under mounting pressure to solve the problem at any cost; this, in turn, will heighten the tendency of states to seek maximum control over contested sources of supply, thereby increasing the risk of conflict between the countries that share or jointly claim a given resource deposit.

In most cases, these conflicts will be resolved without recourse to violence, as the nations involved arrive at a negotiated solution to their predicament. Global market forces will tend to encourage such an outcome: the perceived economic benefits of compromise are generally much greater than the likely costs of war, and so most states will choose to pull back from their maximum demands if they can be assured of a reasonable slice of the resource pie. But negotiations and market forces will not work in every instance. In some cases, the materials at stake will be viewed as so essential to national survival or economic well-being that compromise is unthinkable. It is difficult, for example, to imagine that the United States will ever allow the Persian Gulf to fall under the control of a hostile power, or that Egypt will allow Sudan or Ethiopia to gain control over the flow of the Nile River. In such situations, national security considerations will always prevail over negotiated settlements that could be perceived as entailing the surrender of vital national interests.

Global market forces can also increase the likelihood of conflict, most notably when a contested resource is seen as being so valuable in monetary terms that none of the claimants involved is willing to accept its loss. This appears to be the case in the Democratic Republic of Congo (formerly Zaire), where several internal factions and foreign powers have been fighting for control over the lucrative gold and copper fields of the south and west.[50] A similar situation has long prevailed in Sierra Leone—in this case, involving internal conflict over the country's valuable diamond fields. Typically, contests of this sort arise in poor and underdeveloped countries where possession of a mineral deposit or oil field is seen as the only viable route to the accumulation of wealth.

The risk of internal conflict over resources is further heightened by the growing divide between the rich and the poor in many developing countries—a phenomenon widely ascribed to globalization. While those at the top of the economic ladder are able to procure the basic necessities of life, those at the bottom are finding themselves increasingly barred from access to such vital commodities as food, land, shelter, and safe drinking water. As supplies contract and the price of many materials rises, the poor will find themselves in an increasingly desperate situation—and thus more inclined to heed the exhortations of demagogues, fundamentalists, and extremists who promise to relieve their suffering through revolt or ethnic partition.

"The distribution of [economic] competitiveness is now uneven," the Institute for National Security Studies observed in 1999. "This pattern raises the disturbing prospect of a 'globalization gap' between winners and losers. . . . Leaders of the losers often blame outsiders or unpopular insiders for economic hardship. Some foment crises to distract domestic attention from joblessness and hunger."[51]

This danger will only grow more acute as increased economic competition and pressure from international lending agencies force the governments of developing nations to eliminate subsidies on food and other basic commodities and to privatize such essential services as water delivery. A foretaste of this was provided in April 2000, when

Bolivia's major cities were paralyzed by protests against a government plan to privatize municipal utilities and impose fees on drinking water. At least five people died in skirmishes with the police, and many more were injured. Order was restored only after President Hugo Banzer declared a state of emergency and ordered army troops to clear major thoroughfares.[52]

Thus, while market forces and globalization can help avert violence in many instances of resource scarcity, there are situations in which they are likely to fail. When this occurs, disputes over access to critical (or extremely valuable) resources may lead to armed conflict. Such encounters can take the form of an internal struggle for control over a particular resource, a territorial dispute over contested border zones or EEZs, a naval contest over critical waterways, or a regional power struggle in areas holding large supplies of critical resources, such as the Persian Gulf and Caspian Sea regions. Whatever form these engagements take, they are best described as *resource wars*—conflicts that revolve, to a significant degree, over the pursuit or possession of critical materials.[53]

Human history has been marked by a long succession of resource wars—stretching all the way back to the earliest agrarian civilizations. After World War II, the relentless pursuit of resources was overshadowed by the political and ideological exigencies of the U.S.-Soviet rivalry; but it has resurfaced with fresh intensity in the current era. Given the growing importance ascribed to economic vigor in the security policy of states, the rising worldwide demand for resources, the likelihood of significant shortages, and the existence of numerous ownership disputes, the incidence of conflict over vital materials is sure to grow.

Resource competition will not, of course, prove the sole source of conflict in the twenty-first century. Other factors—ethnic hostility, economic injustice, political competition, and so on—will also lead to periodic outbreaks of violence. Increasingly, however, these factors will be linked to disputes over the possession of (or access to) vital materials. However divided two states or societies may be over matters of politics or religion, the likelihood of their engaging in mutual combat becomes considerably greater when one side believes that its essential supply of water, food, or energy is threatened by the other. And with the worldwide availability of many key resources facing eventual decline, the danger of resource disputes intruding into other areas of disagreement can only increase.

2

Oil, Geography, and War:
The Competitive Pursuit of Petroleum Plenty

Of all the resources discussed in this book, none is more likely to provoke conflict between states in the twenty-first century than oil. Petroleum stands out from other materials—water, minerals, timber, and so on—because of its pivotal role in the global economy and its capacity to ignite large-scale combat. No highly industrialized society can survive at present without substantial supplies of oil, and so any significant threat to the continued availability of this resource will prove a cause of crisis and, in extreme cases, provoke the use of military force. Action of this sort could occur in any of the major oil-producing areas, including the Middle East and the Caspian basin. Lesser conflicts over petroleum are also likely, as states fight to gain or retain control over resource-rich border areas and offshore economic zones. Big or small, conflicts over oil will constitute a significant feature of the global security environment in the decades to come.

Petroleum has, of course, been a recurring source of conflict in the past. Many of the key battles of World War II, for example, were triggered by the Axis Powers' attempts to gain control over petroleum supplies located in areas controlled by their adversaries. The pursuit of greater oil revenues also prompted Iraq's 1990 invasion of Kuwait, and this, in turn, provoked a massive American military response. But combat over petroleum is not simply a phenomenon of the past; given the world's ever-increasing demand for energy and the continuing possibility of supply interruptions, the outbreak of a conflict over oil is just as likely to occur in the future.

The likelihood of future combat over oil is suggested, first of all, by the growing buildup of military forces in the Middle East and other oil-producing areas. Until recently, the greatest concentration of military power was to found along the East-West divide in Europe and at other sites of superpower competition. Since 1990, however, these concentrations have largely disappeared, while troop levels in the major oil zones have been increased. The United States, for example, has established a permanent military infrastructure in the Persian Gulf area and has "prepositioned" sufficient war matériel there to sustain a major campaign. Russia, meanwhile, has shifted more of its forces to the North Caucasus and the Caspian Sea basin, while China has expanded its naval presence in the South China Sea. Other countries have also bolstered their presence in these areas and other sites of possible conflict over oil.

Geology and geography also add to the risk of conflict. While relatively abundant at present, natural petroleum does not exist in unlimited quantities; it is a finite, nonrenewable substance. At some point in the future, available supplies will prove inadequate to satisfy soaring demand, and the world will encounter significant shortages. Unless some plentiful new source of energy has been discovered by that point, competition over the remaining supplies of petroleum will prove increasingly fierce. In such circumstances, any prolonged interruption in the global flow of oil will be viewed by import-dependent states as a mortal threat to their security—and thus as a matter that may legitimately be resolved through the use of military force. Growing scarcity will also result in higher prices for oil, producing enormous hardship for those without the means to absorb added costs; in consequence, widespread internal disorder may occur.

Geography enters the picture because many of the world's leading sources of oil are located in contested border zones or in areas of recurring crisis and violence. The distribution of petroleum is more concentrated than other raw materials, with the bulk of global supplies found in a few key producing areas. Some of these areas—the North Slope of Alaska and the American Southwest, for example— are located within the borders of a single country and are relatively free of disorder; others, however, are spread across several countries—which may or may not agree on their common borders—and/ or are located in areas of perennial unrest. To reach global markets, moreover, petroleum must often travel (by ship or by pipeline) through other areas of instability. Because turmoil in these areas can easily disrupt the global flow of oil, any outbreak of conflict, however minor, will automatically generate a risk of outside intervention.

That conflict over oil will erupt in the years ahead is almost a foregone conclusion. Just how much violence, at what levels of intensity, and at which locations, cannot be determined. Ultimately, the frequency and character of warfare will depend on the relative weight and the interplay of three key factors: (1) the political and strategic environment in which decisions over resource issues are made; (2) the future relationship between demand and supply; and (3) the geography of oil production and distribution.

THE POLITICS OF OIL SECURITY

Many resources are needed to sustain a modern industrial society, but only those that are viewed as being vital to national security are likely to provoke the use of military force when access to key supplies is placed in jeopardy.* There is no question that oil has enjoyed this distinctive status in the past. Ever since the introduction of oil-powered warships at the beginning of the twentieth century, petroleum has been viewed as essential for success in war. Before that time, petroleum had largely

---

*In 1998, the U.S. National Security Council defined "vital interests" as those interests "of broad, overriding importance to the survival, safety, and vitality of our nation. Among these are the physical security of our territory and that of our allies, the safety of our citizens, our economic well-being, and the protection of our critical infrastructures. We will do what we must to defend these interests, including—when necessary—using our military might unilaterally and decisively" (*A National Security Strategy for a New Century*, October 1998).

been used to provide illumination, most commonly in the form of kerosene. (Indeed, many of the major oil companies of today, including Exxon, Mobil, and Royal Dutch/Shell, were initially established in the nineteenth century to produce and market kerosene to the growing urban populations of Europe and North America.) The critical turning point came in 1912, when the British Admiralty—then led by First Lord of the Admiralty Winston Churchill—decided to convert its combat vessels from coal to oil propulsion.[1]

The transition from coal to oil provided British ships with a significant advantage in speed and endurance over the coal-powered vessels of its adversaries, especially Germany. But it also presented London with a significant dilemma: while rich in coal, Britain possessed few domestic sources of petroleum and so was vitally dependent on imported supplies. With a war about to begin, and the reliability of overseas suppliers in question, the cabinet decided—on a strict national security basis—to endow the government with direct responsibility for the delivery of oil. On June 17, 1914, Parliament voted to approve the government's acquisition of a majority stake in the Anglo-Persian Oil Company (APOC), a London-based firm that had recently discovered petroleum in southwestern Persia. With this vote, it became British policy to protect APOC's oil concession area in Persia—thus, for the first time, making the security of overseas petroleum supplies a major state responsibility.[2]

The link between oil and military policy was made even more substantial during World War I itself, when all of the major belligerents employed oil-driven vehicles for combat, reconnaissance, and logistics. The airplane and the tank—oil-powered machines that were to revolutionize the conduct of warfare—were introduced during the conflict. Scarcely less important was the widespread use of motor vehicles to carry troops and supplies to the battlefield: over the course of the war, the British army's fleet of trucks grew from 10,000 to 60,000; the American Expeditionary Force brought with it another 50,000 motor vehicles.[3] It is with this in mind that Lord Curzon, former viceroy of India and soon-to-be foreign secretary, told a group of government and industry officials in London that the Allies had "floated to victory upon a wave of oil."[4]

This perception continued to influence strategic thinking after World War I and in the years leading up to World War II. Believing that the next major conflict would see an even greater reliance on oil-powered weapons than the last, many governments followed the British example by creating state-owned oil companies and by seeking control over foreign sources of petroleum. Britain, for its part, expanded its oil interests in the Persian Gulf area and strengthened its dominant position in Iran (the new name for Persia). France established a state-owned firm, the Compagnie Française des Pétroles, and obtained concessions in the Mosul area of northwest Iraq. Germany and Japan—both of which lacked domestic sources of petroleum—laid plans to acquire their supplies from Romania and the Dutch East Indies, respectively.[5]

Once war broke out, the competitive pursuit of oil by all sides had a significant impact on the tempo and trajectory of battle. In the Pacific, Japanese efforts to gain control over the petroleum supplies of the Dutch East Indies produced mounting alarm in Washington and led, in 1941, to the imposition of a U.S. embargo on oil exports to Japan. This, in turn, persuaded Japanese officials that a war with the United States was inevitable, propelling them to seek an initial advantage through a surprise attack on the U.S. naval base at Pearl Harbor. In the European theater, Germany's desperate need for oil helped trigger its 1941 invasion of Russia. Along with Moscow and Leningrad, a major target of the invasion was the Soviet oil center at Baku (in what is now Azerbaijan). Both efforts ended in failure: the Japanese plan to import East Indian oil was foiled by American air and submarine attacks on tanker ships, while the German drive on Baku was thwarted by stubborn Soviet resistance. With their supplies of oil becoming increasingly scarce, Japan and Germany were unable to mount effective resistance to Allied offensives and so were eventually forced to concede defeat.[6]

After the war, petroleum continued to be seen by military planners as a vital combat necessity. With military organizations placing even greater emphasis on the role of airpower and armored forces, the need for reliable oil supplies became more critical than ever. This influenced the strategic thinking not only of the European powers, which had long been dependent on imported supplies, but also of the United States, which for the first time began to acquire significant supplies of petroleum from outside the country. Fearing that the Soviet Union would seek control over the Persian Gulf area—rapidly becoming the leading source of Western oil imports—Washington established a modest military presence in the region and sought to integrate Iran, Iraq, Saudi Arabia, and other key oil-producing states into the Western alliance. Both the Truman Doctrine (1947) and the Eisenhower Doctrine (1957) included promises of U.S. military aid to any state in the region that came under attack from Soviet or Soviet-backed forces.[7]

Initially, American moves in the Middle East were governed by classical military considerations: to prevent a hostile power from gaining control over a vital resource needed for the effective prosecution of war. With the outbreak of the October 1973 Arab-Israeli conflict, however, the perception of oil as a strategic commodity took on an entirely new meaning. To punish Washington for its support of Israel and to build worldwide pressure for an acceptable outcome to the conflict, the Arab states cut off all petroleum deliveries to the United States and imposed rolling cutbacks on deliveries to other countries. At the same time, the Organization of Petroleum-Exporting Countries (OPEC) announced a fourfold increase in the price of oil. Occurring at a time when petroleum supplies were already under pressure from rapidly growing demand, the oil embargo and OPEC price increase sent a powerful shock wave through the global economy: oil shortages developed in many areas, industrial output declined, and the world plunged into a prolonged economic recession. From this time on, oil was seen not only as an essential military commodity but also as a prerequisite for global economic stability.[8]

The Arab oil embargo was rescinded in March 1974, and the economic crisis gradually receded. Nevertheless, the events of 1973–74 left a profound and lasting impact on the perceived link between oil and the national security of the major industrialized powers. Worried that significant supply disruptions could occur again, the oil-importing countries sought to minimize their vulnerability by searching for new petroleum deposits in more secure locations (the North Sea and the North Slope of Alaska, for example) and by storing large quantities of oil in special reservoirs. The United States, for its part, stored hundreds of millions of barrels of oil in its newly established Strategic Petroleum Reserve.

The American response to the "oil shocks" of 1973–74 was not limited to defensive measures. For the first time, senior officials began talking of using force to protect vital petroleum supplies in peacetime, to guarantee the health of the economy. Specifically, policy makers began to consider American military intervention in the Middle East to prevent any interruption in the flow of Persian Gulf oil. Initially private, these deliberations became public in 1975 when Henry Kissinger, then secretary of state, told the editors of *Business Week* that the United States was prepared to go to war over oil. Although reluctant to employ force in a dispute over prices alone, he stated, Washington would have no such hesitation "where there's some actual strangulation of the industrialized world."[9]

This formulation of Western security interests has governed American military planning ever since. When, in 1979, the shah of Iran was overthrown by militant Islamic forces and the world experienced a second major "oil shock," President Carter was quick to threaten the use of force against any adversary that might seek to impede the flow of oil from the Persian Gulf area. On January 23, 1980, in the statement cited in chapter 1, Carter declared that any attempt by a hostile power to constrict the flow of oil in the Gulf "will be repelled by any means necessary, including military force."[10] In line with this principle, known since as the Carter Doctrine, the United States commenced a military buildup in the Persian Gulf area that has continued to this day. This principle has, moreover, periodically been put to the test. During the Iran-Iraq war of 1980–88, when the Iranians stepped up their attacks on oil shipping in the Gulf (presumably to punish Kuwait and Saudi Arabia for their financial support of Iraq), the United States agreed to "reflag" Kuwaiti tankers with American flags and provide them with a U.S. naval escort.[11]

The Carter Doctrine was next invoked in August 1990, when Iraqi forces occupied Kuwait and positioned themselves for an assault on

Saudi Arabia. Concluding that Iraqi control of both Kuwaiti and Saudi oil fields would pose an intolerable threat to Western economic security, President Bush quickly decided on a tough military response—dispatching large numbers of American forces to defend Saudi Arabia and, if need be, to drive the Iraqis out of Kuwait. "Our country now imports nearly half the oil it consumes and could face a major threat to its economic independence," he told the nation on August 7. Hence, "the sovereign independence of Saudi Arabia is of vital interest to the United States."[12] A number of other concerns, including Iraq's burgeoning weapons capabilities, also figured in the U.S. decision to employ force in the Gulf, but senior administration officials always placed particular emphasis on the threat to Western oil supplies and the continued health of the American economy.[13]

Since Desert Storm, American leaders have continued to stress the importance of unhindered oil deliveries to the health and stability of the global economy. "America's vital interests in the [Persian Gulf] region are compelling," General J. H. Binford Peay III, commander in chief of the U.S. Central Command (CENTCOM), declared in 1997. "The unrestricted flow of petroleum resources from friendly Gulf states to refineries and processing facilities around the world drives the global economic engine."[14] In accordance with this outlook, the United States has beefed up its forces in the Gulf and taken other steps to protect friendly powers in the area. At the same time, Washington has enhanced its capacity to intervene in the Caspian Sea region and in other areas holding large supplies of oil. (These efforts will receive a close look in chapters 3 and 4.)

A similar perspective regarding the role of oil in maintaining economic stability also governs the security policies of other states, including China and Japan. Both of these countries have bolstered their capacity to protect vital petroleum supplies: China has tightened its hold on Xinjiang (a potential source of oil and the site of a rebellion by members of the Muslim Uighur ethnic group) and the islands of the South China Sea (another potential source of oil); Japan has extended the reach of its air and naval forces to better protect its sealanes. (For more on this, see chapter 5.)

For oil-importing countries, the safe delivery of oil is the basis of their economic security. For oil exporters, however, the *possession* of oil dominates economic thinking. Even at the depressed prices of the late 1990s, the sale of oil was enormously lucrative for those countries; as demand grows and prices rise, the monetary value of oil reserves will climb even higher. In 1997, for instance, the U.S. Department of State placed the value of untapped Caspian Sea oil supplies at a staggering $4 trillion—and oil prices were then considerably lower than they are today.[15] It is therefore not surprising that any state possessing some piece of this latent wealth will view its protection as a vital aspect of national and economic security.

THE DYNAMICS OF GLOBAL OIL CONSUMPTION

Another key factor in determining the frequency and character of oil conflict is the relationship between supply and demand in the petroleum market. If global supplies continue to outpace the demand for oil, as was largely the case during the 1990s, the risk of conflict will prove relatively low because importers will be able to compensate for supply interruptions in one producing area by seeking additional supplies from others. If, however, demand outpaces supply or if production in relatively secure areas (like the United States and the North Sea) goes into permanent decline, the probability of friction and conflict is likely to rise.

Global Demand Patterns

It is risky, of course, to make predictions about the future demand for oil. Much can happen in the years ahead to increase or decrease global requirements. Nevertheless, all available information suggests that the worldwide demand for petroleum will rise at a steady rate of approximately 2 percent per year between now and 2020. Using Department of Energy projections, this means that oil use will rise from about 77 million barrels per day (mbd) in 2000 to 85 mbd in 2005, 94 mbd in 2010, 102 mbd in 2015, and 110 mbd in 2020.[16] At that point, oil consumption will be half again as great as it was in 1996, twice the level for 1975, and about five times the rate for 1958.

Largely driving the demand for petroleum is its use as a source of energy for electrical power generation, heating, and transportation. No other form of energy is as widely or intensively used in the global economy today. As suggested by oil expert Edward L. Morse, "Petroleum is the most versatile fuel source ever discovered [and is] situated at the core of the modern industrial economy. . . . Despite competition from [natural] gas and nuclear energy, it has maintained its prominence largely because it is the only energy source that can be used across the board—in space heating, as an industrial fuel supply, and as a means to generate electricity—and because it continues to be unrivaled in the transportation sector."[17] At the end of the twentieth century, oil accounted for about 39 percent of total world energy consumption; coal, the second major source of energy, accounted for only 24 percent.[18] The remaining 37 percent of global energy consumption was divided between natural gas (22 percent), nuclear energy (6 percent), hydropower, and "traditional" fuels like wood and animal waste.

Most experts believe, moreover, that petroleum will remain the world's leading source of energy during the first decades of the twenty-first century. Of the estimated 612 quadrillion BTUs ("quads") of energy that will be consumed worldwide in 2020, 225 quads, or 37 percent, will be provided by petroleum. Natural gas—like oil, a hydrocarbon-based substance—jumps to second place in this projection, edging out coal and eating slightly into oil's enormous lead.* Together, oil and natural gas will account, by this estimate, for two-thirds of world consumption in 2020; coal will account for 22 percent, and all other sources for 12 percent.[19] (See Table 2.1.)

Oil, like these other sources of energy, is used to generate electricity and to provide power for industry or agriculture. It alone, however, fuels the world's transportation systems. At present, petroleum in its various forms—gasoline, diesel fuel, jet fuel, and so on—accounts for 95

---

*Some analysts believe that the growing popularity of natural gas will diminish the strategic importance of petroleum. But while it is true that gas is outstripping oil in the generation of electricity, it is far less useful as a source of fuel for motor vehicles. Like petroleum, moreover, natural gas is a nonrenewable resource that is likely to be fully depleted before the end of the twenty-first century. On top of this, gas is usually found in the same locations as oil, and so is subject to identical strategic considerations.

Table 2.1: World Energy Consumption by Fuel, 1996–2020 (In quadrillion BTUs)							
		Projections					Average Annual Percentage Change, 1996–2020
Fuel Type	Actual, 1996	2000	2005	2010	2015	2020	
Oil	145.7	157.7	172.7	190.4	207.5	224.6	1.8
Natural Gas	82.2	90.1	111.3	130.8	153.6	177.5	3.3
Coal	92.8	97.7	107.1	116.0	124.8	138.3	1.7
Nuclear	24.1	24.5	24.9	25.2	23.6	21.7	−0.4
Other	30.7	32.7	38.3	41.9	45.6	49.7	2.1
Totals	375.5	402.7	454.3	504.2	555.1	611.8	2.1

Source: U.S. Department of Energy, *International Energy Outlook 1999*, Table A2. Note: totals may not equal sum of components due to independent rounding.

percent of all transportation energy consumed in the world today. As the number of automobiles and trucks on the road increases and as more people fly for business or pleasure, the amount of petroleum devoted to transportation uses will grow substantially. In the year 2020, transportation activities will account for an estimated 52 percent of worldwide petroleum consumption, up from 43 percent in 1996.[20]

Largely driving the increased use of petroleum in transportation is what the U.S. Department of Energy terms the "motorization" of the world—the acquisition of private automobiles by more and more individuals and private companies. Per capita car ownership is already very high in the industrialized world, approaching 775 vehicles per thousand people in the United States and about 600 per thousand in Canada and Japan; the rate is lower in the developing countries, but rising at a very rapid pace. "In the urban centers of the developing world, car ownership is often seen as one of the first symbols of emerging prosperity," the DoE observed in 2000. As a result, "per capita motorization in much of the developing world is projected to more than double between 1997 and 2020." And because almost all of these added vehicles will be powered by oil, the global demand for petroleum will continue to expand throughout this period.[21]

Petroleum is also used as a feedstock for the manufacture of other materials, including lubricants, plastics, and artificial fibers. According to the American Petroleum Institute, approximately 7 percent of all oil consumed by the United States—the equivalent of 450 million barrels per year—is used in the production of these materials.[22] As in the field of transportation, the use of petroleum as a raw material for other products is expected to grow in the years ahead.

Although the twenty-first century is likely to bring many changes in the way we live, there is, at present, no indication that the world will cut back on its need for oil as a source of energy, as fuel for transportation, as a feedstock for other materials, or as a critical resource in warfare. Indeed, it is likely that we will see a continuing rise in the consumption of petroleum on a global basis. Such growth will be evident in every part of the world but will be especially pronounced in the developing areas of Asia and Latin America, where rapid industrialization is generating an enormous need for energy and transportation fuel. As shown by Table 2.2, oil consumption in the developing world is expected to grow at two or three times the rate in the industrialized countries. Of particular significance is the surging demand for petroleum in developing Asia—according to the DoE, oil consumption in China and India will rise by a brisk 3.8 percent per year.[23] (For discussion of the strategic significance of rising energy demand in Asia, see chapter 5.)

It is possible, of course, that future developments will soften the demand for oil in the years ahead. It has been suggested, for example, that the spread of computers and high-speed communications will reduce the need for travel and other energy-consuming activities. However, the arrival of the Computer Age has not, in fact, been accompanied by any noticeable decline in the demand for petroleum; rather, the opposite is true—spurred by growing private automobile use, oil consumption is rising in the United States and in other countries that possess large numbers of computers. The rapidly exploding use of the Internet, moreover, has produced a surge in demand for electricity—and this, too, has generated an increased need for oil and natural gas.[24] It seems unlikely, then, that the proliferation of computers and related systems will lead to a near-term decline in the demand for petroleum.

Table 2.2:
World Oil Consumption by Region, 1990–1996, and Projections, 2000–2020
(Million barrels per day)

Region and Country	Actual		Projected					Annual Percentage Change, 1996–2020
	1990	1996	2000	2005	2010	2015	2020	
Industrialized countries, total	39.0	42.7	44.9	47.4	50.1	52.3	54.5	1.0
North America, total	20.4	22.0	23.6	25.5	27.4	28.8	30.2	1.3
United States	17.0	18.3	19.5	21.2	22.7	23.7	24.7	1.2
Western Europe	12.5	13.7	14.4	14.8	15.3	15.6	16.0	0.7
Industrialized Asia, total	6.2	7.1	6.8	7.1	7.5	7.9	8.3	0.7
Japan	5.1	5.9	5.6	5.7	6.0	6.3	6.6	0.5
Eastern Europe and former USSR	10.0	5.7	6.0	6.1	6.4	6.6	6.9	0.8
Developing countries, total	17.0	23.1	26.2	31.4	37.0	42.9	48.7	3.2
Developing Asia, total	7.6	11.9	13.6	15.5	18.5	21.8	24.3	3.0
China	2.3	3.5	4.6	5.0	6.4	8.1	8.8	3.8
India	1.2	1.7	1.9	2.6	3.1	3.5	4.1	3.8
Middle East	3.9	4.8	5.2	6.5	7.5	8.5	9.8	3.0
Africa	2.1	2.4	2.7	3.0	3.5	4.1	4.7	2.8
South and Central America	3.4	4.0	4.8	6.3	7.4	8.5	10.0	3.9
World, total	66.0	71.5	77.1	84.8	93.5	101.8	110.1	1.8

Source: U.S. Department of Energy, *International Energy Outlook 1999*, Table A4. Figures for 2000–2020 are for the "reference case," which assumes modest but not major increases in the price of oil. (Note: because of rounding, totals may not add up exactly.)

It is also possible that the introduction of new types of vehicular engines will reduce the use of petroleum in transportation. In the short term, oil consumption could be reduced by the use of cars propelled by "hybrid" engines that combine an electrical power system with a conventional gasoline-fueled motor. Hybrid automobiles of this sort went on sale in the year 2000. Even greater savings are expected in coming years from the introduction of vehicles powered by "fuel cells," devices that obtain energy from an electrochemical reaction. However, there is no evidence as yet that hybrid cars will be sold in large numbers, or that fuel cells (which in their present form are costly and bulky) will prove economical for the propulsion of private automobiles.[25] Under these circumstances, the U.S. Department of Energy foresees no slowdown in the steadily rising use of petroleum in transportation.[26]

It appears, then, that the global demand for oil will continue to rise in the years ahead, pushing daily consumption rates to ever higher levels. The big question thus becomes: will the oil industry be able to satisfy rising demand, or will significant shortages emerge? To answer this, we must turn to an examination of global supplies.

The Global Supply Equation

Until now, the global energy industry has largely succeeded in satisfying the worldwide demand for oil at an affordable price. To do so, oil producers have increased their output from approximately 10 million barrels per day in 1950 to 73 mbd in 1999. At some point, however, the petroleum industry will lose its ability to keep pace with soaring demand. This is because the world possesses only a certain amount of conventional (liquid) petroleum, and when half of this supply has been consumed—a critical milestone that is likely to be reached during the first or second decade of the twenty-first century—producers will encounter significant difficulties in increasing the rate of extraction. The result, eventually, will be recurring shortages of oil.

Just exactly *when* these shortages will emerge depends on the size of the world's remaining petroleum supply and the annual rate of extraction. The evolution of oil technology also figures in this equation: with the introduction of new and improved modes of production, it should be possible to extract a higher percentage of the oil found in any given reservoir and to exploit petroleum sources lying farther offshore or deeper underground. Obviously, it is impossible to calculate *exactly* how much oil will ultimately prove available for human use or when this supply will begin to run out; it is possible, however, to speculate with some accuracy when significant shortages are likely to arise.

To do this, the amount of oil that remains available for human use must be calculated. According to BP Amoco, the world possessed "proved" reserves holding an estimated 1,033 billion barrels of conventional petroleum at the end of 1999. These are reserves that, "with reasonable certainty," can be recovered "from known reservoirs under existing economic and operating conditions."[27] In addition, most analysts believe that the earth harbors an additional, "unproven" quantity of petroleum, with estimates of these reserves ranging from 200 to 900 billion barrels.* This leaves an untapped supply of approximately 1,250 to 1,950 billion barrels of petroleum at the start of the twenty-first century.

There is considerable debate among geologists as to whether the upper or the lower range of these estimates is the more accurate. Each side in this debate has brought persuasive arguments to bear. Those who favor the upper range maintain that exploration teams continue to find new sources of petroleum and that advances in oil-drilling technology will permit the exploitation of remote and deep-underground deposits that were once considered inaccessible.[29] Supporters of the lower figure argue that few new *major* deposits of petroleum have been discovered since the 1970s, and that the magnitude of many existing fields has been exaggerated for a variety of reasons—for example, to enable OPEC members to raise their annual production quotas (which are based on the size of a producer's declared reserves).[30] It appears sensible, therefore, to settle on an estimate that falls midway between the two extremes: an approach that gives us an untapped supply (in the year 2000) of approximately 1,600 billion barrels.[31]

---

*These figures are derived from calculations regarding the world's original (predrilling) supply of conventional petroleum. According to the various estimates of this supply, the earth possessed somewhere between 2,100 and 2,800 billion barrels of conventional petroleum before the onset of systematic drilling in the nineteenth century. Of this amount, approximately 850 billion barrels were consumed by 1999.[28]

At current rates of production—approximately 73 million barrels per day in 1999, or 26.6 billion barrels per year—the residual world supply of 1,600 billion barrels could theoretically satisfy global needs for another sixty years. This may prove to be welcome news for many people, suggesting that the problem of oil scarcity will not arise for many decades to come. But there are a number of problems with this estimate. To begin with, global consumption will not remain static but is likely to grow at a steady pace in the years ahead. If one accepts the DoE's prediction that worldwide consumption will rise by 1.9 percent per year between 1997 and 2020, reaching 113 million barrels per day (41 billion barrels per year) at the end of this period, the world will have devoured another 800 billion barrels of oil by 2020. This means that the remaining supply at that time will amount to about 850 billion barrels, or enough oil at the then-current rate of consumption to last another twenty-one years—bringing the moment of total depletion back to 2040, instead of 2060.

But even this somewhat reassuring calculation is subject to further skepticism. It is wholly unrealistic to assume that oil producers will be able to extract every last gallon of petroleum from known and unknown reservoirs. Some deposits are too small or too deep underground to justify the expense of extraction. Furthermore, because producers tend to exploit the easiest-to-reach supplies first and to leave the harder-to-reach reserves until later, eventually most of the world's easily exploited deposits will have been consumed, leaving only the hard-to-reach supplies.[32] Many geologists believe, in fact, that the rate of production of any given oil deposit begins to decline soon after the halfway point in exploitation has been passed. Looking at the global supply as a whole, the year when half the earth's original endowment of 2,450 billion barrels has been exhausted will be 2010, give or take a couple of years. This does not mean that significant shortfalls will begin to occur in 2011; it does mean, however, that the remaining petroleum could prove far more difficult to extract.[33]

Of course, much could happen between now and 2010 to alter this equation. A global economic crisis would significantly reduce the demand for oil, as would the widespread introduction of hydrogen-powered or hybrid vehicles. Alternatively, the supply of oil could be affected by the discovery of new deposits or the introduction of new oil-extraction technologies. As supplies dwindle, moreover, the price of oil will rise, thus increasing the incentive for exploitation of hard-to-reach petroleum deposits, as well as development of unconventional sources of energy such as the manufacture of liquid fuels from oil shale and tar sands.* It is possible, then, that oil will prove to be as plentiful in 2015 and 2020 as it is today, even if demand has risen significantly.[35] On the other hand, the global supply of petroleum could prove less abundant than originally assumed, if, for example, global reserves were found to be smaller than believed, or if future exploration efforts fail to locate major new sources of petroleum.[36]

Whether shortages occur sooner or later, the world economy, as presently constituted, remains hostage to the easy availability of petroleum at an acceptable cost. So long as oil flows in sufficient quantities, states will be able to expand their economies and otherwise meet the needs of growing and increasingly affluent populations. If oil supplies dwindle, however, or if prices rise above a tolerable level, many economies will suffer and large numbers of people will experience significant hardship. (A small taste of this was experienced in the spring of 2000, when gas prices in parts of the United States climbed over two dollars a gallon and angry truckers converged on Washington, D.C., to express their outrage; similar protests, on an even more massive scale, engulfed much of Europe in the early fall of that year.) In such circumstances, the governments of oil-importing nations will come under enormous pressure to do something: subsidize oil imports, impose mandatory rationing, release fuel from their strategic reserves, or employ force to remove any obstacles to the global flow of petroleum.[37]

---

*The world possesses substantial supplies of such materials. If they can be converted into usable liquids at a reasonable cost and without significant damage to the environment, the risk of future oil shortages will be significantly reduced. However, existing procedures for such conversion are costly, energy-intensive, and environmentally unfriendly. (The production of oil from tar sands, for example, requires a large quantity of water—itself a limited resource—and produces vast amounts of tailings, or waste materials.) Barring some future breakthroughs in technology, therefore, it does not seem prudent to rely on these materials as a convenient substitute for conventional petroleum.[34]

THE INESCAPABLE CONSTRAINTS OF GEOGRAPHY

As older fields are depleted, the global competition for oil will focus increasingly on those few areas of the world that still contain significant supplies of petroleum. These areas will automatically acquire increased strategic importance, as will the transit routes used for carrying oil to distant markets. Clearly, any instability or disorder in these critical areas could impede the continued flow of oil, thus provoking outside intervention. The relative likelihood of conflict is therefore closely related to the geography of oil distribution and to the political environment in key producing and transit regions.

The most significant fact about petroleum, from a world security point of view, is that so much of it is concentrated in a few major producing areas. As shown by Table 2.3, fourteen countries—Saudi Arabia, Iraq, the United Arab Emirates (UAE), Kuwait, Iran, Venezuela, Russia, Mexico, the United States, Libya, China, Nigeria, Norway, and the United Kingdom—jointly possess all but 10 percent of the known world supply. Among these fourteen, the possession of oil is even more highly concentrated, with the five leading producers—Saudi Arabia, Iraq, the UAE, Kuwait, and Iran—together holding nearly two-thirds of global reserves.

The high concentration of petroleum in a handful of major producing areas means that the global availability of oil is closely tied to political and socioeconomic conditions within a relatively small group of countries. When war or political turmoil erupts in these countries, and the global flow of oil is subsequently disrupted, the rest of the world is likely to experience significant economic hardship.[38] This was made painfully evident in 1973–74, when the Arab oil embargo produced widespread fuel shortages and triggered a prolonged economic recession; the same message was delivered again in 1979–80, following the revolution in Iran. A close look at Table 2.3 suggests, moreover, that such traumas can occur again in the future: a majority of the countries listed in this group have experienced war or revolution during the past ten to twenty years, and many continue to face internal or external challenges.

Table 2.3: Global Reserves and Production of Petroleum (As calculated in 1999)			
Producer (in order by reserves)	Estimated Reserves (bbl)	Percent of World Reserves	Production, 1998 (mbd)
Saudi Arabia	261.5	24.8	9.2
Iraq	112.5	10.7	2.2
United Arab Emirates	97.8	9.3	2.7
Kuwait	96.5	9.2	2.2
Iran	89.7	8.5	3.8
Venezuela	72.6	6.9	3.3
Russia	48.6	4.6	6.2
Mexico	47.8	4.5	3.5
United States	30.5	2.9	8.0
Libya	29.5	2.8	1.4
China	24.0	2.3	3.2
Nigeria	22.5	2.1	2.2
Norway/United Kingdom (North Sea)	16.1	1.5	6.0
Total	949.6	90.1	53.9

Source: BP Amoco, *Statistical Review of World Energy 1999.*
bbl = billion barrels
mbd = million barrels per day

The epicenter of all this disorder is, of course, the Middle East. That so many of the world's leading oil producers are located in this fractious region has long been a matter of grave concern for leaders of the major importing nations. Even before the discovery of oil, the states in this region were torn by internal divisions along ethnic and political lines, and by the historic rift between Sunni and Shiite Muslims. Once the flow of petroleum began, these divisions were further strained by disputes over the ownership of oil fields and the distribution of oil revenues. This fiery cauldron has been further heated in recent years by the rise of Islamic fundamentalism, the endurance of authoritarian regimes, and deep frustration (among many Arabs) over Israel's treatment of the Palestinians.[39]

Because the Middle East has so often been convulsed by social and political unrest, the major consuming nations have sought to reduce their dependence on Persian Gulf oil by developing alternative sources elsewhere. This is the impulse that led to the rapid development of North Sea and North Slope reserves in the 1970s and, more recently, to the establishment of new production areas in Africa, Latin America, and the Caspian region. "We are undergoing a fundamental shift away from reliance on Middle East oil," the National Security Council optimistically reported in 1998. "Venezuela [has become] our number one foreign supplier and Africa supplies 15 percent of our imported oil."[40]

But while shifting production to these other areas may diminish the importers' reliance on the Middle East, this does not guarantee that the new sources of petroleum will be any less free of disorder and conflict. Colombia and Nigeria, for example, have experienced considerable internal violence over the past few years, while Venezuela is going through a painful and potentially disruptive political transition. Nor is the Caspian Sea area likely to prove any less unstable than the Persian Gulf (a point to which we will return in chapter 4). It is true that the development of multiple producing areas allows consuming nations to switch from one source of oil to another when a crisis erupts in any individual area, but the number of such sources are few, and those among them that are entirely free of conflict (or the risk of conflict) are fewer still.

It is clear, then, that a strategy of diversification can succeed for only so long. Ultimately, the oil-importing countries will be forced to rely on the same group of unreliable suppliers in the Persian Gulf, the Caspian, Latin America, and Africa. Like it or not, major importing countries will have to pay close attention to political developments in key producing areas and will have to intervene—in one way or another—whenever local and regional turmoil threatens to disrupt the flow of petroleum.

The same is true of areas that do not themselves possess large supplies of petroleum but that are used for the *shipment* of oil—whether by tanker or by pipeline. Several such areas—the Strait of Hormuz (connecting the Persian Gulf to the Indian Ocean), the Red

Sea, the South China Sea, and Transcaucasia—lie astride or encompass areas of recurring conflict, and thus are likely to be the subject of continuing concern to the major importing countries. To highlight this point, the Department of Energy has produced a list of six "world oil-transit chokepoints" that are said to be at risk of closure; together, these six constricted passageways carry some 30 million barrels of oil per day—over 40 percent of total world consumption.[41] (See Table 2.4.)

Ensuring the safe transport of petroleum through such areas has become a matter of increasing concern to the major importing countries, especially the United States and Japan. Any attempt by a hostile power to block the flow of oil through these transit routes would almost certainly provoke a military response from Washington, and perhaps from other capitals as well. The United States has been particularly emphatic about its determination to resist any blockage of the Strait of Hormuz and has warned against the interdiction of oil routes in the South China Sea and other vital passageways. Tokyo has also expressed concern about the safety of oil traffic through the South China Sea and, like the United States, has built up its capacity to conduct naval operations in the area. (See chapters 3 and 5.)

Armed conflict is also possible in the case of disputed border zones or contested offshore areas that are believed to contain large deposits of petroleum. Many promising sources of oil are located in uninhabited border zones with poorly defined or contested boundaries, or in disputed maritime regions. Saudi Arabia, for instance, has yet to reach agreement with its neighbors over the exact location of key interior boundaries—many of which straddle important oil-bearing areas.[42] The establishment of exclusive economic zones in accordance with the United Nations Convention on the Law of the Sea has also produced disagreement over the location of offshore boundaries in a number of key energy-producing areas, including the Persian Gulf, the Caspian Sea, the Red Sea, and the South China Sea. (See Appendix for a list of territorial disputes that derive from or affect the ownership of vital petroleum reserves.)

The perceived value of these contested supplies is certain to rise as the demand for oil grows and other, more accessible sources of

	Table 2.4: World Oil Transit "Chokepoints"		
Chokepoint	Location	Oil Flow in 1998 (mbd)	Comments
Strait of Hormuz	At the mouth of the Persian Gulf, between Iran and Oman	15.4	A site of repeated clashes in the past; closure would prevent the flow of Persian Gulf oil to much of the world
Strait of Malacca	Between Malaysia and the Indonesian island of Sumatra; connects the Indian Ocean with the South China Sea	9.5	Closure would severely disrupt the flow of oil from the Persian Gulf to Japan, China, Taiwan, and South Korea
Bab el Mandeb	At the mouth of the Red Sea, between Yemen and Eritrea/Djibouti	3.3	Closure would prevent tankers from the Persian Gulf from reaching the Suez Canal and the Sumed pipeline
Suez Canal and Sumed Pipeline	Northeast Egypt; connects the Red Sea with the Mediterranean	3.1	A site of repeated clashes in the past; closure would severely disrupt the flow of oil from the Persian Gulf to Europe
Bosporus/Turkish Straits	The boundary between European and Asian Turkey; connects the Mediterranean to the Black Sea	1.7	Much of the oil from the Caspian is expected to flow through this passageway; it remains the main export route for Russian oil
Panama Canal	Central Panama; connects the Atlantic Ocean and the Caribbean with the Pacific Ocean	0.6	Closure would disrupt the flow of oil between the Atlantic and the Pacific

Source: U.S. Department of Energy, "World Oil Transit Chokepoints," August 1999.

petroleum are depleted. This, in turn, will surely increase the potential for friction and conflict between states claiming the same piece of territory and seeking to reap the maximum economic benefit from it. In most cases, such disputes will be confined to the immediate nations involved; they could, however, expand to include outside powers if the stakes were to appear particularly critical. Operation Desert Storm—which followed Iraq's invasion of Kuwait over a long-simmering border dispute—is a case in point.

In the future, intervention of this sort is especially likely in the Caspian region and the South China Sea, both of which are sites of resource-driven disputes over the ownership of offshore economic zones. In the Caspian, five states—Azerbaijan, Iran, Kazakhstan, Russia, and Turkmenistan—are contesting the location of offshore boundaries; in the South China Sea, seven states—Brunei, China, Indonesia, Malaysia, the Philippines, Taiwan, and Vietnam—are locked in a similar dispute. A serious outbreak of violence in either area could threaten the vital interests of many nations, inviting intervention by the United States and other oil-importing countries.

THE STRATEGIC TRIANGLE

Clearly, all three of these key factors—the politics of oil security, the dynamics of demand and supply, and the constraints of geography—will play a significant role in determining the likelihood and location of future conflict over oil. Each is sufficient in its own right to raise the specter of bloodshed, but it is the combination of all three that produces the high risk of war.

This danger will be present in most oil-producing areas, but the risk of significant conflict will be greatest in those areas where the supply of oil coincides with the competitive interests of the United States and major regional powers. As the twenty-first century commenced, this danger was most acute in a vast triangular region stretching from the Persian Gulf in the west to the Caspian Sea in the north and the South China Sea in the east. Within this "Strategic Triangle" can be found some of the world's largest concentrations of petroleum, along with numerous territorial disputes and the clashing security interests of powerful states.

Incorporated within the Strategic Triangle are three major oil-producing areas: the Persian Gulf, possessing approximately 65 percent of the world's known petroleum reserves; the Caspian Sea basin, producing little petroleum at present but possessing huge reserves of oil and natural gas; and East Asia, containing a number of existing fields and housing potentially large reserves in the South China Sea. Also located in this region are a number of secondary sources of hydrocarbons, including the Tarim basin of western China and the Yadana gas field in the Andaman Sea, off the west coast of Burma. Together, these three areas account for approximately 49 percent of current world oil production and 74 percent of currently identified reserves.[43]

Given the importance of the Strategic Triangle to global energy supplies and the high risk of conflict within, it is appropriate to begin this study of resource conflict with an assessment of conflict dynamics in this critical region.

3

Oil Conflict in the Persian Gulf

Of all the world's major oil-producing areas, the Persian Gulf region is the one most likely to experience conflict in the next century. Possessing nearly two-thirds of global petroleum supplies, the Gulf is certain to remain the focus of intense worldwide competition as energy demand rises in the decades ahead. In addition, the region is riven by a multitude of power rivalries, religious schisms, and territorial disputes. These divisions have often triggered violence in the past and are likely to do so again in the future. And because any such upheaval can jeopardize the global supply of oil, intervention by outside powers—especially the United States—is an ever-present possibility.

Many factors contribute to the likelihood of war in the Gulf area, not all of which are connected to oil. Political ambition, religious differences, and greed regularly provoked conflict in the years before 1908, when the first significant deposits of petroleum were found in Iran. But the presence of vast supplies of energy in the Gulf is likely to increase both the frequency of warfare and its relative destructiveness. For one thing, many important energy reserves lie in areas that are claimed by two or more states or in featureless border regions with no established boundaries. Because the possession of these disputed areas can produce billions of dollars in annual oil and gas revenues, the various claimants may choose to seize the territory through force rather than allow a rival to obtain all or part of these royalties. Conflict can also arise in situations where a large oil reservoir spans the border between two countries or when one state attempts to extract a disproportionate share of the total supply. (Iraq accused Kuwait of taking more than its rightful measure of the shared Rumaila field in the late 1980s; this provided a pretext for the Iraqi invasion of 1990.)

The presence of large reserves of oil in the Gulf has increased the likelihood and potential intensity of interstate conflict in another manner, by giving the nations of the region the means to procure vast quantities of modern weapons. Ever since the OPEC oil price rises of 1973–74 brought them added income, the Gulf countries have jointly spent hundreds of billions of dollars on imported arms—in many cases, obtaining the most sophisticated and lethal systems available. The acquisition of so much advanced weaponry has inevitably fueled the expansionist impulses of certain Gulf leaders, including the former shah of Iran (who intervened in the Omani civil war in the mid-1970s) and Saddam Hussein of Iraq. Many analysts believe that Hussein's 1990 invasion of Kuwait was triggered in part by a belief that his forces were so well armed that no outside power would contest Iraq's annexation of the emirate.[1] Whenever warfare has broken out, moreover, the presence of large numbers of modern weapons has naturally elevated the scale and intensity of the fighting. (The Iran-Iraq war of 1980–88, for example, produced an estimated one million casualties and over $100 billion in property damage.)

Increased oil income has also increased the risk of *internal* conflict in the Gulf, particularly in those countries where the bulk of such funds have gone to a small princely or business elite. Although most of these countries have attempted to avert domestic strife over the distribution of petroleum revenues by providing extraordinary benefits to their citizens (including free education and medical care and subsidized food, housing, and energy), the accumulation of so much wealth in the hands of a prominent elite has naturally aroused a certain amount of resentment on the part of those who are less privileged. When this resentment has been fused with other sources of discontent—whether of a religious, political, or ideological nature—the results have often proved explosive.

Many of these factors, of course, can be found in other regions that harbor large supplies of petroleum. What sets the Persian Gulf apart from these other areas is the fact that the great powers, including Great Britain and the United States, have chosen to intervene in local disputes when they perceived a threat to the free flow of oil. Britain played a key role in Gulf affairs from before World War I until the early 1970s; the United States has been a major regional actor since the 1950s. Acting on the belief that access to Persian Gulf energy was essential to their nations' security, leaders of both countries have regularly sanctioned the use of force to overcome what were seen as impediments to continued production and supply.

Great Britain no longer exercises a major military role in the Gulf. The United States, however, has steadily expanded its military presence in the region. Even as U.S. troop strength has been diminished in other potential theaters of war, such as Europe and the Far East, additional forces have been deployed in the Gulf. In ordering these deployments, American officials have been very clear about their intentions: the United States will not permit a hostile state to acquire the ability to obstruct the free flow of oil from the Gulf to major markets in the West. This principle—first articulated by President Carter in January 1980—was invoked on several occasions in the 1980s and '90s to justify the use of force by American troops in the Gulf; it is likely to trigger additional U.S. interventions in the decades ahead.

American officials claim that the conspicuous presence of U.S. troops in the Gulf and the demonstrated willingness of successive administrations to endorse the use of force will reduce the risk of conflict by deterring potential adversaries from obstructing the flow of oil.[2] But while American might may well have discouraged some potential challengers from playing a more assertive role in the Gulf area, the very magnitude of the American military presence—along with Washington's periodic use of force—has also *provoked* opposition to U.S. policies. This is especially evident in Saudi Arabia, where the growing deployment of American troops has aroused fierce hostility from militant Islamic leaders who resent the presence of non-Muslims on their soil and decry America's close ties with Israel. Similarly, continuing U.S. air strikes on Iraq have alienated many pro-Western Iraqis who might otherwise direct their ire toward Saddam Hussein. The recurring attacks on Iraq, coupled with continuing economic sanctions, have also angered people in neighboring countries who have come to believe that the United States is more likely to employ force against Arabs and Muslims than against other likely foes.

Taken together, these factors are a recipe for recurring violence. The question, then, is not whether there will be conflict in the Persian Gulf, but when and of what sort. This chapter will examine the critical stakes at risk in the Gulf, the trajectory of U.S. military strategy in the area, and the myriad sources of potential strife.

THE UNIQUE STATUS OF THE GULF

The signal importance of the Persian Gulf area to global conflict dynamics is entirely the product of geology: an estimated 65 percent of the world's untapped petroleum reserves are located in this area, and many geologists believe that future discoveries will add to the region's net supply. The Gulf's oil deposits are also highly concentrated and located close to the surface, meaning that they are among the easiest to find and develop. While it is possible that new supplies of petroleum will be found in the North Atlantic or Siberia, or in other remote locations, the Gulf area alone can provide the vast amounts of hydrocarbons that will be needed to satisfy rising demand in the twenty-first century.

The Persian Gulf oil-producing region comprises five major and several secondary suppliers. Heading the list of the major producers is Saudi Arabia, with an estimated 263.5 billion barrels (bbl) in proven reserves, representing approximately 25 percent of the world

Table 3.1: Oil Production and Reserves in the Persian Gulf Area, 1999				
Country	Production, mbd	Percent of World Total	Proven Reserves, bbl	Percent of World Reserves
Iran	3.55	5.1	89.7	8.7
Iraq	2.58	3.6	112.5	10.9
Kuwait	2.03	2.9	96.5	9.3
Oman	0.91	1.3	5.3	0.5
Qatar	0.72	1.0	3.7	0.4
Saudi Arabia	8.60	11.9	263.5	25.5
UAE	2.51	3.2	97.8	9.4
Yemen	0.40	0.6	4.0	0.4
Other	0.10	0.1	0.2	–
Total	21.40	29.7	673.2	65.1

Source: BP Amoco, *Statistical Review of World Energy 2000.*
bbl = billion barrels
mbd = million barrels per day

total. Next in line are four other states with very large reserves: Iraq (with 112.5 bbl in reserves), the United Arab Emirates (97.8 bbl), Kuwait (96.5 bbl), and Iran (89.7 bbl). Also included are a number of secondary suppliers, notably Bahrain, Oman, Qatar, and Yemen. Together, these nine countries produced an average of 21.3 million barrels of oil per day in 1999, or 30 percent of total world production; they also possessed an estimated 673 billion barrels of untapped oil, representing 65 percent of total world reserves.[3] (See Table 3.1.)

The key factor here is *reserves.* With proven reserves of 673 billion barrels of oil, plus an unknown quantity of uncharted supplies, the Gulf states can continue to extract oil from the ground for several decades to come at current or even higher rates of production— without depleting their available reservoirs. Other major producers have smaller reserves to begin with and tend to exploit their available supplies at a faster rate. The United States, for example, is currently producing oil at the rate of about 2.8 billion barrels per year; if that rate is maintained in the years ahead and no new deposits of oil are discovered, U.S. reserves—estimated at 28.6 billion barrels in 2000—

will be fully depleted by 2010. In the Gulf, however, existing reserves are so vast that even with a projected increase in the rate of production—from 20 to 40 million barrels per day—a substantial supply of oil will remain in the ground in 2010 and beyond.

In considering the matter of reserves, special mention must be made of Saudi Arabia. This desert kingdom is not only the world's leading producer of oil—extracting 8.6 million barrels per day in 1999, or 12 percent of total worldwide production—but is also the paramount owner of untapped supplies. With proven reserves of 264 billion barrels, Saudi Arabia alone harbors more oil than North America, South America, Europe, and the former Soviet Union combined. Most geologists believe, moreover, that continued exploration will result in the discovery of additional reserves, thus enhancing Saudi Arabia's status as the world's leading supplier of petroleum.[4]

The fact that Saudi Arabia and the other major Gulf suppliers possess such vast reserves of oil also means that they alone can expand production on a large enough scale to satisfy the anticipated increase in global demand. If worldwide oil consumption increases by 55 percent between 1997 and 2020, as predicted by the U.S. Department of Energy, a significant share of the additional petroleum will have to come from the Gulf—there simply is no other pool of oil large enough to sustain an increase of this magnitude. It is for this reason alone that all projections of future supply and demand assume that the Persian Gulf will account for an ever-expanding share of the world's oil requirements: from 27 percent in 1990 to 33 percent in 2010 and 39 percent in 2020.[5]

As the century proceeds, the oil-importing states will become ever more dependent on energy supplies from the Gulf. According to the DoE, global imports of Persian Gulf petroleum will more than double between 1997 and 2020, from 16.3 to 36.4 million barrels per day. Not every country is expected to experience a big rise in imports from the Gulf area, but for some the increase will be substantial: Chinese imports, for example, are predicted to jump by 960 percent over the next two decades, from 0.5 to 5.3 mbd; imports by developing Asia will rise by 114 percent, from 4.2 to 9.0 mbd; and imports by the North American countries will rise by 105 percent, from 2.0 to 4.1 mbd, according to projections.[6] (See Table 3.2.)

The industrialized world's growing dependence on Persian Gulf energy will exacerbate many of the pressures described earlier in this chapter. Oil and gas deposits located in contested areas will become increasingly valuable, and so the claimants to these reserves will face greater temptation to seize and occupy them through the use of force. Similarly, ambitious leaders could be tempted to expand their oil holdings by annexing neighboring countries, as Saddam Hussein tried to do in 1990. The further concentration of petroleum income in the hands of ruling elites could also provoke an increase in revolutionary fervor among those less fortunate. Any of these developments, moreover, could jeopardize the free flow of oil, leading to military intervention by the United States.[7]

Increased international dependence on Persian Gulf energy will also generate new sources of conflict. As more and more nations come to rely on the Gulf for their essential imports of petroleum, the competition for access to the available supply will intensify. Market forces will, of course, help alleviate these pressures by allowing better-off countries to procure what they need through the payment of higher fees, and by compelling less-wealthy states to somehow dampen demand. But some importing countries may seek alternative means of satisfying their requirements, such as forming military alliances with local powers and trading weapons and other forms of assistance for oil. Such arrangements have already been tried in the Gulf—France maintained ties with Saddam Hussein before 1990, while China is said to have formed such a relationship with Iran[8]—and could become more common in the years ahead. With many states competing for access to oil in this manner, relations between rivals within the region will become more strained and the risk of combat between them will grow. In a worst-case scenario, this could lead to a clash between the external backers of rising Gulf powers.[9]

Market forces can also fail in another way: by causing oil prices to rise to such a level as to create widespread economic hardship in importing countries, and so lead to demonstrations, strikes, riots, and other forms of civic strife. In such an environment, political leaders are bound to consider extreme measures to restore public order. This

Table 3.2: Global Imports of Persian Gulf Oil, 1997 and 2020
(In millions of barrels per day)

Importing Region and Country	Actual Imports, 1997	Estimated Imports, 2020	Percent Increase, 1997–2020
North America*	2.0	4.1	105
Western Europe	3.5	3.7	6
Developed Asia**	4.8	5.5	15
China	0.5	5.3	960
Developing East and Southeast Asia	4.2	9.0	114
All others	1.3	8.8	577
Total, all countries	16.3	36.4	123

Source: U.S. Department of Energy, *International Energy Outlook 2000*, Table 13.
*The United States, Canada, and Mexico
**Japan, Australia, and New Zealand

could mean the imposition of gasoline rationing, price controls, or the declaration of martial law. It could also include military action abroad. Such action has, in fact, been contemplated by American strategists in the past, and could emerge as the favored response to future crises of this sort.[10]

THE EVOLUTION OF U.S. STRATEGY

In the pursuit of what are viewed as vital national interests, American leaders have persistently argued that the United States must be able to employ military power if needed to ensure the continued flow of oil from the Persian Gulf producers to markets in the West. "America's vital interests in [the Gulf] are long-standing," General Anthony C. Zinni, then commander in chief of the U.S. Central Command (CENTCOM), told Congress in 1999. "With over 65 percent of the world's oil reserves located within the Gulf states," the United States and its allies "must have free access to the region's resources."[11] But while U.S. objectives have remained consistent over a long period of time, the strategies employed to achieve this goal have changed with the trend toward an ever-increasing commitment of American military power.

American policy makers first articulated the principle of securing Gulf oil supplies in 1943, when President Franklin D. Roosevelt authorized the delivery of U.S. military assistance to Saudi Arabia. Believing that the Western powers would become highly dependent on Persian Gulf oil after the war, administration officials concluded that the United States—which until that point had paid little attention to the Gulf—would have to exercise a more conspicuous role in the area. This led to the establishment of diplomatic relations with Saudi Arabia and, in 1945, to a face-to-face meeting between President Roosevelt and King Abdel-Aziz Ibn Saud, the founder of the modern Saudi state.[12] The designation of Persian Gulf oil as a vital security interest did not, however, lead to the immediate buildup of American forces in the area; instead, U.S. strength was built up over time, reflecting changes in the orientation of national strategy.

Initially, in the early Cold War period, the United States maintained a relatively low profile in the Gulf. Rather than station large numbers of American soldiers there, Washington chose to rely on Great Britain—the traditional hegemon in the area—to maintain regional stability. This changed in 1968, however, when then Prime Minister Harold Wilson announced that London would withdraw its military forces from "East of Suez" by the end of 1971. Convinced that the withdrawal of the British would produce a dangerous vacuum in the Gulf, American strategists determined that Washington would have to assume primary responsibility for the maintenance of stability. Following an intensive review of American interests in the Gulf by the National Security Council—then headed by Henry Kissinger— President Nixon signed National Security Decision Memorandum No. 92, mandating an expanded U.S. presence in the region.[13]

Coming when it did, the decision to upgrade U.S. involvement in the Gulf posed a significant dilemma for senior policy makers. With the fighting in Vietnam then at its peak, and the American public reluctant to endorse another major military commitment in a Third World area, the administration was unable to deploy large numbers of U.S. troops in the Gulf. To resolve this dilemma, Washington adopted what came to be known as the "Surrogate Strategy"—a policy of utilizing friendly local powers to serve as the "guardians" of Western interests with substantial U.S. military assistance and strategic guidance from Washington. "What we decided," Under Secretary of State Joseph J. Sisco later explained, "is that we would try to stimulate and be helpful to the two key countries in this area—namely, Iran and Saudi Arabia—that . . . they could become the major elements of stability as the British were getting out."[14]

The surrogate policy governed American strategy in the Gulf for most of the 1970s. Between 1970 and 1978 alone, Washington sold Iran over $20 billion worth of sophisticated weaponry—producing what Representative Gerry E. Studds of Massachusetts termed "the most rapid buildup of military power under peacetime conditions of any nation in the history of the world."[15] But while American weaponry helped Iran defend itself against its foreign enemies, it proved far less useful in protecting the shah, Mohammad Reza Pahlavi, against his domestic opponents. Indeed, the shah's conspicuous ties with Washington were seen by many in the country—especially among the Muslim clergy—as evidence of his pernicious and heretical embrace of the West. By late 1978, domestic opposition to the shah had reached massive proportions, and on January 16, 1979, he fled the country; within months, Iran had fallen under the control of a radical Islamic regime headed by Ayatollah Ruholla Khomeini.

The fall of the shah and the rise of Khomeini forced a thorough reassessment of American strategy in the Gulf. Of the two key "pillars" of the Surrogate Strategy, Iran and Saudi Arabia, the former was by far the stronger and the latter was much too weak to protect vital Western interests on its own. Although Washington attempted to bolster Saudi defenses through massive infusions of American weaponry, it was evident to senior policy makers that the surrogate approach was no longer viable and that, as a consequence, the United States would have to assume *direct* responsibility for stability in the Gulf. It is against this backdrop that President Carter issued his famous statement of January 1980 in which he described the Gulf as a "vital interest" of the United States and warned that an attack on this area "will be repelled by any means necessary, including military force."

To invest this pronouncement with credibility, President Carter established the Rapid Deployment Force (RDF)—a group of combat units based in the United States but available for use in the Gulf when the need arose. Carter also initiated the acquisition of new U.S. military bases in the region, upgraded existing bases, and authorized an expanded navy presence in Middle Eastern waters. This included the deployment of a permanent U.S. naval force in the Gulf, with its headquarters in Bahrain. Although widely derided at the time, these moves laid the foundation for the much enhanced U.S. capability now deployed in the region.[16] (In 1983, the RDF was reconstituted as the U.S. Central Command, or CENTCOM, and assigned additional responsibilities; the naval force at Bahrain later formed the nucleus of the U.S. Fifth Fleet.)

Initially, the RDF/CENTCOM was intended to protect the Gulf area against a hypothetical Soviet invasion. By the late 1980s, however, American policy makers had begun to worry about the growing military might of Iraq. Triumphant in its eight-year war with Iran (1980–88) and well-equipped with modern French and Soviet weapons, Iraq began issuing threats to its southern Gulf neighbors, particularly Kuwait and Saudi Arabia. Fearing that domination of the area by Saddam Hussein would jeopardize Western access to vital petroleum supplies, U.S. strategists turned their attention from the Soviet Union to Iraq. In late 1989, the chairman of the Joint Chiefs of Staff, General Colin Powell, authorized the newly appointed commander in chief of CENTCOM, General H. Norman Schwarzkopf, to prepare a blueprint for all-out combat with the Iraqis.[17]

General Schwarzkopf and his staff labored throughout the first five months of 1990 to develop such a blueprint. As reported in the media, the resulting document—known officially as Operational Plan (OpPlan) 1002–90—called for the deployment of several armored and mechanized divisions to the Gulf along with a powerful array of air and naval forces. To test this blueprint, CENTCOM conducted an elaborate "command post exercise" based on a hypothetical U.S.-Iraqi engagement in mid-July 1990. The exercise was barely completed when, on August 2, Saddam Hussein commenced the invasion of Kuwait. Schwarzkopf was immediately summoned to a crisis meeting with top White House officials at Camp David, Maryland; two days later he was ordered by President Bush to begin preparations for the actual implementation of OpPlan 1002–90. The result, six months later, was Operation Desert Storm.[18]

AFTER DESERT STORM

The 1991 Gulf conflict set an important precedent for U.S. military involvement in the region. Up until that point, American strategy had been designed to minimize the direct involvement of U.S. troops in any regional conflict; in Operation Desert Storm, however, the United States contributed the overwhelming majority of the forces involved. Once the war was concluded, moreover, senior American officials made it clear that Washington was prepared to assume the lead role again or, if required, to act entirely on its own. "The U.S. will continue to use a variety of means to promote regional security and stability [in the Gulf], working with our friends and allies," Assistant Secretary of Defense Joseph Nye declared in 1995. But it "will remain prepared to defend vital U.S. interests in the region—*unilaterally if necessary*" (emphasis added).[19]

Operation Desert Storm also established the prevailing model for American military intervention in the Gulf: a rapid buildup of air, sea, and ground forces followed by a crushing offensive employing high-tech weaponry. Every imaginable U.S. advantage in firepower, mobility, intelligence, and communications was to be employed in an effort to shatter enemy defenses with a minimum loss of American lives. "The ability to project overwhelming and decisive military power is key to CENTCOM's theater strategy as well as our ability to shape the battlefield," General Zinni told Congress in 1999.[20] These two principles—a commitment to unilateral intervention in the Gulf and a war-fighting doctrine of "decisive victory"—are the key features of prevailing U.S. military strategy in the region.

Table 3.3: U.S. Naval Forces in the Persian Gulf, January 1998			
Type of Warship	Vessel	Principal Armament	Crew
Aircraft carriers	USS *Nimitz*	14 F-14 fighters; 36 F/A-18 fighters; 4 EA-6B electronic warfare planes; 23 other aircraft	5,500
	USS *George Washington*	14 F-14 fighters; 36 F/A-18 fighters; 4 EA-6B electronic warfare planes; 21 other aircraft	5,500
Cruiser	USS *Normandy*	Tomahawk cruise missile, Standard missile, Harpoon missile	358
Destroyers	USS *Carney*	Tomahawk cruise missile, Standard missile, Harpoon missile	339
	USS *John Young*	Tomahawk cruise missile, Standard missile, Harpoon missile	339
	USS *Barry*	Tomahawk cruise missile, Standard missile, Harpoon missile	300
	USS *Ingersoll*	n/a	300
Guided missile frigates	USS *Reuben James*	Standard missile, Harpoon missile	200
	USS *Samuel B. Roberts*	Standard missile, Harpoon missile	200
Attack submarines	USS *Annapolis*	Tomahawk cruise missile, Mk-48 torpedo	133
	USS *L. Mendel Rivers*	n/a	107
Mine warfare ships	USS *Dextrous*	Mine Neutralization System	81
	USS *Ardent*	Mine Neutralization System	81

Source: U.S. Navy (electronic communication, January 12, 1998).
n/a = not available

These principles have been put to the test on several other occasions. In January and February of 1998, and then again in November and December of that year, the United States deployed a substantial force in the Gulf to conduct sustained air and missile attacks on Iraq. (See Table 3.3.) The first round of attacks was called off at the last minute, after Saddam Hussein agreed to open up suspected Iraqi weapons sites to U.N. inspection; the second round was initiated in December 1998 when he refused all further cooperation with the

United Nations. In neither of these instances did the United States receive significant support from the international community.[21] Nevertheless, American officials continue to state that U.S. forces are prepared to conduct further strikes against Iraq whenever such action is deemed appropriate.[22]

Since then the United States has further bolstered its strength in the Persian Gulf area. Because it is not feasible to station large numbers of American soldiers in the region on a permanent basis—the costs would be enormous, and none of America's local allies are keen to house a sizable force of non-Muslims on their territory—the Department of Defense is relying instead on deploying troops there quickly when a crisis erupts. To accomplish this, the Pentagon has "prepositioned" vast supplies of heavy equipment at depots in the region and acquired new ships and aircraft to carry a substantial combat force from the United States to the Gulf.[23] The army has already stored sufficient weaponry for an entire brigade in Kuwait, and is constructing a second such facility in Qatar. In addition, the Marine Corps has stored the heavy equipment for an expeditionary force of 15,000 soldiers aboard prepositioning ships in the area, and the air force has stockpiled sufficient hardware to establish a "bare bones" fighter base on very short notice.[24]

American strategy also seeks to strengthen the military capabilities of friendly powers, especially Kuwait and Saudi Arabia, and to reduce (or "degrade") the capabilities of hostile states, notably Iraq and Iran.

To boost the fighting capacity of its allies, the United States has provided vast quantities of modern arms to member states of the Gulf Cooperation Council (GCC), a loose alliance of Bahrain, Kuwait, Oman, Qatar, Saudi Arabia, and the United Arab Emirates. The aim is not to make these states militarily self-sufficient but rather to improve their ability to assist American forces in the event of a major conflagration. "The GCC states will not be able to repel external aggression from either Iraq or Iran," the Pentagon's Institute for National Security Studies noted in 1998. However, with sufficient U.S. assistance, "their forces could make a distinct contribution to a joint effort with the United States."[25]

Washington has sold the GCC countries some of its most capable and sophisticated weapons systems, including F-15 and F-16 fighter aircraft, M-1 tanks, AH-64 Apache attack helicopters, and the Patriot air-defense missile. Between 1990 and 1997 alone, the United States provided these countries with arms and ammunition worth over $42 billion—the largest and most costly transfer of military equipment to any region in the world by any single supplier in recent history.[26] (See Tables 3.4 and 3.5.) The Department of Defense has also provided training to thousands of friendly military personnel, and U.S. forces regularly engage in joint military exercises with GCC member states.

The close relationship between U.S. arms transfers and the broader goals of American strategy in the Gulf is especially evident in the March 2000 sale of eighty upgraded F-16 fighters to the United Arab Emirates. The fighter deal, worth an estimated $7 billion, is unusual in several respects. To begin with, the aircraft sold to the UAE—the so-called Block-60 variant of the F-16—are to be equipped with electronic and radar systems far more sophisticated than those installed on the F-16s supplied to the U.S. Air Force.[27] Even more significant, the sales arrangement allows the United States to operate its own aircraft from the fighter base being built by the UAE to house its F-16s and to preposition military equipment there. Pentagon documents further suggest that the F-16 transaction is intended to lead to other forms of cooperation with the UAE, including the use of its ports by American naval vessels.[28] "U.S. forces could respond to the region quicker and more effectively if bases, ports, and the infrastructure they require were available [in the UAE]," the air force told Congress on March 7, 2000.[29]

To degrade the capabilities of Iran and Iraq—an approach known as "threat reduction"—the United States has imposed economic and trade sanctions and, in the case of Iraq, has conducted air and missile strikes against military installations and arms-production facilities. These policies aim to diminish Iran and Iraq's capacity to manufacture nuclear, chemical, and biological munitions—so-called weapons of mass destruction (WMD)—and ballistic missile delivery systems.*

---

*Iraq is subject to comprehensive trade sanctions in accordance with U.N. Security Council Resolution 687 of March 1991 and other Security Council resolutions; Iran is subject to a U.S.-imposed ban on foreign investment under the Iran-Libya Sanctions Act of 1996.

Table 3.4:
U.S. Arms Transfer Agreements with Selected Persian Gulf States, 1990–97
(In millions of current U.S. dollars)

Recipient	1990–93	1994–97	Total, 1990–97
Bahrain	300	300	600
Kuwait	3,700	500	4,200
Oman	100	0	100
Saudi Arabia	32,000	4,200	36,200
UAE	600	300	900
Total	36,700	5,300	42,000

Source: Congressional Research Service, *Conventional Arms Transfers to Developing Nations, 1990–1997*, July 31, 1998, p. 51.

Measures of this sort are viewed as an important part of the policy of "dual containment," under which the United States has sought to constrain the political and military influence of Iran and Iraq.[30]

While sanctions remain the preferred mechanism for eroding the military power of hostile states, the United States has also engaged in direct military action to accomplish this purpose. The goal of the December 1998 bombing campaign against Iraq, known as Operation Desert Fox, was, according to President Clinton, to cripple "Iraq's nuclear, chemical, and biological weapons programs and its military capacities to threaten its neighbors."[31] Since Desert Fox, the United States has continued to strike at military installations in Iraq as part of a systematic effort to degrade Iraqi capabilities.

All of these endeavors—the expansion of U.S. basing and logistical capabilities, the strengthening of allied forces, and the degradation of adversary strength—are part of a consistent, integrated policy aimed at bolstering American military dominance in the Persian Gulf area. Indeed, securing such dominance in the Gulf has been one of the most important and persistent goals of American strategy since 1980, when the Rapid Deployment Force was first established. All signs indicate that this goal will continue to govern U.S. strategy in the opening decades of the twenty-first century.

Table 3.5: Major U.S. Arms Transfers to Persian Gulf States, 1990–98

Recipient	Year	Value	Quantity and Item
Bahrain	1997	$303 million	20 F-16A/B aircraft
Kuwait	1992	$2.5 billion	6 Patriot air-defense fire units with 450 Patriot missiles; 6 Hawk air-defense missile batteries with 342 Hawk missiles
	1993	$4.5 billion	256 M-1A2 Abrams tanks; 125 M-113 APCs, 52 M-577 command post carriers; 130,000 rounds of 120mm tank ammunition
	1994	$692 million	16 AH-64 Apache attack helicopters with 500 Hellfire antitank missiles
	1995	$461 million	16 UH-60L Blackhawk helicopters
	1998	$609 million	48 M109A6 howitzers, 18 M88A2 recovery vehicles, and 24 M-113A3 APCs
Oman	1991	$150 million	119 V-300 Commando armored vehicles
Saudi Arabia	1990	$3.4 billion	1,117 Light Armored Vehicles, 2,000 TOW antitank missiles, and related base construction for the SANG
	1990	$206 million	150 M-60A3 tanks
	1990	$2 billion	24 F-15C/D Eagle fighter aircraft
	1990	$300 million	12 AH-64 Apache attack helicopters with 150 Hellfire antitank missiles
	1990	$984 million	6 Patriot air-defense fire units with 384 Patriot missiles
	1990	$3.1 billion	150 M-1A2 Abrams tanks, 200 M-2 Bradley Infantry Fighting Vehicles, 207 M-113 APCs
	1991	$3.3 billion	12 Patriot air-defense fire units with 758 Patriot missiles and support gear
	1992	$9 billion	72 F-15XP Eagle fighter aircraft plus 900 Maverick AGM missiles, 300 Sidewinder AAM missiles, and 300 Sparrow AAM missiles
	1995	$690 million	195,000 rounds of 90mm ammunition and other items for the SANG
	1997	$1.4 billion	Maintenance and construction services for 5 E-3 AWACS aircraft and 7 KE-3A aerial refueling tankers; 130 90mm turret weapons systems for Light Armored Vehicles
United Arab Emirates	1991	$682 million	20 AH-64 Apache attack helicopters with 620 Hellfire antitank missiles
	1994	$330 million	10 AH-64 Apache attack helicopters with 360 Hellfire antitank missiles

Table 3.5 (*continued*)			
Recipient	Year	Value	Quantity and Item
	1998	$7 billion	80 F-16C/D fighter aircraft with 491 AMRAAM missiles, 267 Sidewinder AAM missiles, 1,163 Maverick AGM missiles, and other bombs and missiles

Source: Arms Control Association (ACA), "ACA Register of U.S. Arms Transfers," ACA, Washington, D.C., May 1997; also ACA lists of pending arms transfers for 1997 and 1998.
AAM = air-to-air missiile
AGM = air-to-ground missile
APC = armored personnel carrier
SANG = Saudi Arabia National Guard

THE THREE-WAR SCENARIO

Military commanders can never be fully certain of the types and locations of the conflicts they will have to fight, so they like to prepare for a wide range of hypothetical contingencies. The American buildup in the Gulf has been carried out with no specific scenario in mind; instead it gives U.S. policy makers the capacity to prevail in any conceivable conflict situation. But American strategists have identified three basic scenarios for combat in the Gulf: (1) a recurrence of the 1990 Iraqi drive on the oil fields of Kuwait and Saudi Arabia; (2) an effort by Iran to close the Strait of Hormuz or otherwise imperil oil shipping in the Gulf itself; and (3) an internal revolt against the Saudi royal family. Under current U.S. policy, American forces must be able to prevail in all three of these scenarios—alone, or in any combination.

In a sense, the United States has been confronting these challenges for some time already. American forces continue to clash with Iraqi military units on a regular basis, U.S. warships patrol the Gulf and adjacent waters throughout the year, and Washington is orchestrating an international campaign against Osama bin Laden and other sworn enemies of the Saudi regime. These activities sometimes lead to violent incidents that are duly noted in the international press. What is missing from such accounts, however, is an understanding of how these individual episodes fit into a larger, more complex set of conflict systems.

Persian Gulf Region

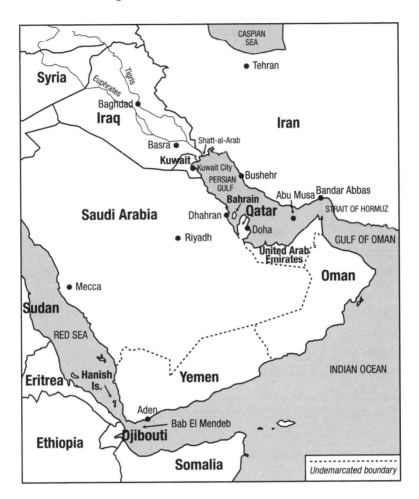

Containing Iraq

At present, the scenario receiving the greatest attention from Washington is the threat of a new Iraqi drive against Kuwait and Saudi Arabia. Although Iraqi forces are much weaker today than they were in 1990 when Saddam Hussein ordered the original invasion of Kuwait, U.S. officials continue to worry about Iraqi designs on the southern Gulf states. "Saddam's history of aggression leaves little doubt that he would resume his drive for regional domination and his quest for weapons of mass destruction if he had the chance,"

Samuel R. Berger, President Clinton's national security adviser, observed in 1998. For this reason, he noted, the United States has taken a variety of steps to constrain Iraqi power and to enhance America's ability to defeat a new Iraqi onslaught with a minimum risk to allied forces.[32]

American efforts to weaken Iraqi power are aimed, in the first instance, at Baghdad's conventional forces. While these forces are much less powerful than those engaged in the 1990 invasion of Kuwait, they remain substantial. According to General J. H. Binford Peay III, the former commander of CENTCOM, "Saddam continues to field the largest army in the region. . . . It is a force that has proven it can mobilize and deploy quickly and continue to threaten Kuwait and Saudi Arabia."[33] Peay and other U.S. officials place particular emphasis on the threat posed by the Republican Guards, a highly mobile force that has spearheaded many Iraqi assaults in the past.

Iraq is also said to possess a residual chemical and biological weapons industry along with ballistic missile delivery systems. The exact dimensions of this capacity are not fully known, as Saddam Hussein has gone to great lengths to hide the remnants of Iraq's once-formidable WMD capabilities. The bulk of these facilities were destroyed by Operation Desert Storm or by the United Nations Special Commission (UNSCOM), the body established in 1991 to oversee the implementation of U.N. Security Council Resolution 687 (which prohibits Iraq from possessing ballistic missiles and weapons of mass destruction). Nevertheless, most Western analysts believe that the Iraqis were able to hide some plans and equipment from UNSCOM inspectors—all of whom were expelled in late 1998—and so could be capable of reconstituting a limited ability to manufacture chemical and biological weapons.[34]

To diminish the threat posed by Iraqi military capabilities, the United States has engaged in a wide range of preventive efforts. These include: economic and trade sanctions, a naval blockade to enforce the trade embargo, the enforcement of a no-fly zone and no-drive zone over southern Iraq, a no-fly zone over northern Iraq, periodic air and missile attacks on Iraqi military installations, the prepositioning of U.S. military equipment in Kuwait and Qatar, and the constant rotation of American combat units through the region. Together, these efforts represent a substantial commitment of U.S. resources, entailing the permanent deployment of over 20,000 American soldiers in the Gulf and the expenditure of many billions of dollars per year.[35]

Except at moments of heightened tension, the most taxing aspects of this costly effort are the enforcement of trade sanctions and the no-fly and no-drive zones.* Maintenance of the southern no-fly zone, which excludes all Iraqi aircraft from the airspace extending southward from the 33rd parallel to the Kuwaiti border, is an especially demanding task. By January 2000, the aircraft assigned to Operation Southern Watch—the Pentagon's name for this effort—had flown over 240,000 individual flights over the exclusion zone.[36] Since December 1998, moreover, the aircraft participating in Southern Watch have encountered increased resistance from the Iraqis and have responded with a steady barrage of missiles.[37]

The United States has also periodically engaged in what Samuel Berger called "disarmament from the air"—the systematic destruction of Iraqi military capabilities through sustained air and missile attack. During Operation Desert Fox, he noted, "We damaged or destroyed much of the machinery that Iraq uses to develop, test, and produce the delivery systems for its WMD. . . . We [also] destroyed the headquarters of the Special Republican Guard, and a number of other Republican Guard headquarters, barracks, and training facilities."[38] Nevertheless, U.S. military planners continue to warn of Iraqi military capabilities. In 1999, General Zinni observed that "due to the destruction of key facilities and specialized equipment, Iraq's ballistic missile program has been set back *one to two years*" (emphasis added).[39] Zinni's assessment implies that a fresh round of attacks will be needed every other year or so to prevent Iraq from rebuilding its missile arsenal. Indeed, it appears that Operation Southern Watch has now taken on this preemptive function: between December 1998 and August 1999, U.S. and British aircraft fired a total of 1,100

---

*To sustain the naval blockade of Iraq, CENTCOM arranged in 1999 for U.S. warships to refuel in the port of Aden in Yemen; on October 12, 2000, an American destroyer, the USS *Cole*, was struck by a terrorist bomb in Aden harbor after being refueled there.

missiles against 359 targets in Iraq—or about three times the number of targets attacked during Operation Desert Fox.[40]

To preserve the combat readiness of American forces, the military conducts frequent training exercises along the Iraq-Kuwait border. The exercises, known as "Operation Desert Spring," are held three or four times a year—providing what CENTCOM calls a "near-continuous" U.S. military presence along the southern edge of Iraq. The United States also conducts periodic air and naval exercises in the region and, through Operations Bright Star (an annual field exercise) and Ultimate Resolve (an annual command post exercise), tests the Pentagon's ability to mount another large multinational campaign on the scale of Desert Storm.[41]

Iran and the Strait of Hormuz

The strategy of "dual containment" also applies to Iran, the other major obstacle to American dominance in the Persian Gulf area. With a long coastline on the Gulf and a large and growing naval capability, Iran is viewed in Washington as the "threat after next"—the nation that is most likely to oppose American oil interests once the risk of an Iraqi invasion has been reduced to marginality. As noted by General Zinni in 1999, "Iran remains potentially the most dangerous threat long-term to peace and stability in the [Persian Gulf] region. In the 20th year of its revolution, Iran's ambitions to be the dominant regional power and leader of the Islamic world remain undiminished."[42]

Iran does not pose a direct threat to Saudi Arabia and the southern Gulf kingdoms—at least not for the time being. However, by building up its navy and deploying antiship missiles along its coasts, Iran may imperil oil shipping in the Persian Gulf and the all-important Strait of Hormuz, the Gulf's narrow opening to the Arabian Sea and the larger world beyond. Although lacking major warships, Iran has acquired three submarines, twenty missile-armed patrol boats, numerous shore-based missile batteries, and a large inventory of antishipping mines. This is enough, General Zinni testified in 1999, to jeopardize "open access to Gulf shipping lanes."[43]

Only six miles wide at its narrowest point, the Strait of Hormuz is described by the U.S. Department of Energy as "the world's most important oil chokepoint" because of the sheer volume of oil—over 15 million barrels per day—that passes through it.[44] With missile batteries deployed at both entrances to the strait, and a large inventory of anti-shipping mines, Iran is in an ideal position to impede shipping through this vital channel. Pentagon strategists suggest, moreover, that Iran will seek to do so in the event of a future clash with the United States.[45]

Iran also seeks to extend its control over Abu Musa and both Greater and Lesser Tunb, a small group of islands that guard the western approaches to the strait. Iran seized the Tunbs from Ras al-Khaimah (part of the United Arab Emirates) in 1971 and has occupied them since. It shared Abu Musa with Sharjah (another UAE component) until 1994, when it took control of the entire island. When pressed by the UAE to submit the dispute over the islands to international mediation, Tehran declared that they were "an inseparable part of Iran."[46] Since then, the Iranians have deployed antiship missiles on Abu Musa and fortified their positions on the Tunbs.[47]

Just as it would resist any new Iraqi assault on Kuwait, the United States would greet any Iranian move to impede Persian Gulf shipping with an immediate and crushing military response. Tomahawk cruise missiles and radar-guided bombs would most likely be used to demolish Iranian ships, missile batteries, airfields, and communications facilities. Ships and aircraft already deployed in the region would carry out most of the attacks, backed up by additional units sent in from the United States and Europe. And while the Iranians might succeed in damaging a number of tankers, their ability to imperil the oil flow would quickly be eliminated by superior American firepower.[48]

The one uncertainty in this equation involves Tehran's intentions to use its ballistic missiles and weapons of mass destruction. Iran is thought to possess several hundred Soviet-type Scud missiles, as well as a number of longer-range Scud variants based on North Korean technology; at least some of these missiles may be armed with chemical warheads. If war broke out in the Gulf, Iran might launch its missiles against the southern Gulf kingdoms in a preemptive attack, or in retaliation for American and Saudi air strikes on Iranian territory. Such a barrage would not, in the end, affect the outcome of the war—this would almost certainly entail the ultimate defeat of Iran—but could result in extensive death and destruction, especially if the missiles were equipped with chemical weapons.[49] To counter this threat, the United States has deployed Patriot antimissile systems in the Gulf and attempted to impede Iran's access to missile and WMD technology.*

Acutely conscious of America's military superiority and desperate to improve the nation's economic performance, a significant faction of the Iranian leadership has sought to reduce tensions in the Gulf and to restore Iran's ties to the West. The most conspicuous advocate for this position is Mohammed Khatami, a moderate Muslim cleric who was elected president in 1997. Although Khatami's power is limited by the Iranian constitution (which reserves ultimate power to senior religious leaders), he has spoken often of his desire to improve relations with the GCC states and the major Western powers.[51] In recognition of his efforts, U.S. Secretary of State Madeleine Albright noted in June 1998 that the United States was ready to devise "a road map leading to normal relations" if Tehran addressed American concerns regarding terrorism and the pursuit of WMD.[52] It is unclear, however, whether Khatami can overcome the influence of hard-line clerics and reverse Iran's current, hostile stance toward the West.

While it is certainly possible that Iran and the United States will mend their relations in the years ahead, it is unlikely that Washington will in any way relax its concern over Iranian military capabilities; nor, for that matter, will it reduce its capacity to defeat Iran in the event of a future clash in the Gulf. As suggested by General Peay, it is Iran's long-term military potential, not its current political orientation, that most worries American strategists. "[Iran] has a population of over 60 million people, large numbers of highly educated engineers and technicians, abundant mineral deposits, and vast oil and gas reserves," he noted. "With such resources, Iran retains the

---

*An even more worrisome scenario involves the acquisition by Iran of nuclear weapons. Although Tehran currently lacks the capacity to manufacture such munitions, many Western analysts believe that it is attempting to build a clandestine nuclear program. (As a signatory to the Non-Proliferation Treaty, Iran has opened its existing nuclear facilities to international inspection.) Much uncertainty exists over the scale and tempo of Iran's nuclear efforts, but most experts believe that Tehran is still a decade or more away from producing operational weapons.[50]

means, over the long-term, to potentially overcome its current economic malaise and endanger other Gulf states and U.S. interests."[53]

Protecting the Saudi Regime

The third scenario that dominates U.S. military planning is an internal threat to the Saudi monarchy. Protection of the Saudi regime has been a basic feature of U.S. security policy since 1945, when President Roosevelt met Ibn Saud and assured him of America's support.[54] At the core of this arrangement is a vital but unspoken quid pro quo: in return for protecting the royal family against its enemies, American companies will be allowed unrivaled access to Saudi oil fields. To defend the monarchy against its external opponents, the United States has fought a war against Iraq and conducted the military buildup described above. Increasingly, however, internal defense is becoming the greater priority.[55]

The threat posed by the antigovernment underground was first revealed in November 1995, when a massive truck bomb shattered the headquarters of the Saudi Arabia National Guard in Riyadh, killing five American servicemen and two Indians working at the facility. Seven months later, on June 25, 1996, another truck bomb killed nineteen American servicemen at the Khobar Towers housing complex in Dhahran, in what proved to be the most deadly attack on U.S. forces since the end of the 1991 Gulf conflict. Although the identity of the bombers has never been fully established, they are widely assumed to be members of militant antigovernment Islamic organizations.[56] Similar groups, linked to Saudi extremist Osama bin Laden, are also thought to be responsible for the August 1998 bombings of the American embassies in Kenya and Tanzania.

Most analysts believe that the ultimate aim of the organizations involved in these and similar attacks is to overthrow the existing Saudi regime and replace it with an even more conservative Islamic government. Such a revolution is needed, Saudi dissidents argue, because the royal family has been so corrupted by its massive oil wealth and its ties to the West that it can no longer be considered worthy to govern. As evidence of such corruption, they point to Saudi Arabia's timid and ineffectual opposition to Israel and the presence, on sacred Islamic soil, of non-Muslim oilmen and soldiers. Reversing these injustices, the dissidents argue, can be accomplished only by eliminating the existing regime through jihad, or holy war. And because the United States is the leading source of protection for the regime, it, too, must be the target of jihad.[57]

For the most part, those who hold such views in Saudi Arabia are content to express them in private, or among the faithful in private religious assemblies. (Open political debate is not permitted in the kingdom, and those suspected of espousing antigovernment views are routinely arrested and confined to prison.)[58] Nevertheless, a small but significant minority within the fundamentalist community favors more vigorous action, including violent attacks on military bases and government offices.[59] "To the extremists, to declare the government as illegitimate makes it an infidel government," explained Jamal Khashoggi, a Saudi journalist. "And the moment they declare a government an infidel government, they believe they have the right to fight against it."[60]

Although driven primarily by religious belief, these groups have also tapped into other sources of discontent. Much of this discontent is of an economic nature: when oil revenues declined in the 1990s, the government cut back on the lucrative benefits provided to all Saudi citizens. Unemployment rose, expectations declined, and many young Saudis became embittered by the loss of privileges once taken for granted. With the open expression of political dissent forbidden, it is not surprising that a certain percentage of these disaffected youths have moved to the political margins.[61]

Despite determined efforts by the Saudi government to suppress dissident organizations, they continue to thrive. This is partly due to their professed religious character, which provides a certain degree of immunity from government surveillance, and partly to the fact that they enjoy the patronage of wealthy Saudi businessmen and senior clerics in Iran, Sudan, and other Muslim countries. Also contributing to the effectiveness and prestige of these organizations is the presence in their ranks of many ex-combatants (of various nationalities) from the anti-Soviet struggle in Afghanistan. "These groups' multinational composition, financial independence, and international ties to other terrorist groups make them an elusive threat," CENTCOM noted in 1997. "Trained as *mujahideen* in the Afghan war against Soviet occupation, members of these groups . . . form small, impenetrable cells to pursue an extremist agenda."[62]

To prevent these efforts from coalescing into a more substantial threat to the Saudi regime, the United States has undertaken a wide range of measures. These include assistance in the creation of a large, efficient, and well-equipped domestic security apparatus. Primary responsibility for internal stability and the protection of the royal family falls on the Saudi Arabia National Guard (SANG), an elite force of 57,000 active-duty combatants equipped with a broad array of modern weapons. From its inception, this force has received most of its training, equipment, and technical support from the U.S. Department of Defense or from American military contractors.[63] In 1990, for instance, U.S. firms were awarded a $3.4 billion contract to supply the SANG with 1,117 Light Armored Vehicles, 2,000 TOW antitank missiles, 27 M-198 towed howitzers, and related services; follow-on contracts, worth $819 million and $690 million respectively, were signed in 1993.[64]

Although it has entrusted the SANG and other Saudi security agencies with primary responsibility for protecting the royal family against internal threats, the United States has taken active measures of its own. These include extensive intelligence-collection activities designed to identify and track the leaders of Saudi extremist organizations—especially Osama bin Laden and his associates—as well as diplomatic efforts to deny them safe haven and banking privileges in neighboring countries.[65] The United States has also made it clear that it will employ military force to punish those implicated in terrorist attacks on U.S. bases and personnel, as it did following the August 1998 bombings of the American embassies in Kenya and Tanzania.*

---

*Claiming that bin Laden's organization was behind the embassy bombings, the United States fired Tomahawk cruise missiles at a guerrilla training base in Afghanistan and a suspected chemical weapons (CW) facility in Sudan. Although the effort was characterized by White House officials as a damaging blow to the terrorist underground, it was later revealed that no senior bin Laden associates were killed in the raids and that evidence for CW production at the Sudanese facility—a well-known pharmaceutical plant—was meager and inconclusive.[66]

Ultimately, the United States is prepared to intervene with its own forces to defend the regime against internal attack. This was made abundantly clear in 1981, when President Reagan declared that the United States would not allow an insurgent movement to overthrow the Saudi monarch, as had occurred in Iran two years earlier. "I will not permit [Saudi Arabia] to be an Iran," he told reporters at the White House.[67]

Direct American involvement in a civil war is, no doubt, the last thing that Washington would like to see happen. To prevent this, great emphasis is being placed on intelligence activities and the disruption of antigovernment organizations. But President Reagan's 1981 statement provides an unambiguous indication of America's determination to protect the Saudi monarchy at all costs. Nor is there any evidence to suggest that this commitment has in any way been diluted since Reagan's time; if anything, the United States is even more closely wedded to the Saudi regime now than it was in 1981. And while it is impossible to predict the exact nature of the U.S. response to any particular threat to the regime, it is likely to be swift, muscular, and lethal.

OTHER SOURCES OF CONFLICT

Other pressures, ranging from political and economic unrest to succession battles and border disputes, could also pose a threat to the free flow of oil and thus provoke American military intervention.

As in Saudi Arabia, political unrest has flared up in several of the smaller GCC sheikhdoms. In each case, opposition to the regime has been fueled by some combination of religious discord, economic unease, opposition to the presence of U.S. forces, or a lack of democratic political expression. Most significant, from a strategic point of view, is the unrest in Bahrain—the home base of the U.S. Fifth Fleet. Unlike the other GCC countries, Bahrain possesses little oil and gas and so cannot provide its citizens with a high level of economic support. Living standards have declined in recent years and unemployment has risen, provoking several antigovernment demonstrations and street riots by disaffected youths—most drawn from the country's

Shiite majority, which tends to be poorer than the Sunni minority.[68] Although these protests have all been crushed by government forces, opposition to the regime continues in Manama, the capital, and among Bahraini exiles in other countries.[69]

At present, none of the dissenting forces in Bahrain or the other Gulf kingdoms is powerful enough to take power. Nevertheless, they are evidence of an underlying discontent that could grow stronger in the years ahead. This danger is compounded, moreover, by the prospect of succession struggles in a number of the GCC monarchies. No clear line of succession has been established in Saudi Arabia, and the departure of the current monarch, King Fahd, could be followed by a power struggle among the many male descendants of Ibn Saud. Similar disputes could break out within the ruling circles of Bahrain, Kuwait, and the United Arab Emirates, providing the spark for popular unrest or civil war.[70]

Conflict could also erupt as a result of territorial disputes. The rift between Iran and the UAE over Abu Musa and the Tunbs is not the only significant territorial contest in the region: several other disputes have arisen over the location of boundaries or the possession of valuable offshore territories.[71] Saudi Arabia and Qatar, for example, have clashed on several occasions over the location of their mutual border. In the most recent skirmish, in 1994, Saudi border guards are reported to have opened fire on Qatari personnel.[72] (Despite efforts by Egypt to mediate between the two countries, the border dispute remains unresolved.) Qatar is also party to a border dispute with Bahrain—in this case, over possession of the Hawar Islands and two sandbars off Qatar's western shore. Although seemingly trivial, this dispute is potentially significant because the territories in question are believed to harbor large supplies of oil and gas, and because it has produced rancor within the ranks of the GCC.[73] (See Appendix for additional information on territorial disputes in the Persian Gulf area.)

The Persian Gulf area is full of political, social, and economic fissures, and long-term stability is likely to prove an elusive goal. The United States—which has taken upon itself the burden of responsibility for maintaining stability in the region—will inevitably be drawn into any future conflict. But however high the cost of U.S. involvement in the Gulf, the Americans will find it difficult to leave. "Withdrawing from the region," General Peay of CENTCOM said in 1997, "is not an option."[74]

4

Energy Conflict in the Caspian Sea Basin

Due north of the Persian Gulf, across the western flank of Iran, lies another major locus of energy-related strife: the Caspian Sea basin. Composed of Russia and Iran, as well as several former republics of the Soviet Union—Azerbaijan, Georgia, Kazakhstan, Kyrgyzstan, Tajikistan, Turkmenistan, and Uzbekistan—the Caspian basin is thought to house the world's second or third largest reserves of petroleum, along with a vast supply of natural gas. Although many states hope to benefit from the development of these reserves, the future development of Caspian Sea energy is clouded by ethnic and political turmoil within the region and the emergence of a new power struggle between the United States and Russia. As the global demand for energy rises and the struggle for control over the Caspian's reserves intensifies, the region will face a growing risk of violent conflict.

The potential for conflict in the Caspian Sea basin derives from many of the same factors encountered in the Persian Gulf area: contested boundaries and territorial disputes, the prevalence of authoritarian regimes, severe economic disparities, long-standing regional rivalries, and a cauldron of ethnic and religious strife. The situation in the basin is further complicated by the fact that the Caspian Sea itself is landlocked, and so any energy supplies sent from the region to markets elsewhere must travel by rail or pipeline through adjacent areas—many of which are themselves engulfed in conflict. On top of this, Russia has a major presence in the Caspian basin, and so many of the internal convulsions now wracking that country are being felt throughout the region.

Just how volatile this area can be was brutally demonstrated in the fall of 1999, when rebel Muslim forces attacked the southern Russian republic of Dagestan and Moscow replied with a full-scale attack on neighboring Chechnya (to which the Dagestani rebels had fled). Fighting also erupted in Uzbekistan and Kyrgyzstan, in each case between government forces and militant Islamic factions.[1] In January 2000, moreover, Uzbek border guards occupied a narrow stretch of Kazakh territory, claiming the land belonged to Uzbekistan.[2] Other states in the region, fearing additional outbreaks of violence, procured new weapons for their armies or sought the protection of Washington or Moscow.[3] With arms pouring into the area and the major powers jockeying for advantage, the Caspian basin appears headed for a recurring cycle of crisis and conflict.

Despite all this, many of the world's leading energy concerns have acquired development rights in the region and have begun to produce significant amounts of petroleum. Major drilling operations are now under way in offshore areas of Azerbaijan and Kazakhstan and will soon commence in several neighboring countries. To ensure that future energy output can be delivered to foreign markets, these firms have stepped up the construction of oil and gas pipelines from the Caspian to ports and refineries in other areas. The first new pipeline, from Baku in Azerbaijan to Supsa on Georgia's Black Sea coast, was opened in 1999; a second line, from the Tengiz field in Kazakhstan to the Russian port of Novorossiysk (also on the Black Sea), is scheduled to open in 2001. An even longer pipeline, of some eleven hundred miles, may someday extend from Baku to Ceyhan on Turkey's Mediterranean coast.

This frenzy of activity is being driven by reports of vast oil and

natural gas deposits lying beneath the Caspian Sea and in the surrounding areas. Energy experts have not yet determined exactly how
much oil and natural gas is sitting in these deposits, but all acknowl-
edge that the amounts are truly substantial—easily surpassing those
of the North Sea area and East Asia. "The Caspian may hold oil and
gas reserves second only to those of the Middle East," Daniel Yergin
and Thane Gustafson of Cambridge Energy Research Associates reported in *The New York Times*.[4] It is not surprising, then, that the
major energy firms are determined to establish a significant stake in
the region. The Caspian basin has become the "new oil El Dorado,"
Foreign Minister Herve De Charrette of France proclaimed in 1996—
the most promising site for future energy development in the world.[5]

The discovery of these new reserves has affected the strategic calculations of every state in the region, along with many outside of it.[6]
Most significant in this regard is the arrival of the United States as a
major actor in the Caspian basin. Eager to reduce Western dependence on Persian Gulf oil, American leaders have placed heavy emphasis on the development of Caspian Sea energy resources. As
discussed in chapter 1, Washington has also enhanced its capacity to
project military force into the region. This, in turn, has aroused immense concern in Moscow, which views the Caspian basin as part of
its traditional sphere of influence. Russian leaders also seek to ensure
that much of the Caspian's oil and gas supplies travel through Russian
pipelines on their way to markets elsewhere, as was the case during
the Soviet era. The stage is being set, therefore, for a long-term power
struggle between the United States and Russia.[7]

The development of the basin's energy resources is also affecting
the political and economic circumstances of the Caspian states themselves. For those nations with significant oil and gas reserves, the
prospect of future energy wealth is serving to accelerate their efforts
to break out of the Russian-dominated, Soviet-style economic system.
Partnerships with Western oil companies can also lead to increased
contact with Western governments, thus enabling them to diminish
their political as well as their economic ties to Moscow. The same is
true of neighboring countries like Georgia and Kyrgyzstan, which

possess little oil and gas of their own but could play an important role in the transportation of Caspian energy to foreign markets. At the same time, these states are fully aware of their relative weakness compared to Russia, and so are reluctant to leave Moscow's orbit altogether.[8]

The interplay between these factors—the emerging U.S.-Russian rivalry and the efforts of local states to manipulate this rivalry to their advantage—is enough to generate considerable instability in the region. But a number of other factors complicate the situation further. These include the efforts of Iran and Turkey to advance their own interests in the region, long-standing ethnic and religious disputes, and widespread social unrest.[9]

The proponents of deep American involvement in the region, including senior government officials, argue that the production and sale of Caspian basin energy supplies will generate enough wealth to satisfy the aspirations of every key actor, thus reducing the risk of regional conflict. "Caspian energy development is not and should not be viewed as a zero-sum game," Under Secretary of State Stuart Eizenstat affirmed in 1997. "All the new independent states can benefit from the region's rapid economic development."[10] But the prevailing concentration of oil wealth in the hands of a small local elite, coupled with widespread ethnic divisions and a history of political strife, is likely to erase the promise of mutual benefit. Far from promoting stability, Professor Martha Brill Olcott of Colgate University observed in 1998, the aggressive pursuit of Caspian Sea energy will exacerbate local tensions and produce "a zone of instability and crisis that could stretch from the Black Sea to the Indian Ocean and from the Ural Mountains to the Tarim Basin [in China]."[11]

THE NEW OIL EL DORADO

The Caspian basin has been producing energy for a very long time— Baku first became a major center of oil production in the early 1900s—but energy experts have yet to agree on the total amount of oil and gas to be found in the region. In 1997, the U.S. Department of State told Congress that the Caspian basin holds as much as

200 billion barrels of oil—about ten times the amount found in the North Sea, and a third of the Persian Gulf's total reserves.[12] The Department of Energy has been equally optimistic about Caspian supplies, reporting in June 2000 that the region possesses proven reserves of 18 to 35 billion barrels of oil and possible reserves of 235 billion barrels.[13] Other analysts have provided different numbers, both higher and lower than the DoE figures; all agree, however, that the final numbers are likely to prove substantial.[14] "While estimates of the size of regional oil and gas reserves vary widely," Under Secretary Eizenstat told a Senate subcommittee, "the Caspian Sea is potentially one of the world's most important new energy producing regions."[15]

What is most significant, however, is not the absolute scale of Caspian reserves but the fact that production in this region is expected to rise in the years ahead while production in many other oil-bearing areas is likely to decline. In 1997, for example, oil production in the Caspian region totaled only 1.1 million barrels per day—a small fraction of worldwide production. By 2010, however, Caspian production is expected to reach 4 mbd and, by 2020, 6 mbd.[16] During this same period, production in the United States is expected to decline from 9.5 to 8.7 mbd, and in the North Sea from 6.3 to 5.9 mbd.[17] These trends are likely to continue in the years that follow, as Caspian production continues to rise and that in many other areas to experience significant decline.*

The Caspian region is also valued for its large reservoirs of natural gas. According to the Department of Energy, Azerbaijan, Kazakhstan, Turkmenistan, and Uzbekistan together possess proven reserves of 236 to 337 trillion cubic feet (tcf) of gas, an amount equivalent to the combined reserves of the United States, Canada, and Mexico. In addition, these countries house *possible* reserves of approximately 328 tcf, bringing total hypothetical reserves to 565 to 665 tcf.[18] If this

---

*Expectations that the region harbors large quantities of untapped petroleum were buoyed in July 2000, when the Offshore Kazakhstan International Operating Co. (OKIOC)—a joint venture of ExxonMobil, Royal Dutch/Shell, BP Amoco, Phillips Petroleum, and several other companies—announced a major oil find in the Kashagan field in the northeastern corner of the Caspian Sea.

Table 4.1: Oil and Gas Reserves in the Caspian Sea Basin				
	Oil		Natural Gas	
Country	Proven Reserves (bbl)	Possible Reserves (bbl)	Proven Reserves (tcf)	Possible Reserves (tcf)
Azerbaijan	3.6–12.5	32.0	11	35
Iran*	0.1	15.0	0	11
Kazakhstan	10.0–17.6	92.0	53–83	88
Russia*	2.7	14.0	n/a	n/a
Turkmenistan	1.7	80.0	98–155	159
Uzbekistan	0.3	2.0	74–88	35
Total	18.4–34.9	235.0	236–337	328

Source: U.S. Department of Energy, Energy Information Administration, "Caspian Sea Region," June 2000.
*Includes only those areas adjacent to the Caspian Sea
bbl = billion barrels
tcf = trillion cubic feet

estimate proves accurate, the Caspian's natural gas reserves would equal those of North and South America combined. (See Table 4.1.)

Even with the uncertainties regarding the ultimate scale of Caspian basin oil and gas supplies, foreign firms have been pouring into the area in pursuit of exploration and development rights. Among the hundreds of companies that have flocked to the region in search of the new "oil El Dorado" are many of the world's leading energy concerns, including Amoco, Chevron, Exxon, Mobil, British Petroleum, Royal Dutch/Shell, Elf Aquitaine of France, Agip of Italy, Statoil of Norway, Lukoil of Russia, and the China National Petroleum Corporation. (Some of these companies have recently combined into even larger concerns, such as BP Amoco and ExxonMobil.) These and other firms had invested billions of dollars in new production and transportation facilities by 1999 and were planning to spend even larger amounts in the early years of the twenty-first century—reaching an estimated $50 billion in total investments by 2010.[19]

In most instances, these companies have joined with local, usually state-owned concerns and with one another to create large exploration and production consortia. The first such enterprise was established in

1993, when Chevron concluded a historic $20 billion joint venture arrangement with the Kazakh government to develop the giant Tengiz oil field on Kazakhstan's Caspian coast. The resulting firm, Tengizchevroil, was later joined by Mobil (now ExxonMobil), which purchased a 25 percent share in the consortium from the Kazakh government in 1996. Another joint venture, the Caspian Pipeline Consortium (CPC), was established by the Tengizchevroil partners and Lukoil to build a nine-hundred-mile, $2.2 billion pipeline to carry Tengiz oil to the Russian Black Sea port of Novorossiysk. Once the pipeline is completed—it's scheduled for 2001—Tengizchevroil hopes to produce and export as much as 750,000 barrels of oil per day.[20]

The next large Caspian consortium was established in December 1994, when Amoco, BP, Lukoil, Unocal, Pennzoil, Statoil, and a number of other firms joined with the State Oil Company of Azerbaijan (SOCAR) to form the Azerbaijan International Operating Company (AIOC). This $8 billion enterprise has exclusive rights to the development of three offshore fields in Azerbaijan's sector of the Caspian Sea, possessing total estimated reserves of 3 to 5 billion barrels of oil.[21] SOCAR has also participated in the formation of several other major projects, including the $4 billion Shah-Deniz project, led by British Petroleum (now BP Amoco), Statoil, Elf Aquitaine, Lukoil, and the National Iranian Oil Company (no U.S. firms are included in this project because of the participation by Iran), and the $2 billion Lenkoran-Talysh Deniz project, led by Elf Aquitaine and Total of France. Another big consortium, the Offshore Kazakhstan International Operating Co. (OKIOC), is drilling for petroleum in the vast Kashagan field in the northeast Caspian.[22]

These projects and others of this magnitude will transform the landscape of the Caspian region and bring substantial wealth to the firms and governments involved. Before all of these endeavors can reach fruition, however, the oil companies and their governmental partners must clear a number of critical roadblocks. To begin with, there is no established legal framework for apportioning offshore territories in the Caspian Sea itself, leaving considerable uncertainty as to ownership of undersea deposits. Considerable effort will also be required to rebuild the energy and transportation infrastructure left behind by the former Soviet Union, much of which is in a condition of serious decay. The most significant problem, however, is the task of moving the energy from the point of production to markets elsewhere: because the Caspian Sea is landlocked, future energy exports will have to travel by land—and with the United States opposing future reliance on the existing, Soviet-era pipeline system (which extends through Russia to eastern Europe), an entirely new set of pipelines will have to be constructed.[23]

To a certain extent, decisions over the location of major pipelines and other such matters will be made by the oil companies involved, in accordance with their respective needs and resources. Increasingly, however, these decisions will reflect the interplay of powerful political forces. Not only are many states competing for the privilege of housing the pipelines (in order to collect tariffs on the throughput of energy), but a number of external powers—including the United States, Russia, Turkey, and China—seek to determine future pipeline routes in accordance with their perceived strategic interests. It is these concerns, rather than the purely financial interests of the oil companies, that will ultimately determine the fate of the Caspian Sea region.

THE "GREAT GAME II": U.S.-RUSSIAN COMPETITION IN THE CASPIAN BASIN

By far the most significant factor in the regional conflict equation is the emergence of a new power struggle between the United States and Russia. Both of these countries seek to gain economic advantage from the development of Caspian Sea energy, and both seek to determine the routes by which this energy will travel to the outside world. Both, moreover, view the Caspian and Central Asia as an important geopolitical prize in the new, post–Cold War redistribution of global power. And senior leaders in both the United States and Russia believe that strategic concerns of this sort take precedence over purely economic considerations when calculating the national interest.[24]

Some analysts have come to describe this competition as the "Great Game II"—a reference to the "Great Game" of the nineteenth century, which pitted imperial Britain against Czarist Russia in a struggle to dominate this very area.[25] "Today's great oil game is just as treacherous [as its predecessor]," Hugh Pope observed in *The Wall Street Journal.* In its present form, "the struggle typically pits Western interests against Russians fighting a rear-guard action in their old backyard."[26]

American officials are reluctant to embrace the "Great Game" analogy in their public statements, suggesting that all states involved can obtain substantial benefits from the development of Caspian Sea energy. There is no question, however, that leaders of both countries view the U.S.-Russian relationship in the Caspian as a high-stakes competition. "Already the United States is declaring that [this area] is in their zone of interest," President Boris Yeltsin observed in 1997. While Russian influence is waning, he added, "the Americans, on the contrary, are beginning to penetrate this zone, and, without reservation, declare this."[27] More recently, in May 2000, the head of the Caspian Sea working group in the Russian Ministry of Foreign Affairs, Andrei Y. Urnov, told an audience in Washington, "It hasn't been left unnoticed in Russia that certain outside forces are trying to weaken our position in the Caspian basin, to drive a wedge between us and other Caspian states."[28] As if to confirm these perceptions, Sheila Heslin of the U.S. National Security Council told a Senate investigating committee that the goal of American policy in the Caspian is "in essence to break Russia's monopoly of control over the transportation of oil from the region."[29]

As in any great-power contest, there are many dimensions to the U.S.-Russian rivalry in the Caspian area. To enhance their political influence, both sides have sought to establish close ties with local leaders by sending high-level delegations to promise various forms of aid and support; both sides have also sought to expand their trade and financial links with the region. At its core, however, this is a struggle for control over the distribution of energy resources: both Washington and Moscow seek to exercise ultimate dominion over the flow of Caspian oil and natural gas to markets in other areas of the world.

Moscow's major objective in this contest is to ensure that a significant portion of the Caspian's energy output travels through the existing Russian pipeline system to the Black Sea and Europe. This would provide the depleted Russian treasury with lucrative transit fees and allow Moscow to exercise some degree of control over the distribution of Caspian energy supplies. At the same time, senior Russian officials—many of whom enjoy close ties to large energy firms like Lukoil and Gazprom—want Russian companies to play a significant role in major Caspian operating consortia like AIOC and CPC, thereby guaranteeing these firms (and their owners) a share of the immense wealth that is expected to be generated.[30]

Washington has two key objectives: first, to develop Caspian basin energy as an alternative to Persian Gulf supplies; second, to ensure that the Caspian oil and gas travel to markets in the West without passing through Russia or Iran.[31] "This is about America's energy security, which depends on diversifying our sources of oil and gas worldwide," Energy Secretary Bill Richardson explained in 1998. "It's also about preventing strategic inroads by those who don't share our values."[32] To bypass Russia and Iran, the United States wants the major oil consortia to build new oil and gas pipelines running beneath the Caspian Sea from Kazakhstan and Turkmenistan to Azerbaijan, and then onward to Georgia and Turkey. Although far more costly than alternative routes through Russia and Iran, such a network is claimed by American officials to be the least susceptible to interdiction by hostile forces.

Both sides in this contest have invested considerable effort in the struggle to achieve their objectives. Russia has put enormous pressure on Azerbaijan and Kazakhstan to send a significant share of their oil exports through southern Russia to Novorossiysk on the Black Sea. These efforts, in turn, have led Russia to place a high premium on stability in Chechnya and Dagestan, as the Azerbaijan-Novorossiysk pipeline route must pass through one or the other. It is not surprising, then, that Moscow responded to the 1999 guerrilla attacks on southern Dagestan with a full-scale invasion of Chechnya, where the guerrillas were based. Moscow is also suspected of promoting instability in Georgia as part of a campaign to reduce the appeal of a pipeline crossing that country on its way to Turkey.[33]

The United States has likewise invested great effort in this contest. President Clinton invited the leaders of Azerbaijan, Kazakhstan, and Turkmenistan to the White House for formal state visits and played a critical role in persuading these states to endorse a new pipeline system connecting the Caspian area with Turkey and the Mediterranean. Clinton also sent his top aides to the Caspian to promote the pipeline project, offering substantial economic and military assistance to all those states that cooperated with the American plan.[34] To counter Russian moves in Georgia, moreover, the United States has voiced strong support for President Eduard Shevardnadze and is helping the country modernize its military forces. (See Table 4.3 on page 96.)

Although both the United States and Russia have made strenuous efforts to prevail in this contest, neither has as yet achieved its principal objectives. Moscow has not been able to dominate the oil flow from the Caspian or to curb American influence in the region; Washington has not been able to discourage the major oil companies from shipping a significant share of their output through Russia. It is likely, then, that both sides will step up their efforts to gain advantage in the Caspian basin. Indeed, Russia's specialist on the Caspian, Andrei Urnov, revealed in May 2000 that the Russian Security Council had recently concluded that Moscow's interests in the area "should be upheld and promoted in a more persistent way."[35] The new U.S. administration will no doubt follow suit, suggesting that the "Great Game II" will continue to play itself out in years ahead.

It is impossible, of course, to predict where all of this will lead. For now, a direct military clash between the United States and Russia in the Caspian area appears unlikely: neither side will knowingly allow their common struggle over energy distribution to reach the point of a violent clash, and neither has deployed sufficient forces in the region to conduct a major conflict. On the other hand, it is certainly possible to envision the periodic outbreak of "proxy" wars in the area— conflicts between local powers that are allied with Russia or the United States and receive considerable military aid and advice from their respective patrons. In fact, the steps now being taken by Moscow and Washington to bolster their allies are entirely consistent with such a scenario.

PREPARING THE BATTLEFIELD

Without attracting very much attention from the outside world, Russia and the United States have engaged in systematic efforts to strengthen their respective military position in the Caspian Sea basin. They have not, however, proceeded on parallel tracks: Russia—as a Caspian state itself and the inheritor of the Soviet military establishment—has been able to build on an existing infrastructure in the region, while the United States lacks military bases in the region and so has had to establish its presence through other means. Despite their different starting positions, however, both have succeeded in establishing a significant presence in the region.

The Russian Military Presence

Russia's military presence in the Caspian basin includes the combat forces that are based on that portion of its territory lying within the region. These forces are assigned to the North Caucasus Military District (M.D.), one of six major military commands in the Russian Federation. At the end of 1999, this command had at its disposal some 80,000 ground troops, divided into two motorized rifle divisions, one airborne division, three motorized rifle brigades, a Spetsnaz (special forces) detachment, an artillery brigade, and a variety of specialized units. Also located within this M.D. is the Fourth Air Army, equipped with some 475 combat planes (mostly MiG-29s, Su-22s, Su-24s, Su-25s, and Su-27s), and a small naval contingent based at Astrakhan on the Caspian itself.[36]

Although the Russian military as a whole has suffered substantial reductions in strength since the breakup of the Soviet Union, it is evident that the Russian leadership has attempted to shield the North Caucasus M.D. from the heaviest personnel and equipment cutbacks.[37] This was especially evident in 1999, when Moscow unleashed a ferocious campaign against anti-Russian forces in Chechnya. Besides committing large numbers of ground troops to the campaign, Russian generals employed a great deal of armor, artillery, and airpower to subdue the rebels—leveling Grozny and other Chechen communities in the process. The use of all these military assets in the subjugation of Grozny was all the more telling because it represented the first significant political act of Russia's new president, Vladimir V. Putin.[38]

Russia also maintains smaller garrisons and military detachments in Armenia, Azerbaijan, Georgia, Kazakhstan, and Tajikistan. In most cases, these forces were deployed in the area during the Soviet era and were permitted to remain there under terms of the Collective Security Treaty signed by members of the Commonwealth of Independent States in 1992. (Although Azerbaijan and Georgia chose to withdraw from the treaty when it was renewed in 1999, Moscow has yet to extract all of its troops or close down its bases in these two countries.) Russian troops also serve with peacekeeping units in Abkhazia and South Ossetia (both in Georgia) and in Tajikistan. As of late 1999, there were at least 22,000 Russian combat troops serving in the Caspian countries, along with significant numbers of specialized military personnel.[39] (See Table 4.2.)

Russia has also sought to extend its influence in the Caspian area through military aid agreements, arms transfers, and other forms of military-to-military contact.[40] Following the breakup of the Soviet Union in 1992, Moscow signed mutual security agreements with most of the Caspian states, allowing for Russian occupation of certain former Soviet bases. Under a 1993 accord with Turkmenistan, for example, Russian officers occupy senior positions in Turkmenistan's armed forces and Russian troops help guard the country's borders with Iran and Afghanistan.[41] A 1995 agreement with Kazakhstan provides for Russian occupation of several missile bases in that country and the formation of joint Russian-Kazakh military units.[42] Similar agreements were signed with Armenia and Georgia in 1995,[43] and with Tajikistan in 1999.[44]

Other forms of military cooperation have also proliferated. In 1996, for example, Russia established an integrated air-defense system with Armenia, Kazakhstan, Kyrgyzstan, and Tajikistan; this system

Table 4.2: Russian Military Bases and Forces in the Caspian Region, 1999		
Country	Forces Deployed	Comments
Armenia	3,100 ground troops; 1 air-defense squadron with 14 MiG-29s	8 additional MiG-29s and a battery of S-300 air-defense missiles deployed in 1999
Azerbaijan		Russians occupy ABM radar station at Gabala
Georgia	5,000 ground troops; 1 air regiment with cargo planes, helicopters	Another 3,000 Russian troops also serve with peacekeeping units in Abkhazia and South Ossetia; Moscow has promised to reduce its force levels in Georgia between 2000 and 2001
Kazakhstan		Russians operate ABM radar station at Balkhash, air-defense missile test range at Emba
Kyrgyzstan		Russian officers command Kyrgyz Border Guard forces
Tajikistan	8,200 ground troops of the 201st MRD plus other units	New troop agreement signed in 1999; Russian officers also command the 14,500-strong Frontier Forces

Source: International Institute for Strategic Studies, *The Military Balance, 1999–2000;* assorted news articles.
ABM = antiballistic missile
MRD = motorized rifle division

was strengthened in 1999 following joint exercises involving all participating countries.[45] Moscow has also established a joint naval command at Astrakhan, equipped with Russian ships and manned by sailors from Russia, Kazakhstan, and Turkmenistan.[46] Equally noteworthy, Russia has begun to transfer significant quantities of arms and ammunition to selected Caspian republics. Although details of these transactions are rarely made public, the International Institute for Strategic Studies (IISS) reported in 1999 that Moscow had provided Kazakhstan with 16 Su-27 fighter planes, 3 fast patrol boats, and a quantity of S-300 air-defense missiles; other arms deliveries included a batch of Mi-24 and Mi-8 helicopters supplied to Tajikistan and 160 BTR-80 armored personnel carriers provided to Uzbekistan.[47]

The Growing American Presence

The United States does not, of course, enjoy the same sort of access to military facilities in the Caspian Sea area as does Russia. There are no American bases in the region, nor are any U.S. troops deployed there on a regular basis. Nevertheless, Washington has begun to establish a significant presence in the Caspian through a combination of diplomatic efforts, military exercises, and military aid agreements.

The Clinton administration placed a particularly high priority on diplomatic contacts with leaders of the Caspian states, regularly bringing these leaders to Washington for meetings with the president and vice president and sending top U.S. officials to meet with them at home.[48] Though these visits were primarily intended to enlist local support for American oil investments and for the adoption of pipeline routes favored by Washington, they were also designed to establish or to bolster U.S. military ties with the countries involved. Thus, in a White House statement on the November 1997 meeting between Bill Clinton and President Nursultan Nazarbayev of Kazakhstan, it was reported that the two leaders "renewed their commitment to regional security cooperation, including enhanced bilateral military-to-military cooperation."[49] Similar agreements have been concluded at meetings with other key leaders from the region.[50]

As a result of these agreements, the United States has begun to provide various forms of military assistance to the Caspian Sea states. These include the sale or transfer of military equipment, periodic visits between senior officers, the training of military personnel, and the sponsorship of joint military exercises. According to the Department of State, total U.S. aid to the eight Caspian basin states (Armenia, Azerbaijan, Georgia, Kazakhstan, Kyrgyzstan, Tajikistan, Turkmenistan, and Uzbekistan) during fiscal years 1998–2000 totaled an astonishing $1.06 billion, of which $175 million was intended for regional security, arms transfers, nonproliferation activities, and military training.[51] (See Table 4.3.)

The principal recipient of U.S. aid, both military and economic, is Georgia. Claiming that "U.S. national security interests are at stake in Georgia," the Clinton administration asked Congress to provide a

Table 4.3:
U.S. Military and Economic Assistance to the Caspian Basin States,
Fiscal Years 1998–2000
(Current dollars in thousands)

Recipient	Regional Security Programs			WMD Counter-proliferation	Economic Development	Other*	Total, All Programs
	Total, All Programs	(FMF Grants)	(IMET Training)				
Armenia	0	0	0	5,347	116,072	119,928	241,347
Azerbaijan	2,000	0	0	0	19,220	71,710	92,930
Georgia	90,741	(10,200)	(1,208)	4,025	87,127	120,142	302,035
Kazakhstan	7,551	(5,850)	(1,701)	14,195	57,840	67,350	146,936
Kyrgyzstan	5,469	(4,450)	(1,019)	7,657	36,482	45,358	94,966
Tajikistan	14,946	0	0	128	9,665	30,704	55,443
Turkmenistan	2,593	(1,650)	(943)	3,637	14,000	14,670	34,900
Uzbekistan	6,292	(4,850)	(1,442)	10,401	34,425	42,335	93,453
Totals	129,592	(27,000)	(6,313)	45,390	374,831	512,197	1,062,010

Source: U.S. Department of State, *Congressional Presentation for Foreign Operations*, Fiscal Year 2000 (Washington, D.C., 1999). Figures for FY 98 are actual; for FY 99, estimates; for FY 00, budget request.
*Includes humanitarian assistance, support for democratization, antidrug activities, health, and environmental protection.
FMF = Foreign Military Financing (arms transfers)
IMET = International Military Education and Training
WMD = weapons of mass destruction

total of $302 million in American aid to that country during the 1998–2000 period.[52] As part of this effort, the Department of Defense is helping modernize and professionalize the Georgian military, with particular emphasis on its border-protection capacity. This focus on Georgia is intended partly to bolster the Shevardnadze government in its efforts to remain independent from Moscow, and partly to ensure the safety of the oil and gas pipelines that cross Georgia on their way from Azerbaijan to the Black Sea and Turkey.[53] Increased American military assistance is essential, Shevardnadze noted in 1999, because the "intensification of transport through the Caucasus" will invite terrorism and other threats to Georgian security.[54]

Energy concerns also govern the U.S. relationship with Azerbaijan and Kazakhstan.[55] Senior American leaders are particularly eager to beef up Azerbaijan's defense capabilities, since the main pipelines to the Black Sea and Turkey will originate in Baku. However, under pressure from the Armenian community in the United States (which seeks to punish Azerbaijan for its continued trade blockade of Armenia), Congress has banned most forms of aid to the Azerbaijani government.[56] To get around this obstacle, the Department of Defense has forged cooperative links with the Azerbaijani military in the nonproliferation field (as allowed by Congress) and included Azerbaijani forces in joint military exercises.[57] Additional military aid and training has been provided to Azerbaijan by Turkey, Washington's strategic partner in the Caspian region.[58]

In the case of Kazakhstan, U.S. military aid has followed several paths. As we have seen, the first CENTRAZBAT exercise was conducted on Kazakh territory, allowing for close cooperation between U.S. and Kazakh military officials. The United States has also given Kazakhstan a fast patrol boat, the *Dauntless,* for maritime security in the Caspian Sea and is providing advanced training to Kazakh military personnel. In 1997, moreover, Secretary of Defense William S. Cohen and Kazakh president Nazarbayev signed a defense cooperation agreement calling for regular contact and exchanges between American and Kazakh officers.[59] These programs enable American officers to develop military-to-military ties with their local counterparts and provide U.S. forces with an opportunity to gain close familiarity with the terrain of the Caspian Sea basin.

Together, these efforts by Russia and the United States are producing a steady buildup of military capabilities in the Caspian region and, if the events of 1999 and 2000 are any indication, a growing inclination by local leaders to rely on military means of resolving regional disagreements. Past experience suggests, moreover, that behaviors of this sort tend to result in a heightened level of regional tension and hostility, greatly increasing the risk of war.

SOURCES OF FRICTION AND CONFLICT

Long before the discovery of major oil and gas deposits, the Caspian Sea area was riven by numerous disputes and internal divisions. Many of these divisions, such as those between the Armenians and the

Azeris, or between the Abkhazians and the Georgians, periodically erupted in violence. The arrival of Western oil companies has only exacerbated many of the existing problems. Among the most significant sources of friction in the Caspian today are: territorial disputes over the ownership of development rights in the Caspian Sea, interstate and separatist conflicts in areas through which pipelines are being built (or are likely to be built), and widespread socioeconomic disorder.

The Contested Caspian

At present, there is no commonly accepted legal framework covering ownership of the Caspian's undersea energy resources. All of the five littoral states—Azerbaijan, Iran, Kazakhstan, Russia, and Turkmenistan—seek to divide up these waters in such a way as to obtain the largest possible territory in which to drill for oil. The resulting confusion over the Caspian's legal status has deterred some firms from bidding on concession rights in deeper waters and soured relations between the littoral states. Until the dispute is resolved, exploitation of the Caspian's offshore deposits will be a source of continuing discord and friction.[60]

Several factors complicate the task of resolving the Caspian Sea territorial dispute. The first is the continuing legacy of the Soviet legal system. Until the collapse of the Soviet Union in 1992, the Caspian lay mostly within the territory of the USSR (except for a section abutting Iran), and decisions regarding its economic development were largely made in Moscow. More concerned with protecting access to the Caspian's valuable sturgeon catch than in drilling for oil, the Soviet Union and Iran signed a treaty in 1921 (reaffirmed by a second treaty in 1940) giving each an exclusive ten-mile-wide coastal fishing zone and providing for shared jurisdiction of all remaining waters. Today Russia—which assumed responsibility for the USSR's treaty obligations—insists that the 1921 and 1940 treaties are still in force. Moscow argues (with some support from Iran) that the new nations are thus entitled to a ten-mile coastal zone of their own but that the main body of water remains under *shared* jurisdiction. The three new nations of the Caspian, on the other hand, want to divide up the entire sea among the littoral states, giving each a substantial slice of undersea territory and excluding Russia and Iran from energy-bearing areas of the central Caspian.[61]

In support of their various positions, the five littoral states offer conflicting interpretations of the Caspian's legal status. Russia and Iran claim that the Caspian is a lake, and thus not subject to the provisions of the United Nations Convention on the Law of the Sea (UNCLOS). Under this interpretation, the 1921 and 1940 Soviet-Iranian treaties would carry considerable weight. However, the other three littoral states insist that the Caspian is a sea, and therefore falls under the jurisdiction of UNCLOS. In this case, international law would support a division of the Caspian's development rights into five national sectors, each extending from the littoral states' coastline to a point or line equidistant between them. This position is also backed by the United States.[62]

There is currently no agreement among the littoral states on resolving these issues. Negotiations have been held on an irregular basis, but it is not clear when—or in what manner—the matter will be concluded.[63] In the meantime, Azerbaijan and Turkmenistan have proceeded as if their interpretation will ultimately prevail, leasing out large sections of their maritime territory to international energy consortia like the AIOC. This, in turn, has led to a bilateral dispute between these two countries over the precise location of the midline between them—a dispute that directly affects the ownership of off-shore oil fields located in the central Caspian. The rights to develop one such field, called Kyapaz by Azerbaijan and Serdar by Turkmenistan, have been auctioned off to competing foreign firms by the two governments, producing a volley of angry charges between them. Both countries have declared that they wish to adopt a negotiated settlement, but no such accord has yet been signed.[64]

The unsettled legal status of the Caspian also jeopardizes a key element of the U.S. plan for energy development in the region: the construction of an oil and gas pipeline beneath the Caspian Sea from Turkmenistan to Azerbaijan. This ambitious project received its initial boost in August 1999, when Turkmenistan gave its approval for construction of the Trans-Caspian Gas Pipeline (TCGP) by Shell Oil, Bechtel, and GE Capital. It is unclear, however, whether the partners in the scheme can raise the necessary start-up funds, estimated at $3 billion.[65] But even if this problem can be overcome, there still remains the unresolved issue of jurisdiction over the pipeline's undersea route.

Instability on the Pipeline Trail

Questions over the production and delivery of Caspian basin energy supplies invariably come back to the central dilemma of transportation. No matter which direction the pipelines may follow—north, south, east, or west—they must cross through one or more areas of instability. Some of these areas may be more unstable than others, and future developments may bring peace to areas now torn by violence. In all likelihood, however, whatever route is selected for the export of Caspian energy will encounter some form of friction or violence.[66] (See map of likely pipeline routes.)

By far the shortest and most expedient routes for carrying Caspian energy to world markets would extend southward from Azerbaijan and Turkmenistan through Iran to existing oil terminals on the Persian Gulf coast. But this route, of course, would clash with the official U.S. policy of isolating the Iranian economy. In 1995, President Clinton signed an executive order that bars American companies from conducting business with Iran. In 1996, moreover, the U.S. Congress adopted the Iran and Libya Sanctions Act, imposing severe penalties on non-U.S. firms that invest more than $40 million in Iran's oil industry. Unless there is a significant sea change in U.S. policy, therefore, none of the major Caspian oil consortia will be able to construct pipelines through Iran.[67]

The next most practical route for the export of Caspian energy supplies extends westward from Azerbaijan and Kazakhstan through remnants of the old Soviet pipeline system to the Russian port of Novorossiysk, from which tankers can proceed across the Black Sea and through the Turkish Straits to the Mediterranean. This route is, in fact, being used for the transport of oil from the Tengiz field in

Caspian Sea Basin

Kazakhstan and for some of the output from the AIOC fields in
Azerbaijan. But the pipeline from Baku to Novorossiysk passes right
through the heart of Chechnya, and has had to be shut down on
occasion because of the fighting there. The line from Kazakhstan to
Novorossiysk circumvents Chechnya to the north but skirts several

other trouble spots, including Dagestan and North Ossetia. Clearly, Russia's determination to control Chechnya and suppress rebel groups in the region is motivated, at least in part, by a desire to protect these vital pipeline routes.[68]

To avoid the turmoil in southern Russia, AIOC and the other Azerbaijan-based consortia intend to ship the bulk of their exports through Georgia, to the port of Supsa on the Black Sea. But this trajectory also entails some degree of risk: in Azerbaijan, the chosen route passes close to the rebellious territory of Nagorno-Karabakh (controlled since 1991 by Armenian separatists); in Georgia, it passes near two contested areas, South Ossetia and Abkhazia. To further complicate matters, Russia has deployed "peacekeeping" forces in both Abkhazia and South Ossetia, and is thought to have aided the Armenians of Nagorno-Karabakh in their struggle with Azerbaijan.[69] What this means, of course, is that any effort by Azerbaijan and Georgia to safeguard the route against rebel incursions could lead to a clash with Russian troops and thus to a much larger conflict.

The United States has been the main proponent of an oil and gas pipeline that would follow the Baku-Supsa route as far as Tbilisi in Georgia and then turn south into northeastern Turkey; one branch of the system would then feed gas into the Turkish network at Erzurum and a second, carrying oil, would cross the middle of the country and terminate at the port of Ceyhan on the Mediterranean coast. This route is especially appealing to U.S. policy makers because it would link Turkey, a key member of NATO, to America's key allies in the Caspian: Azerbaijan and Georgia. "This is not just another oil and gas deal, and this is not just another pipeline," Secretary Richardson declared in 1999. "It is a strategic framework that advances America's national security interests."[70]

Development of this "framework" was one of the most important policy objectives of the Clinton administration. To generate support for the Baku-Ceyhan pipeline (as this enterprise is known), the White House pledged various forms of economic assistance and worked closely with the governments involved to draft the required protocols.[71] The November 1999 signing of a legal document by the leaders of Azerbaijan, Georgia, and Turkey to allow work on the pipeline was hailed by Richardson as a "major foreign policy victory" for the administration and was witnessed by the president himself.[72]

But while the Baku-Ceyhan pipeline project enjoys strong support in Washington, it must still overcome a number of significant obstacles—not the least of which is oil company reluctance to shoulder the immense cost of its construction, estimated at $2.4 billion. Some of the companies would reportedly prefer to rely on the shorter Baku-Supsa line, or to bide their time until improvements in the U.S.-Iranian relationship allow for the transit of Caspian Sea energy to the Persian Gulf, where extensive storage and port facilities are already in place.[73] The Baku-Ceyhan line would also pass through an area that has experienced bitter fighting between the Turkish army and Kurdish insurgents belonging to the PKK (Kurdish Workers' Party). Although the PKK called for a cease-fire in 1999 after the capture of its supreme leader, Abdullah Ocalan, Turkish repression of the Kurds has continued apace, and so there is every likelihood of renewed fighting in the area.[74]

The other potential pipeline routes—those running eastward from the Caspian, rather than westward—face an equal or even greater risk of conflict. Of these proposals, none is more fraught with hazard than the plan to build a natural gas pipeline from the Dauletabad field in eastern Turkmenistan to Multan in Pakistan—a route that passes right through the center of war-torn Afghanistan. Improbable as this seems, several companies, including Unocal of the United States, have secured approval from the Taliban—Kabul's current masters—for construction of such a pipeline.[75] Although eager to proceed with this project, Unocal has had to suspend operations in the area because of continued fighting between the Taliban and rebel forces of Ahmad Shah Massoud, a former leader of the anti-Soviet mujahideen. In 1999, moreover, Afghanistan was subjected to U.N. economic sanctions because of Kabul's refusal to extradite Osama bin Laden to the United States for prosecution in connection with the August 1998 bombings of the American embassies in Kenya and Tanzania—thus precluding further cooperation between U.S. oil firms and the Taliban.[76]

The final pipeline route under consideration is also the most

ambitious: a Chinese plan to transport Caspian oil and gas from Kazakhstan and Turkmenistan to eastern China, a distance of some four
thousand miles. Aside from the various geographical impediments to
this project—much of the terrain along this route is harsh and mountainous—the proposed pipeline would pass through several areas of
instability, including China's remote Xinjiang province. The only part
of China (other than Tibet) in which non-Chinese peoples form the
majority, Xinjiang has long been torn by fighting between government
troops and Uighur separatists who seek to establish an independent
"East Turkestan."[77] Despite this, Beijing secured an agreement from
Kazakhstan in 1997 for the construction of an eighteen-hundred-mile
pipeline from the Aktyubinsk oil field to Xinjiang. Future plans call
for the addition of a natural gas pipeline that would draw on supplies
in Kazakhstan and Turkmenistan and proceed onward to coastal
China.[78]

The various pipeline routes leading out from the Caspian are likely
to remain periodic sites of conflict for a long time to come. Once the
pipelines are built and large quantities of oil and gas are regularly
flowing through them, these routes undoubtedly will be invested with
considerable strategic importance by the leaders of the countries
though which they pass; accordingly, opponents of the regime in
question are likely to view attacks on these assets as the perfect means
for weakening the government and depleting its coffers. A permanent
low-grade war along the various pipeline routes in the Caspian area
could result. And if the governments involved fail in their efforts to
protect the pipelines, they are certain to turn for help to their external
allies—leading to increased involvement by Washington and Moscow
and, in a worst-case situation, to the deployment of American and
Russian combat troops.

Social and Political Unrest

The future stability of energy production in the Caspian region is also
threatened by widespread discontent and unrest within the area's
newly independent states. These countries were ruled until very recently by a self-perpetuating bureaucratic elite—the Soviet *nomen-*

klatura—trained by and loyal to the Communist Party leadership in Moscow. When the Soviet system collapsed, local Communist elites, now recast as nationalist leaders, seized the reins of government and established local principalities on a Soviet-inspired, authoritarian model. For the most part, these regimes have embraced a market-type economy and at least the trappings of democracy. However, several of the states have resorted to authoritarian methods to retain power, a development that has alienated many sectors of society.[79]

The paramount leaders of the new Caspian states—Presidents Aliyev of Azerbaijan, Nazarbayev of Kazakhstan, Saparmurat Niyazov of Turkmenistan, and Islam Karimov of Uzbekistan—seem firmly entrenched in power. All have legitimized their autocratic rule through some form of democratic process—some would say "democratic window dressing"[80]—and all appear to enjoy some degree of popular support. Aliyev and Nazarbayev, for instance, won extended terms of office through tightly controlled elections in 1998 and 1999, respectively.[81] But none of these autocrats has allowed opposition parties or a critical press to flourish, and all rely on state security organs (often remnants of the KGB) to suppress dissent.[82]

Despite the repression, social and political unrest is growing throughout the region. Opposition parties have sprouted in many countries, labor movements are gaining strength, and antigovernment demonstrations have erupted on a number of occasions. Even more significant is the emergence of militant Islamist movements inspired by, and often supported by, their counterparts in the Persian Gulf and Southwest Asia.[83] Although most such groups are concerned with religious and educational matters, some have taken up arms against what they see as alien, hostile regimes. Islamic militants in Uzbekistan have attacked government offices there and in Kyrgyzstan, and insurgents in Tajikistan have been fighting an on-again, off-again conflict with government forces (and their Russian allies) since the early 1990s. In 1999, as mentioned, a rebel army invaded southern Dagestan with the declared intent of establishing an Islamic republic.[84]

The potential for instability is further heightened by the legacy of the Soviets' crazy-quilt pattern of administrative borders. To diffuse nationalist impulses and to otherwise promote its interests, the Soviet leadership created interrepublic borders that often bore little relationship to the actual distribution of ethnic groups. For example, Moscow incorporated the Armenian-populated enclave of Nagorno-Karabakh within Azerbaijan instead of Armenia. Similarly, a largely Tajik-inhabited area was incorporated into Uzbekistan, and a number of Uzbek-populated areas were assigned to Tajikistan and Kyrgyzstan.

These territorial allocations were relatively unimportant during the Soviet era. But they assumed great significance in 1992 when the various internal borders became the outer perimeters of sovereign states. In this new situation, some ethnic constituencies have wound up as minority groups in states controlled by other, unfriendly groups. This has led to the outbreak of separatist conflicts in some areas (notably in Abkhazia and Nagorno-Karabakh) and to periodic flare-ups of ethnic unrest in others.[85] Although cease-fires have been arranged in some areas of fighting, including Abkhazia, Nagorno-Karabakh, and Tajikistan, none of the major disputes have been fully resolved, and the potential for renewed combat appears substantial.[86]

Tensions are being exacerbated, moreover, by the growing gap between rich and poor in the Caspian region. Although the signing of new oil and gas contracts has produced instant wealth for a small number of favored entrepreneurs—most of whom enjoy close links to the governing elite—economic activity as a whole has declined since 1990, and most people have suffered a sharp drop in their living standard.[87] "Frequent travelers to the region are struck almost immediately by the pervasive bitterness and the growing sense of deprivation that most citizens feel about their deteriorating lives," Professor Olcott of Colgate University observed in 1998. "The countries are being deeply divided from within, between those whom the transition process has benefitted and those whom it has impoverished."[88]

Political instability provides ample opportunity for outside powers to manipulate developments in the region and to force local governments into military alliances or other security arrangements they would prefer to avoid. Such alliances may cause neighboring states to feel a greater sense of insecurity—and make them more likely to seek new military linkages of their own. It is in such an environment that proxy wars are most likely to erupt. As in Central America during the 1980s, both Washington and Moscow have a significant vested interest in the survival of particular Caspian regimes. When these regimes are threatened by internal unrest or the spillover of conflicts from neighboring countries, their great-power patrons are likely to respond with increased offers of aid and assistance. Given the capricious location of many Caspian borders, and the ethnic and ideological linkages between various rebel factions, any outbreak of fighting is likely to appear threatening to several governments and thus invite stepped-up involvement by both major powers. This, in turn, can lead to an arms-supply contest between Washington and Moscow, with each side attempting to outdo the other in the delivery of weaponry and military equipment—accompanied, as always, by the deployment of military advisers and technicians.

THE SMOLDERING CASPIAN

Even without the involvement of Russia and the United States, the Caspian Sea basin would be prey to periodic upheavals and violence in the period ahead. The most likely outcome of such friction, as noted, is the outbreak of proxy conflicts involving local governments and insurgent groups backed by a major power. Such antagonisms could take the form of all-out combat but are more likely to involve persistent but low-grade warfare in border zones and embattled ethnic enclaves. To protect vital pipelines against recurring attack and sabotage, regional leaders may be forced to deploy their armies along vulnerable sections for an indefinite period. History suggests that low-grade conflicts of this sort can last for many years without producing dramatic change in the battlefield equation. But it is also possible for such contests to experience sudden escalation leading to deeper involvement by outside powers.

Clearly, neither Washington nor Moscow wants to be drawn into regional conflicts. But the fact that both of these powers are strengthening their military ties in the area and providing arms to local governments is a cause for alarm. Neither power can control social and political developments in the Caspian or prevent the outbreak of violence. As a result, they may find themselves in a situation where their vital interests appear at risk and direct military involvement seems to offer the only solution. In this manner, the Caspian could prove the setting for a major regional conflagration.

5

Oil Wars in the South China Sea

Clear across the broad width of Asia, on the western fringe of the Pacific Ocean, lies the third anchor of the Strategic Triangle: the South China Sea. Bordered on the north by Taiwan and China, on the east by the Philippine Islands, on the south by Indonesia and Malaysia, and on the west by Vietnam, the South China Sea adjoins some of the most dynamic and powerful states in Asia. Long important as a crossroads for seaborne commerce, these waters are also thought to sit atop substantial reserves of oil and natural gas. While much larger than the Persian Gulf and the Caspian Sea, the South China Sea is like them in two critical respects: its undersea resources are subject to overlapping and contested claims, and the states involved in these maritime disputes appear prepared to employ military force in the defense of what they view as vital national interests.

Driving the struggle for control over the South China Sea's subsea energy reserves is the extraordinary economic growth of the Asia-Pacific region. Until the economic crisis of 1997–99 engulfed the region, the economies of the Pacific Rim countries were expanding at spectacular rates of growth, in some cases exceeding 10 percent per year. Although the crisis slowed or reversed economic growth in a number of these countries, its effects proved relatively short-lived. In China and Taiwan, the crisis produced only a modest dip in what had been very high rates of expansion—over 11 percent per year in the case of China. Economic expansion was predicted to resume its brisk pace throughout East Asia in the early years of the twenty-first century, restoring this area's status as the premier dynamo of the world economy.[1]

For decades, economic growth in Asia has required ever-expanding amounts of energy. For most of the 1990s, energy consumption in East Asia's ten leading economic centers (China, Hong Kong, Indonesia, Japan, Malaysia, the Philippines, Singapore, South Korea, Taiwan, and Thailand) grew by a rate of 5.5 percent per year—approximately ten times the rate of the rest of the world.[2] The rate of growth in Asia's energy consumption is expected to moderate slightly in the early decades of the twenty-first century, but, at 3.7 percent per year, would still be likely to exceed the rates prevailing in other parts of the world. By the year 2020, Asia is expected to account for approximately 34 percent of total world energy consumption, compared to 24 percent for North America, 13 percent for western Europe, and 12 percent for the former Soviet Union and eastern Europe.[3] (See Table 5.1.)

Asia's growing need for energy will generate an especially strong demand for oil and natural gas. If current projections prove accurate, the nations of Asia will rely on these materials for approximately half of their total energy supply in 2020. In the case of petroleum, this means that Asia's daily consumption would rise from 19 million barrels per day (the rate in 1997) to 33 million barrels at the end of this period. The added amount of oil—some 14 million barrels per day—is equivalent to current consumption by Latin America, the Middle East, and the former Soviet Union combined. Asia's supply of natural gas will have to increase by an even more substantial amount to meet anticipated demand in 2020.[4]

The acquisition of all this additional oil and gas will prove especially arduous for the nations of Asia because the region lacks adequate hydrocarbon reserves of its own. Although several countries,

Table 5.1: Projected Energy Consumption in Asia, 1990–2020 (Quadrillion BTU)							
	History		Projections				Average Annual Percentage Change,
Region/Country	1990	1997	2005	2010	2015	2020	1997–2020
Developing Asia, total	51.4	75.3	105.0	126.4	144.3	172.6	3.7
China	27.0	36.7	55.0	68.1	79.2	97.3	4.3
India	7.8	11.8	17.0	20.4	23.1	27.3	3.7
South Korea	3.7	7.5	9.3	10.7	11.9	13.4	2.6
Other	13.0	19.3	23.7	27.2	30.1	34.7	2.6
Industralized Asia, total*	23.0	27.1	29.2	31.1	32.2	33.1	0.9
Japan	18.1	21.3	22.6	24.1	24.8	25.4	0.8
World, total	346.7	379.9	449.0	500.2	544.4	607.7	2.1

Source: U.S. Department of Energy, *International Energy Outlook 2000*
*Includes Australia and New Zealand

including China and Indonesia, possess modest supplies of petroleum and natural gas, none possesses truly significant quantities, such as those found in the Persian Gulf and the Caspian areas. At the end of the 1990s, Asian countries produced approximately 7 million barrels of oil per day but consumed 19 million barrels; by 2020, the gap between production and consumption will have doubled, with net imports reaching 25 million barrels per day.[5] A similar situation prevails with natural gas: although Asia currently produces about as much gas as it consumes, it will become increasingly dependent on imported supplies as time passes.

The growing demand for energy in Asia will affect the South China Sea in two significant ways. First, the states that border on the area will undoubtedly seek to maximize their access to its undersea resources in order to diminish their reliance on imports. Second, several other East Asian countries, including Japan and South Korea, are vitally dependent on energy supplies located elsewhere, almost all of which must travel by ship *through* the South China Sea. Those states will naturally seek to prevent any threat to the continued flow of resources. Together, these factors have made the South China Sea the fulcrum of energy competition in the Asia-Pacific region.[6]

So far, energy competition in the region has provoked only minor outbreaks of violence, in most cases involving clashes between the naval forces of neighboring states. These outbreaks have largely arisen from competing claims to the Spratly archipelago, a large chain of reefs, shoals, and islands that stretches for hundreds of miles across the region. Because possession of the islands could be used to legitimize claims to surrounding waters—and to their subsea resources— interested nations have attempted to assert control over as many of these bodies as possible. At least five states (China, Malaysia, the Philippines, Taiwan, and Vietnam) have established military bases or naval stations in the Spratlys, and fighting has erupted on several occasions when one or another of these states has sought to expel the forces of another. By 1999, thirteen such incidents had been reported, and the intervals between them appeared to be growing shorter.[7] (See Table 5.3.)

These incidents are worrisome for several reasons. Although the states involved have thus far managed to avoid a major military engagement, there are signs of growing tension in the region. China has become increasingly assertive in the area, and a regional arms race has broken out. In addition, the Philippine government has invoked its mutual defense treaty with the United States to obtain American support for efforts to dislodge Chinese forces from islands claimed by Manila. Japan has also sought to bolster its position in the area, and it, too, has appealed for American military support. A future clash in the Spratlys could trigger a much larger conflict, involving the forces of several major powers.

The South China Sea is not the only area in Asia that could witness the outbreak of a major conflict in the years ahead. The region also faces the possibility of war between China and Taiwan, and between North Korea and South Korea. But these disputes, which originated during the early Cold War period, have lost some of their immediacy and venom. (In fact, the Koreas appear to be considering reunification.) The dispute over the South China Sea, however, is likely to grow more intense as the regional competition over vital energy supplies increases.

ENERGY GEOPOLITICS IN ASIA

The need for additional supplies of energy will prove to be one of the most demanding challenges facing Asian leaders in the decades to come. Growing national wealth will, of course, provide many of these states with the funds needed for new domestic energy projects and, where necessary, the procurement of imported supplies. As demand continues to rise, however, domestic reserves will be exhausted and the competition for imported supplies will intensify. This, in turn, will have a profound impact on politics within the region and on the relationships between these countries and the world at large.

The linkages between energy demand and foreign policy will be especially strong in the case of China and Japan, the two most powerful states in the region and the two leading consumers of energy. Both countries hope to attain high levels of economic growth in the twenty-first century, and both will need to secure additional supplies of energy to make this possible. China's energy use is expected to double between 2000 and 2020, rising from 44 to 97 quadrillion BTUs ("quads") per year; Japan's consumption will rise by about 25 percent, from 20 to 25 quads. If these projections prove accurate, China and Japan together will account for one-fifth of total world energy consumption in 2020—about the same amount as western Europe and Latin America combined.[8] (See Table 5.2.)

Securing all of this energy is bound to prove a major challenge for Chinese and Japanese leaders. China is in a somewhat better position than Japan in this regard, because it possesses significant domestic supplies of oil, natural gas, and coal. Until 1993, China exported more oil than it imported, and it currently obtains the bulk of its petroleum and natural gas from domestic sources. It is in the possession of coal, however, that China is especially fortunate: in 1999, BP Amoco estimated that China's reserves of coal stood at 114.5 billion metric tons, or about 12 percent of the total world

Table 5.2: Projected Energy Consumption in China, Japan, and South Korea by Fuel Type, 1990–2020

Region/Fuel Type	History 1990	History 1997	Projections 2005	Projections 2010	Projections 2015	Projections 2020	Average Annual Percentage Change, 1997–2020
China							
oil (mbd)	2.3	3.8	5.4	7.1	8.8	9.5	4.1
natural gas (tcf)	0.5	0.7	2.4	3.9	5.8	8.6	11.2
coal (mst)	1,124	1,532	2,161	2,584	2,882	3,658	3.9
Japan							
oil (mbd)	5.1	5.7	5.8	6.0	6.2	6.3	0.4
natural gas (tcf)	1.9	2.3	2.9	3.2	3.4	3.7	2.0
coal (mst)	125	143	164	168	173	175	0.9
South Korea							
oil (mbd)	1.0	2.3	2.7	3.1	3.4	3.6	2.0
natural gas (tcf)	0.1	0.5	0.8	1.1	1.5	2.4	6.8
coal (mst)	42	65	71	81	87	89	1.4

Source: U.S. Department of Energy, *International Energy Outlook 2000*.
mbd = million barrels per day
tcf = trillion cubic feet
mst = million short tons

supply.[9] Beijing intends to rely to an increasing degree on its abundant supply of coal for its energy requirements; according to the U.S. Department of Energy, coal's share of China's total energy consumption will rise from 74.5 percent in 1995 to approximately 77.4 percent in 2015.[10]

China's heavy reliance on domestic supplies of coal has obvious economic advantages but also significant long-term problems. To begin with, the extensive burning of coal for electric power generation and industrial use is producing dangerous levels of air pollution in many parts of the country, causing massive environmental damage and severe, costly health problems. In addition, the heavy use of coal is releasing large amounts of carbon dioxide into the upper atmosphere, substantially increasing China's contribution to the buildup of heat-trapping "greenhouse" gases. At present, China accounts for 13 percent of world carbon emissions, compared to 24 percent for the United States; by 2020, China's share is expected to rise to 21 percent, while the U.S. share will drop to 20 percent.[11] This surge in China's carbon emissions will make it much harder to implement the 1992 U.N. Framework Convention on Climate Change, which calls on all states to cooperate in reversing the accumulation of greenhouse gases.

A heavy dependence on coal will also hinder further development of China's transportation infrastructure, which increasingly relies on motor vehicles and air travel. At present, there are only about two automobiles per one hundred people in China, compared to about forty per one hundred people in the older industrialized countries; however, car ownership in China is rising at a rate of 12 to 14 percent per year and could grow even faster in coming years as more and more Chinese aquire a middle-class standard of living.[12] Air travel is also growing at an astonishing rate, in recent years averaging more than 20 percent per year.[13] All of this, combined with the continuing expansion of industries using petroleum feedstocks, will produce a steadily rising demand for oil.[14]

To satisfy these needs and to reduce the use of coal in metropolitan areas, China will require a huge increase in its consumption of oil and natural gas. According to the DoE, China's consumption of oil will rise from an estimated 3.8 million barrels per day in 1997 to 9.5 million barrels in 2020, an increase of 150 percent. At the same time, consumption of natural gas will rise by about 1,129 percent, from 0.7 to 8.6 trillion cubic feet per year.[15] It is highly doubtful that domestic production of these hydrocarbons will keep pace with the growth in demand. As of 1999, China was producing 3.2 million barrels of oil per day and consuming about 4.4 million barrels, an import gap of 1.2 million barrels per day;[16] by 2020, the gap between output and consumption will rise to an estimated 5.9 million barrels per day.[17] Imports of natural gas will also have to grow significantly over this period.

Hoping to minimize its dependence on imported oil, China has sought to increase production at its domestic fields. Despite strenuous efforts, however, Beijing has not been able to extract increased supplies of petroleum from existing deposits, many of which are substantially depleted. Chinese officials had hoped to compensate for declining reserves at older sites through accelerated development of the Tarim basin in western China, but oil production in this remote area has not matched expectations. Recognizing that China's onshore fields will not be able to yield significantly increased supplies of petroleum, and reluctant to become heavily dependent on foreign sources of energy, Beijing has begun to emphasize the development of offshore sources. This, in turn, has led to growing Chinese interest in the energy potential of the East and South China Seas.[18]

At present, most of China's offshore drilling operations are concentrated in coastal areas, especially the Gulf of Chihli (off northeastern China) and the mouth of the Pearl River (near Hong Kong and Macao). Increasingly, however, China is turning its attention to promising fields in deeper waters. In 1992, Beijing announced its formal claim to the Spratly and Paracel Islands and to all subsea resources lying in adjacent areas of the South China Sea. On this basis, China then awarded drilling concessions to a number of Western firms for energy production in areas off of Vietnam.[19] To protect its new strategic interests in the area, China has also expanded its military presence there.

For Japan, the challenge of obtaining sufficient energy is likely to prove even more demanding, given the country's marked scarcity of domestic reserves. Oil, which provides 56 percent of Japan's total energy requirements, must be obtained from foreign sources, as domestic reserves are infinitesimal—about 60 million barrels, or enough for ten days' consumption. Japan possesses slightly larger reserves of coal and natural gas, but it still relies on foreign sources for 99 percent of its annual coal consumption and 97 percent of its gas consumption. Nuclear energy and hydropower generate some of Japan's electricity, but imported supplies of oil, coal, and gas currently satisfy about four-fifths of the country's primary energy requirements.[20]

The Japanese government has attempted to reduce the country's dependence on imported supplies of energy by investing heavily in nuclear power: it now has fifty-one power reactors on line—more than any other country except the United States and France—and is building another ten. However, Japanese efforts to become self-sufficient in the production of nuclear energy through the development of plutonium-powered breeder reactors have, until now, proved an embarrassing failure. Tokyo will, therefore, remain heavily dependent on imported sources of energy for the foreseeable future.[21]

Japan's continuing dependence on imported energy has obvious geopolitical implications. The country currently obtains about 75 percent of its oil from the Persian Gulf,[22] and this percentage is expected to rise in the years ahead as other sources of petroleum begin to dry up. Virtually all of this oil travels by tanker across the Indian Ocean, through the Strait of Malacca (separating Indonesia from Malaysia), and diagonally across the South China Sea. The latter part of this route is also used by many of the ships bringing coal from Australia and liquified natural gas from Indonesia. Protection of tanker movement through these passageways will, therefore, constitute a major strategic priority for Japan.[23]

While China and Japan will account for a very large share of the energy consumed in Asia, they are not the only states with a growing appetite for oil and gas. Several other countries, including Indonesia, Malaysia, the Philippines, South Korea, Taiwan, Thailand, and Vietnam, will also require increased supplies of energy. Although some of these states can satisfy current needs with domestic reserves (Indonesia, Malaysia, and Vietnam possess oil; Indonesia also possesses coal and natural gas), all will need to supplement local supplies with imported energy. All, moreover, rely on seaborne commerce for imports and exports of vital resources. Most significant, all but South Korea have established claims to extensive offshore development zones in the South China Sea, making them potential rivals of China and one another in the exploitation of seabed energy resources.

The acquisition of increased energy supplies will prove particularly challenging for South Korea and Taiwan—both of which, like Japan, possess very few energy sources of their own and so rely to a great extent on imported supplies. Together, these two countries consumed 2.9 million barrels of oil per day in 1999—about the same amount as Germany—along with substantial quantities of coal and liquified natural gas.[24] From a strategic perspective, both countries find themselves in a position similar to Japan's: highly dependent on oil imports from the Middle East, most of which travels by ship through the South China Sea.

Indonesia, Malaysia, Thailand, and Vietnam occupy a somewhat different geostrategic position. All possess some domestic supplies of energy and export a portion of their output to other countries in the region. All but Indonesia, however, are dependent on imported supplies for at least some portion of their energy consumption, and even Indonesia will be joining the ranks of oil importers in the early twenty-first century. Like South Korea and Taiwan, therefore, they share a vital interest in the security of maritime trade routes. Their concern over maritime security is further magnified by the fact that a large share of their oil and gas reserves are located in offshore fields—primarily in the South China Sea and adjacent waters. Not surprisingly, the development of these fields has led the nations involved to place much greater emphasis on the protection of their offshore territories.

What makes this situation so unstable is the fact that many of these states' exclusive economic zones (EEZs) overlap with one another, producing complex territorial disputes. The lucrative oil and gas fields of the Gulf of Thailand, for instance, are located in areas claimed by Cambodia, Malaysia, Thailand, and Vietnam; the rich natural-gas field in the Natuna Island area is claimed by China, Indonesia, Malaysia, and Vietnam. As the demand for energy rises, the value attached to these areas by the nations that claim them is bound to increase. Under these circumstances, disputes over the possession of offshore EEZs are likely to become increasingly heated and fractious. This will be true of all such disputes—but none is more likely to produce outright conflict than the struggle for control of the resources of the South China Sea.

CONFLICTING CLAIMS IN THE SOUTH CHINA SEA

Long important as a major artery for international shipping, the South China Sea has acquired added significance in recent years because of

expectations that it harbors large reserves of energy. Just how extensive these reserves will prove to be is still a matter of some conjecture:
because so little drilling has been conducted in the area, experts lack
sufficient data to make reliable assessments of untapped supplies.
China's Ministry of Geology and Mineral Resources has reported that
the South China Sea holds as much as 130 billion barrels of oil—an
amount greater than the combined reserves of Europe and Latin
America.[25] Although confirmation of these and other estimates will
require extensive survey work, many countries in the region are sufficiently impressed with its potential to make ambitious territorial
claims. They are also prepared to defend their parcels against rival
claimants.[26]

The legal regime covering possession of offshore energy resources
is relatively new and untested, allowing for widespread disagreement
over its application. Under the U.N. Convention on the Law of the
Sea, nations that border an ocean or sea can claim an EEZ covering
coastal waters out to two hundred miles from the shoreline; when
such a zone overlaps with that claimed by a neighboring state, each
nation may claim an EEZ extending out to a line equidistant between
them. This principle works reasonably well if there are no islands or
other offshore features in the area or if the states involved agree on
the ownership of these features. When, however, the waters under
consideration are populated by many islands, or when ownership of
these islands is contested, the potential for discord and conflict is
great.[27]

With its highly irregular coastal boundaries and numerous clusters
of islands, the South China Sea is a nightmare for the determination
and adjudication of EEZ boundaries. China and Vietnam, for example, have sparred over their maritime border in the Gulf of Ton-
kin; Malaysia and the Philippines both claim areas off of eastern
Borneo; and Malaysia and Vietnam have wrangled over their mutual
border in the Gulf of Thailand. These disputes are complicated
enough. But overshadowing all of these other disputes is China's
claim to the *entire* Spratly archipelago. By claiming these islands,
China seeks to establish an EEZ covering most of the South China
Sea—a stance that puts it in direct conflict with Brunei, Indonesia,

South China Sea Area

Malaysia, the Philippines, Taiwan, and Vietnam, each of which has also laid claim to significant segments of the Spratlys and their surrounding waters.[28]

In large measure, the energy conflict in the South China Sea is a dispute over the Spratly Islands. This collection of four hundred or so islets, cays, reefs, and rocks—many visible at low tide only—are distributed over some eighty thousand square miles of ocean. Although too small to support a permanent population, these islands are claimed in whole or in part by six states: Brunei, China, Malaysia, the Philippines, Taiwan, and Vietnam. China and Taiwan, citing historic links to the area, claim the entire Spratly chain; the Philippines and Vietnam claim significant segments of the chain; and the others claim individual islands falling within their two-hundred-mile coastal EEZs.[29] (See map.)

China bases its claim to the Spratly chain (which it calls the Nansha Islands) on continuous Chinese administration of the archipelago since the Tang dynasty (618–907). To bolster this assertion, Chinese officials cite various accounts of Chinese naval and maritime operations in this area over the succeeding centuries. Most Western experts believe, however, that such operations were both sporadic and largely confined to fishing expeditions.[30] Nevertheless, China's top legislative body, the Standing Committee of the National People's Congress, formally proclaimed Chinese sovereignty over the entire Spratly archipelago in 1992. This measure, known as the Law on the Territorial Waters and Their Contiguous Areas, also empowered the People's Liberation Army (PLA) to employ force if required to defend the islands against foreign attack or occupation.[31]

In support of its claims, China has engaged in a variety of activities intended to demonstrate its intent to occupy and eventually control the entire area. These activities include the establishment of military outposts on unoccupied islands, periodic naval maneuvers, awarding exploration and development concessions to international oil companies in contested waters, and occasionally making a show of force.[32] And while Beijing has agreed to discuss the future of the Spratlys with other states in the area and even to negotiate joint development schemes, it has never abandoned its contention that the entire area falls under Chinese sovereignty.[33]

China's title to the Spratlys has been contested by the other claimants to the islands, all of whom cite historical factors and UNCLOS to advance their positions. Until now, the most assertive of these has been Vietnam, which, like China, bases its claim to the Spratlys on long-term use and occupation (principally by fishermen who establish temporary quarters on the islands). Vietnam was also the first state in the area to award oil exploration contracts to foreign energy firms for development of the South China Sea's underwater resources—a practice that began under the old, U.S.-backed South Vietnamese government and has been continued by the present regime. To protect these operations and to further assert its territorial claims in the face of mounting Chinese pressure, Vietnam has deployed its naval forces in the Spratlys and established military posts on twenty or so reefs and islands.[34]

Taiwan, in its guise as the Republic of China, also claims the entire Spratlys region. Although much less assertive in this regard than Beijing, Taipei has used the same historical arguments to support its contention that the majority of the South China Sea falls within its territorial waters. (Indeed, there is evidence that Taipei and Beijing—despite their sharp differences on many other issues—have collaborated in the development of a common position on the Spratlys dispute.)[35]

A substantial segment of the archipelago is also claimed by the Philippines, which lies just to the east of the main Spratlys formation. Manila calls its cluster of reefs and islands Kalayaan ("Freedomland") and, like the other claimants, has established small posts on a number of these bodies. The government has also awarded development contracts to foreign oil firms seeking access to promising offshore fields in the area between Palawan Island and the main Spratlys chain.[36]

Finally, parts of the southern Spratly region are claimed by Brunei and Malaysia. Neither of these claims compares in scope to those advanced by China, Vietnam, Taiwan, and the Philippines, but both intrude into areas claimed by these other states. The Sultanate of Brunei, a small state on the north coast of Borneo, claims a narrow EEZ extending two hundred miles into the South China Sea. Malaysia claims an EEZ adjacent to the Natuna area, at the southern edge of the South China Sea, and another off Sabah, on Borneo's northeastern tip. To support its position in these areas, Malaysia has established military posts on several of the islands.[37]

ARMED CLASHES IN THE SOUTH CHINA SEA

Although the claimants to the Spratly Islands have generally chosen to avoid military confrontation with one another, there have been a number of violent clashes over the control of particular islands and reefs. For the most part, these incidents have involved the pursuit and capture of fishermen from one country said to be trawling in areas controlled by another. On several occasions, however, these incidents have amounted to something more significant.[38]

The first major incident occurred in March 1988, when Chinese forces seized control of six islands in a section of the chain long claimed by Vietnam.[39] A brief naval engagement followed, in which three Vietnamese vessels were sunk and seventy-two sailors were killed. This marked the first use of military force by Beijing in the Spratly chain, and also the first action in which Chinese naval forces operated in an offensive mode outside of China's coastal waters.[40] (See Table 5.3.)

Since 1988, China has seized a number of other islands in the Spratly chain claimed by Vietnam and established small military installations on several of them. Most of these bases are in the vicinity of the Wananbei-21 block, a promising energy concession leased by China to the Crestone Energy Corporation of Denver in 1992. This concession lies well within the EEZ claimed by Vietnam, and adjacent to other exploration blocks leased by Hanoi to a group of American and Japanese oil companies. To deter any outside interference with Crestone's drilling operations, Beijing has let it be known that it would defend the area with whatever level of force was thought necessary.[41] "I was assured by top Chinese officials that they will protect me with their full naval might,"[42] Randall C. Thompson, the chairman of Crestone, reported in 1992.

Clearly, this was not just empty rhetoric. China has regularly stationed naval vessels in the area and has beefed up its military presence on the islands it seized from Vietnam. Chinese warships have also menaced vessels belonging to Vietnam on several occasions when they have moved into drilling areas claimed by Beijing. In 1994, for instance, Chinese ships prevented the Vietnamese from resupplying a small drilling rig they had moved into the Wananbei block, presumably as a test of Chinese resolve.[43]

The Mischief Reef Incident

Until 1995, all of the clashes in the South China Sea involving military force pitted China against Vietnam. Most Western analysts concluded

Table 5.3: Military Clashes in the South China Sea, 1988–99

Year	Countries Involved	Military Action
1988	China, Vietnam	Chinese and Vietnamese navies clash at Johnson Reef in the Spratly Islands. Several Vietnamese boats are sunk and 72 sailors killed.
1992	China, Vietnam	Vietnam accuses China of drilling for oil in Vietnamese waters in the Gulf of Tonkin and of landing troops on Da Luc Reef. China seizes almost 20 Vietnamese cargo ships transporting goods from Hong Kong.
1994	China, Vietnam	China and Vietnam have naval confrontations within Vietnam's internationally recognized territorial waters over oil exploration blocks 133, 134, and 135. Chinese claim area as part of their Wananbei-21 block.
1995	China, Philippines	China occupies Philippine-claimed Mischief Reef and establishes a small military post there. Philippine ships attempting to reach the island are driven off by Chinese warships.
1995	Taiwan, Vietnam	Taiwanese artillery on Itu Abu fire on a Vietnamese supply ship.
1995	China, Malaysia	Malaysian patrol boats fire on a Chinese trawler off Sarawak, injuring four Chinese crew members.
1996	China, Philippines	Three Chinese vessels engage in a 90-minute gun battle with a Philippine navy gunboat near Campones Island.
1997	China, Philippines	Philippine navy orders a Chinese speedboat and two fishing boats to leave Scarborough Shoal in April; Philippine fishermen remove Chinese markers and raise their flag. China sends three warships to survey Philippine-occupied Panata and Kota Islands.
1998	China, Philippines	Philippine navy arrests Chinese fishermen off Scarborough Shoal.
1998	Philippines, Vietnam	Vietnamese soldiers fire on a Philippine fishing boat near Tennent (Pigeon) Reef.
1999	China, Philippines	Three Chinese fishing boats are attacked by a Philippine gunboat near Scarborough Shoal, one of which is rammed and sunk; all of the fishermen are rescued, but Beijing delivers an angry protest to Manila.
1999	Philippines, Vietnam	Vietnamese forces on Tennent Reef fire at a Philippine Air Force reconnaissance plane flying over the island.
1999	Malaysia, Philippines	Air force planes from Malaysia and the Philippines nearly clash over a Malaysian-occupied reef in the Spratly chain.

Source: U.S. Department of Energy, Energy Information Administration, "South China Sea Region," January 2000. Additional information from the BBC News Online Network.

from this that Beijing would confine its military activities in the area to attacks on the Vietnamese—still at that time isolated from the rest of the international community—while avoiding armed confrontation with the other claimants to the Spratlys.[44] In early 1995, however, the Philippines discovered that China had constructed a small military post on Mischief Reef, an islet located less than 150 miles from Palawan Island and well within the EEZ claimed by Manila. This provoked a series of naval clashes and a diplomatic crisis that altered the entire strategic equation in the South China Sea.

The aptly named Mischief Reef incident erupted on February 8, 1995, when the Philippines accused China of building a permanent military installation on the island and demanded that Beijing withdraw its forces from the area. Chinese officials denied the accusations, claiming that the structures on Mischief Reef were merely shelters for fishermen; they refused, however, to abandon the facility. Shortly thereafter, a group of ships sent into the area by Manila to investigate was driven off by Chinese warships.[45]

Lacking adequate military strength to drive the Chinese out of the area on its own, Manila appealed for international support. As a first step, it called on Washington to honor the U.S.-Philippines Mutual Defense Treaty of 1951 by supporting military efforts to dislodge the Chinese from Mischief Reef. Although Washington declined to provide direct support for such an operation—asserting that the Spratlys lay outside the territory covered by the 1951 treaty—it did agree to supply the Philippines with additional military aid and training. Washington also sent a strong note to Beijing, protesting the introduction of military forces into the area.[46]

Manila then sought to mobilize diplomatic support for its efforts to reclaim Mischief Reef, primarily by appealing to the Association of Southeast Asian Nations (ASEAN), many of whose members also claimed portions of the Spratlys, or had other reasons for fearing Chinese incursions into the region. At a meeting in Brunei in July, the leaders of ASEAN condemned the use of military force in the South China Sea and called on all states involved to settle their differences through diplomatic effort. In response, China promised to pursue a negotiated solution to its dispute with the Philippines and to avoid any further use of force. At the same time, however, China reaffirmed its sovereignty over the Spratlys and eschewed any inclination to surrender Mischief Reef (or any other island under its control) to rival claimants.[47]

Since 1995, Chinese officials have met on several occasions with their Philippine counterparts to discuss the status of Mischief Reef and other islands claimed by both countries. These meetings have resulted in numerous expressions of goodwill and repeated promises to refrain from the use of force in resolving these disputes. Nevertheless, China has continued to occupy Mischief Reef—reinforcing it in 1998 with additional military structures—and has established a presence on islands even closer to established Philippine territory. These moves have inevitably led to further clashes in the South China Sea, including one incident in which a Philippine gunboat rammed and sank a Chinese fishing vessel.[48]

STRATEGIC RESPONSES TO THE SPRATLYS CONFLICT

The Mischief Reef incident of 1995 forced many states in the region, and others with an interest in the area, to recalibrate their policies regarding China and the South China Sea. Until then, most analysts had assumed that China would confine its use of force to its ongoing dispute with Vietnam and use diplomacy to resolve its disagreements with other states in the area. By forcefully intruding into the territory of an ASEAN member state, however, Beijing indicated that it would not be bound by such limitations. Although China has been relatively circumspect in its use of force since then, it has continued to establish military outposts in the Spratlys and to deploy its warships in areas claimed by the ASEAN states.[49] Thus, while many questions remain about China's ultimate objectives in the Spratlys area, there can be little doubt that Beijing regards the use of military force as a viable option in its pursuit of vital national interests.[50]

China's apparent willingness to use military force to achieve its objectives in the South China Sea is given further credence by the continuing buildup of Chinese naval, amphibious, and air-attack capabilities. Between 1985 and 1997, Chinese military spending increased by about 30 percent, from $28.2 billion to $36.5 billion (in constant 1997 dollars).[51] Much of this was devoted to China's ground forces, which constitute the bulk of the People's Liberation Army, but a very significant proportion was allocated to the PLA navy and air force, and to other units with responsibility for "power projection" in areas distant from the Chinese mainland. In particular, great emphasis has been placed on bolstering the navy's capacity to conduct sustained operations on the high seas.[52]

That China is building up its air and naval forces does not necessarily mean that it is committed to a military solution to the Spratlys dispute. Indeed, many experts on Asian affairs believe that the Chinese will eventually agree to a negotiated settlement of all disputed territories.[53] But at this point there is no evidence that Beijing is prepared to abandon its exclusive claim to the entire archipelago or to renounce the use of force in protecting its offshore possessions. It is possible, then, to imagine a scenario in which a series of minor clashes—like those recorded in Table 5.3—lead to a more sustained military engagement between China and one (or more) of the other claimants. Such a contest could, moreover, jeopardize international shipping through the South China Sea, thus precipitating armed intervention by Japan and/or the United States.[54]

The Naval Arms Race in the South China Sea

While it is difficult to discern China's intentions regarding the use of force in the South China Sea, one thing can be stated with certainty: Beijing has systematically bolstered the capabilities of its navy, transforming a large but unimpressive coastal-defense fleet into a significant deep-water force. While the PLA navy (PLAN) still retains many small coastal vessels, it also boasts a growing flotilla of large, oceangoing warships equipped with modern Russian and Western missile systems. This, in turn, has helped spur other states in the region to build up their own naval capabilities. As a result, Southeast

Asia now finds itself embroiled in a naval arms race that shows little sign of slowing down.[55]

The transformation of the PLAN began in the mid-1980s, following a decision by the Central Military Committee to shift the emphasis of Chinese military planning from all-out war with the Soviet Union to regional conflict on China's southern and eastern periphery. Under the leadership of Admiral Liu Huaqing, commander in chief of the PLAN from 1982 to 1987, the navy embraced a strategy of "offshore active defense," which bolstered its capacity for sustained combat operations on the high seas.[56] According to Liu, implementation of "offshore active defense" meant that "the Chinese Navy should exert effective control of the seas within the first island chain"—that is, the waters bounded on the east by the Japanese archipelago, Taiwan, the Philippines, and Borneo (and encompassing the East and South China Seas).[57]

To exercise such control, Beijing has had to replace its older, Korean War–vintage vessels with modern warships capable of operating on the high seas for extended periods of time. Lacking many of the technologies to accomplish this, China has sought to acquire Western electronics and missiles for ships produced in its domestic shipyards while turning to Russia for transfers of ready-made warships.[58] Since 1985, the PLAN has introduced two new classes of surface combatants: the *Luhu*-class destroyer and the *Jiangwei*-class missile frigate, both of which are furnished with advanced Western navigation gear and, in the case of the *Luhu,* the French-built Crotale surface-to-air missile.[59] To further expand its high-seas combat power, Beijing has purchased two fully equipped *Sovremenny*-class destroyers from Russia and is considering the acquisition of two more.[60]

The Chinese have also procured other systems intended for use in offshore power projection. These include several types of amphibious assault vessels plus a variety of naval support ships. To provide these vessels with adequate air cover, China has purchased several dozen Su-27 Flanker combat planes from Russia and plans to build another hundred or so in domestic factories. (Significantly, the first group of Su-27s were deployed on Hainan Island, on the edge of the South China Sea.)[61] China has also sought air-refueling technology from Iran and Russia and is exploring the development (with Russia) of a modern aircraft carrier.[62]

It is no doubt true that these moves are motivated, at least in part, by China's determination to regain control over Taiwan—through force if necessary. Obviously, naval and amphibious forces of these types would be needed for any Chinese attempt to invade and occupy Taiwan. At the same time, it is evident from official government statements and from the actual deployment of Chinese forces that Beijing also intends to use them in southern waters, to enforce Chinese claims to the Spratlys and associated drilling areas. This is evident, for example, in the basing of Su-27s on Hainan Island and in the rotation of modern warships in and out of the area. Whatever China's ultimate intentions, other states in the region have interpreted the Chinese naval buildup as a drive for military dominance in the South China Sea, and have built up their own forces accordingly.[63]

As recently as fifteen years ago, the nations of Southeast Asia possessed few deep-sea warships. Since the late 1980s, however, these countries have engaged in costly efforts to equip their navies with modern vessels capable of operating on the high seas. Although intended for a variety of purposes, these ships are clearly designed to provide their owners with a capacity to protect vital sea-lanes and their extensive EEZs in the South China Sea.[64]

Leading the way is Malaysia. An increasingly affluent nation of 24 million people, Malaysia has sought to develop the largest and most potent navy in Southeast Asia. In 1995, it purchased four fully equipped missile corvettes from Fincantieri of Italy; originally built for Iraq (but never delivered because of successive arms embargoes), these 750-ton vessels are armed with a 76mm gun and Otomat anti-ship missiles. Malaysia has also acquired two F 2000 frigates from Yarrow Shipbuilders of Glasgow and fitted them with a panoply of advanced European gun and missile systems. And, in its most ambitious project yet, Malaysia has contracted for the production, in domestic shipyards, of up to twenty-seven Meko-100 patrol ships, making this the largest multiship naval construction program now under way in Asia.[65]

Thailand and Indonesia, in differing ways, have also endeavored to assemble a significant deep-sea navy. Thailand has sought prominence by acquiring the region's first aircraft carrier, the *Chakri Naruebet.* Built by EN Bazán of Spain, the 11,500-ton, $360 million carrier is intended to carry up to twelve medium helicopters or fifteen vertical-takeoff-and-landing (VTOL) planes.[66] The Thais have also purchased two *Knox*-class frigates from the United States and three 545-ton patrol boats from Australia.[67] Indonesia, meanwhile, attempted to jump-start its naval expansion plans by buying the entire navy of the former East Germany. Included in this thirty-nine ship deal, concluded after German reunification in 1991, were sixteen corvettes, nine minesweepers, and a variety of support ships. On top of this, Indonesia has purchased six surplus frigates from the Netherlands and three from the United Kingdom.[68]

Even the smaller states of the region have invested in new naval capabilities. Singapore, with a population of only three million, has acquired six *Victory*-class missile corvettes from Germany and is building a fleet of twelve *Fearless*-class offshore patrol vessels; the Philippines has acquired two ex–Royal Navy patrol boats from the former British naval base at Hong Kong; and Brunei has ordered three missile-armed corvettes from Yarrow Shipbuilders in Scotland.[69]

While it may be some years before all of these efforts reach fruition, the various naval acquisition programs now under way in China and Southeast Asia will add as many as one hundred new surface combatants to the rosters of regional powers over the next ten to fifteen years—a buildup unmatched in any other area of the world. The escalation of the naval arms race is accompanied, moreover, by significant additions to the region's air forces: all of these countries have acquired long-range patrol planes, as well as fighter craft equipped with sophisticated antiair and antiship missile systems. These and other initiatives have substantially enhanced the ability of these states to conduct sustained military operations on and above the South China Sea.[70]

Japan and the United States

While the most immediate effects of the Mischief Reef incident were felt in the Philippine Islands and neighboring states, significant aftershocks were also felt in Japan and the United States. Neither is directly involved in the Spratlys dispute itself, but both saw in this episode a potential threat to other vital interests, notably the free flow of merchant and naval traffic through the South China Sea. To protect these interests, both countries have placed a higher priority on their ability to project force and control events in the region.

Japan's interests in the South China Sea are directly tied to its dependence on imported energy supplies: approximately three-quarters of its oil passes through the area on its way from the Persian Gulf, as does much of its imported coal and liquified natural gas. Although it would be possible to bypass the South China Sea if the need arose—by rerouting tankers and other ships through the western Pacific—the resulting slowdown in deliveries would wreak havoc on the Japanese economy. To avoid this, Tokyo has sought to promote a peaceful resolution to the Spratlys dispute while at the same time building up its capacity to protect vital sea-lanes against hostile attack.[71]

The new Japanese outlook was first articulated in the "National Defense Program Outline" adopted in 1996, the first major revision of Japanese security policy in twenty years. Without referring to China or the ASEAN countries by name, the program notes that "many countries in the region are expanding or modernizing their military capabilities," posing new threats to Japanese interests. To offset these threats, the document calls for "qualitative improvements" in Japanese forces, particularly those aimed at maritime defense in "areas surrounding Japan."[72]

Japan has invested considerable resources in the enhancement of its naval and air-patrol capabilities. To bolster its navy—officially, the Maritime Self-Defense Force (MSDF)—Japan has introduced several new classes of warships. These include the *Kongo*-class missile destroyer, equipped with the U.S.-supplied AEGIS air-defense system, and the smaller, *Murasame*-class missile frigate. Japan has also begun construction of a new class of amphibious assault ships, the *Osumi*.

(With its large flight deck, the *Osumi* looks to some observers like the prototype for a future Japanese aircraft carrier.[73]) To further enhance its maritime security, Japan has ordered 100 P-3C Orion naval patrol planes from the United States and is exploring the acquisition of airborne refueling equipment for these and other military aircraft.[74] Together, these initiatives will provide Japan with one of the most formidable naval forces in the Asia-Pacific region.

Like Japan, the United States perceives a vital interest in the safety of South China Sea shipping lanes. Although little oil travels to North America via this route, the United States is obliged by treaty to ensure the security of Japan, and this, in turn, entails an obligation to protect Japan's vital supply routes. As noted earlier, the United States is also bound by treaty to help defend the Philippines; even if Washington does not include the Spratlys in its understanding of Philippine territory, a future clash between China and the Philippines could escalate to the point where the United States would become involved. American warships also traverse the South China Sea when sailing between U.S. bases in Japan and the Persian Gulf area. Finally, U.S. officials assert a general interest in discouraging Chinese adventurism in the Asia-Pacific region.[75]

Despite these varied interests, U.S. officials were relatively unconcerned about developments in the South China Sea until the outbreak of the Mischief Reef crisis. Before that, Washington had assumed that Chinese naval activity was aimed exclusively at Vietnam. The discovery of a Chinese military presence on islands claimed by the Philippines came as something of a shock, therefore, and precipitated a fresh review of American policy in the region.[76] This review resulted, on May 10, 1995, in the release of America's first formal public comment on the Spratlys dispute. The U.S. statement condemned "unilateral actions" by any parties to the Spratlys dispute, noting that Washington "strongly opposes the use of force to resolve competing claims." (Although China was not mentioned by name, the reference to "unilateral actions" was widely understood to refer to China's occupation of Mischief Reef.) The statement further declared that "maintaining freedom of navigation is a fundamental interest of the United States"—a clear indication that Washington would resist any effort by China or any other power to impede the free passage of shipping through the South China Sea.[77]

In the characteristically vague language of diplomacy, the May 10 statement did not indicate what steps the United States was prepared to take in protecting its "fundamental interest" in the unhindered passage of international shipping. Five weeks later, however, Assistant Secretary of Defense Joseph S. Nye told a group of Japanese journalists that the United States was prepared to employ military force in keeping the sea-lanes open. Any threat to freedom of navigation in the South China Sea, he said, would jeopardize the flow of essential goods to Japan and other U.S. allies and thus "infringe on an important American interest." This being the case, U.S. forces "would be prepared to escort" ships traveling through the area and to "make sure that free navigation continues."[78]

Faced with such pressure, Beijing declared in May 1995 that it had no intention of interfering with international shipping in the South China Sea.[79] This has not, however, erased all concern in Washington over the safety of vital shipping routes. American officials have continued to affirm that freedom of navigation in these waters is a "fundamental interest" of the United States, and have warned against the "unilateral" use of force by claimants to the Spratly Islands.[80] The United States has also maintained a powerful naval force in the region—the U.S. Seventh Fleet, based in Yokosuka, Japan—and has conducted regular military maneuvers in the South China Sea area. (See Table 5.4.)

The seriousness with which Washington views this issue was given fresh emphasis in 1999. In an interview aboard the aircraft carrier *Kitty Hawk,* following maneuvers in the western Pacific, Rear Admiral Timothy J. Keating, the commander of the Seventh Fleet, noted, "The sea routes are very important to us. A lot of Japanese oil comes though the Straits of Malacca, turns left, and heads through the South China Sea to Japan. So it's the uninterrupted flow of commerce through those waters that is of critical importance to the U.S." Although speaking in general terms, Admiral Keating made it clear that his remarks were largely intended for Chinese ears. "For the U.S. Navy, it's important to sail anywhere in international waters. And if

Table 5.4: Major Surface Combatants in the U.S. Seventh Fleet
(As of January 2000)

Ship Type	Ship	Crew Size	Notable Features
Aircraft carrier	USS *Kitty Hawk*	4,714	Carries 85 aircraft, consisting of F/A-18, F-14, S-3, EA-6, and E-2 fixed-wing aircraft and H-60 helicopters
Cruiser	USS *Vincennes*	358	AEGIS combat control system, Tomahawk missile, Standard ASM/SAM
	USS *Mobile Bay*	358	AEGIS combat control system, Tomahawk missile, Standard ASM/SAM
	USS *Chancellorville*	358	AEGIS combat control system, Tomahawk missile, Standard ASM/SAM
Guided-missile destroyer	USS *Curtis Wilbur*	303	AEGIS combat control system, Tomahawk missile, Standard ASM/SAM
	USS *John McCain*	303	AEGIS combat control system, Tomahawk missile, Standard ASM/SAM
Destroyer	USS *O'Brien*	339	Tomahawk missile, Harpoon ASM
	USS *Cushing*	339	Tomahawk missile, Harpoon ASM
Guided-missile frigate	USS *Gary*	290	Standard ASM/SAM, Harpoon ASM
	USS *Vandegrift*	290	Standard ASM/SAM, Harpoon ASM
Amphibious command ship	USS *Blue Ridge*	1,059	Flagship for the U.S. Seventh Fleet; provides command and control for Seventh Fleet ships on the high seas
Amphibious assault ship	USS *Belleau Wood*	950	Houses 1,703 embarked troops plus their combat gear; can carry up to 9 CH-53 or 12 CH-46 helicopters
Amphibious landing ship	USS *Juneau*	388	Can embark an additional staff of 900, plus helicopters
	USS *Germantown*	340	Houses 338 embarked troops plus their combat gear
	USS *Fort McHenry*	340	Houses 338 embarked troops plus their combat gear

Source: U.S. Seventh Fleet, "Seventh Fleet Ships," electronic document accessed at www.c7f.navy.mil/ships on January 3, 2000; U.S. Navy, "Navy Fact File," electronic document accessed at www.chinfo.navy.mil/navpalib/factfile on January 4, 2000.
ASM = antiship missile
SAM = surface-to-air missile

that happens to be in an area where a particular country is showing a lot of interest, we are not going to let that deter us from exercising our right to sail in international waters. And so we'll return home to our port in Japan by sailing through the South China Sea. It's international waters, and the U.S. is going through."[81]

To achieve its objectives, the United States has steadily strengthened its position in the South China Sea. In 1998, a new "Visiting Forces Agreement" was signed with the Philippines, allowing U.S. warships to participate in joint military exercises with the Philippine navy and to dock at Philippine bases.[82] (Prior to this, American warships had avoided the Philippines because of the 1992 decision by the Philippine Senate to terminate the U.S. lease to Subic Bay Naval Base and other military facilities.) The United States has also arranged to use a new naval base in Singapore that will be made large enough to accommodate American aircraft carriers.[83]

Washington has also sought greater military cooperation with Japan—its principal ally in the region and a significant naval power in its own right. Beginning in 1995, at the time of the Mischief Reef crisis, U.S. and Japanese officials met on a regular basis to establish ground rules for joint military action.[84] These efforts culminated, in September 1997, in the adoption of a new version of the Guidelines for U.S.-Japan Defense Cooperation, the basic agreement governing military relations between the two countries.[85] This text reaffirmed many of the features of the original, 1978 version, but placed special emphasis on what was termed "Cooperation in Situations in Areas Surrounding Japan That Will Have an Important Influence on Japan's Peace and Security." Without going into specifics about the nature of these "situations," the guidelines call for extensive Japanese support of U.S. forces engaged in regional military operations, including "such activities as intelligence gathering, surveillance, and minesweeping" in areas around Japan.[86]

American and Japanese officials have gone out of their way to assert that the new guidelines, and other manifestations of improved U.S.-Japanese military cooperation, are not aimed specifically at China or at any particular conflict, such as the Spratly Islands dispute.[87] But it is impossible to read these documents without concluding that both Washington and Tokyo had China and the South China Sea in mind. Certainly China, and all other states in the area, will assume that the guidelines are intended to lay the foundation for joint military action in the event of any future clash in the Asia-Pacific region.[88]

RESOURCE CONFLICT IN ASIA

The South China Sea is not the only area in East and Southeast Asia where armed conflict could erupt over the possession or flow of vital oil and gas supplies. For example, tension between China and Japan may increase over possession of the Diaoyu Islands (Senkaku in Japanese), a group of uninhabited reefs and islets in the East China Sea that have been the site of low-key air and naval clashes over the past few years.[89] (Like the Spratlys, these islands are of interest only insofar as they establish ownership over a large stretch of water that is believed to sit on top of valuable oil and gas deposits.) Conflict could also erupt between Indonesia and its neighbors over the contested Natuna Island area, which sits astride a vast pool of natural gas.[90]

Nevertheless, the South China Sea is the area most likely to witness large-scale warfare, because all of the factors associated with resource conflict are concentrated here. There is the evidence of untapped reserves of oil and natural gas, along with a complex mosaic of overlapping territorial claims. All of the states involved in these disputes seek to maximize their exploitation of maritime resource zones, and all have demonstrated a willingness to employ force in the protection of offshore interests. All, moreover, have beefed up the capabilities of their air and naval forces. On top of this, three of the world's leading military powers—the United States, China, and Japan—possess vital interests in the area and are prepared to defend these interests with military means if necessary. As with the Persian Gulf and the Caspian Sea, therefore, the South China Sea harbors all of the ingredients for a major military confrontation.

Any such confrontation is likely to commence as a naval incident sparked by competing claims to one of the Spratly Islands. In one such scenario, Chinese warships might sink a Philippine vessel seeking to gain access to Mischief Reef or one of the other Philippine-claimed islands occupied by China. In retaliation, the Philippines would bomb Chinese positions on the islands, provoking Chinese air and missile strikes against military installations in the Philippines. The United States would respond to this crisis by sending an aircraft carrier battle group into the area, intending to intimidate China and preserve the "freedom of the seas." If China refused to back down under these circumstances and attempted to block the American fleet, a Sino-U.S. conflict might erupt, entailing strikes against each other's naval forces. From there, one can imagine a wide variety of escalatory steps leading to a much larger regional conflict.

This is by no means the only scenario that would entail a significant risk of escalation in the South China Sea. Increased friction between China and Japan, for example, could lead to the interdiction of Japanese oil tankers by Chinese warships in the area. Such a move might provoke the use of Japanese and, eventually, American warships to repel (or sink) any Chinese vessels engaged in the operation. Fighting between local powers in the Strait of Malacca—the main oil transit route between the Indian Ocean and the South China Sea—could also provoke intervention by the United States and/or Japan. In all of these cases, and many others, it is the conspicuous *convergence* of vital energy, economic, and strategic interests that contributes to the high risk of armed conflict.

6

Water Conflict in the Nile Basin

Water may appear an unlikely source of strife. But conflict over water has, in fact, been a feature of human behavior throughout history.[1] In the Old Testament, for example, it is recorded that the Israelites could not enter the "Promised Land"—the fertile valleys of the Jordan River basin—until they expelled its original inhabitants. "Go up to a land flowing with milk and honey," God told Moses, who was camped out in the Sinai desert. "I will send an angel before you, and drive out the Canaanites, the Amorites, the Hittites, the Perizzites, and the Jebusites" (Exodus 33:2–3). Later, when Moses' successor Joshua leads the twelve tribes of Israel across the Jordan, God commands him to slay the inhabitants of Jericho and other settlements in the area. There follows one pitched battle after another until the Israelites control the entire region.

For centuries, warfare has been associated with the protection and destruction of vital water systems. Because early civilizations depended for their survival on a complex system of dikes and canals, such works were often the target of attack during outbreaks of combat. When, for instance, Sennacherib of Assyria attacked Babylon (in

689 B.C.) as retribution for the death of his son, he destroyed the city's irrigation works and diverted floodwaters into the city center. "Through the midst of that city," he declared, "I dug canals, I flooded the site with water, and the structure of its very foundations I destroyed. . . . So that in days to come, the site of that city and its temples and its gods might not be remembered, I completely blotted it out with water-floods and made it like a meadow."[2]

The modern era has known its share of water wars as well. One of the defining moments of the British Empire, for instance, occurred in 1885, when General Charles Gordon and his troops were slain by Sudanese followers of Muhammad Ahmad (the Mahdi) in Khartoum, the strategic city at the junction of the two key branches of the Nile River. Thirteen years later, in 1898, Britain and France nearly went to war over another strategic outpost on the Nile: Fashoda, in southern Sudan.[3]

Although often overshadowed by other events, conflict over water also erupted during the Cold War era. The Arab-Israeli War of 1967, for example, was largely triggered by fighting over control of the tributaries of the Jordan River. Iraq and Syria almost went to war in 1975, when Syria began filling up Lake Assad and reduced the flow of the Euphrates River as it emptied into Iraq. The Euphrates again figured in a major crisis in 1990, when Turkey blocked the river's flow in order to fill up one of its own reservoirs. Similar crises occurred in other parts of Asia and the Middle East.[4]

Now, at the dawn of the twenty-first century, conflict over critical water supplies is an ever-present danger. In a vast area stretching from North Africa to the Near East and South Asia, the demand for water is rapidly overtaking the existing supply. Because many key sources of water in this area are shared by two or more countries and because the states involved have rarely agreed on procedures for dividing up the available supply, disputes over access to contested resources will become increasingly heated and contentious. This danger is particularly acute in areas where rainfall is scant and several countries depend on a single major source of water—the Nile River, the Jordan, the Euphrates, and so on—for their basic needs. Unless ways are found to reduce these states' per capita use of the available supply, any increase in utilization by one country in the system will result in less water being available to the others—a situation that could lead to the outbreak of war.[5]

A number of other factors are likely to increase the frequency and severity of water disputes in the decades ahead. As population grows, societies need more water for both daily human use and for food production (usually through increased irrigation). To complicate matters, global population growth is heavily concentrated in those areas of the world—North Africa, the Middle East, and South Asia—where the supply of water is already proving inadequate for many human needs. Rapid urbanization in these areas and the expanding use of water in industrial processes are also contributing to an increase in demand. This means that the stakes in future clashes over the distribution of shared resources will rise and the price for losing out in such a contest will become even more severe.

Global climate change will further complicate the water-supply equation. As greenhouse gases accumulate in the atmosphere, the world's average temperature will rise, and precipitation patterns will be altered in many parts of the world. This could lead to higher levels of rainfall in some areas and lower levels in others. Scientists cannot yet determine exactly how individual regions will be affected, but it is believed that many warm inland areas like northeast Africa (through which the Nile passes) and southwest Asia (through which the Tigris and Euphrates flow) will be left with smaller supplies of water.[6]

Future shortages of water in these regions need not, of course, lead to war. In areas where states enjoy good relations with one another and have a history of resolving differences through peaceful negotiations, disputes over shared sources of water can be addressed without recourse to violence. However, some of the most acute disputes over such supplies have arisen in regions where intergovernmental relations are fractious and where competition over water and other vital resources has led to fighting in the past. In these areas, future shortages are likely to inflame local tensions and increase the risk of war—especially if one party to a dispute believes that another is appropriating more than its rightful share of water.[7]

Typically, in regions where water is scarce, states view combat over vital sources of supply as a legitimate function of national security. As suggested earlier, governments normally eschew the use of force in resolving international disputes unless they believe that critical security interests are at stake. Where water is plentiful, as in the temperate zones of Europe and North America, conflict is unlikely. In areas where water is rarely sufficient, however, its availability is considered a matter of national survival. "Water for Israel is not a luxury," former prime minister Moshe Sharett once asserted. "It is not just a desirable and helpful addition to our natural resources. Water is life itself."[8] Under these conditions, any threat to the continued delivery of water supplies will be considered a justifiable cause of war if other means prove unavailing.[9]

The acquisition and protection of water has long been viewed as a fundamental task of government in areas where supplies are limited. Indeed, the rise of the first true states in Egypt, Mesopotamia, and China is closely associated with the development of canal and irrigation schemes by early pharaohs, kings, and emperors.[10] In more modern times, the development of dams and waterworks was considered an essential function of the colonial powers and, when they departed, by the nationalist regimes that succeeded them. For President Gamal Abdel Nasser of Egypt, for example, construction of the Aswan High Dam on the Nile was the most important task facing the country.[11] Other modern leaders of the Middle East and Asia have also undertaken major water projects and otherwise sought to enhance their countries' water supply. And when other states have threatened action that would reduce this supply, these leaders have been quick to warn of a military response.

A region in which states must compete for access to vital water supplies and in which leaders believe that they must not fall behind in this contest is likely to be a very unstable region indeed—especially if population is rising and the per capita supply of this vital resource is declining. "As [water] becomes increasingly rare," UNESCO Director-General Klaus Toepfer observed in 1999, "it becomes coveted, [and] capable of unleashing conflicts." More than over land or oil, he noted, "it is over water that the most bitter conflicts of the near future may be fought."[12] A similar view was expressed by Israeli Prime Minister Yitzhak Rabin: "If we solve every other problem in the Middle East but do not satisfactorily resolve the water problem, our region will explode."[13]

To fully appreciate the severity of this risk, it is necessary to examine the dynamics of global water use—its supply and demand, its principal uses, and the distribution of available supplies.

A DISPUTED RESOURCE

From a resource perspective, water bears many similarities to oil. It is essential for a wide range of human activities, and it exists in relatively finite amounts. Once the available supply is exhausted, moreover, additional quantities can be acquired only through heroic and costly efforts. Increased population and rising affluence are inflating global demand of both materials, bringing the point of worldwide scarcity closer with every passing day. And, most significant, important sources of water—no less than of oil—are found in areas that overlap national boundaries and may thus become the focus of territorial or ownership contests between neighboring states.

At the most fundamental level, water is absolutely essential to human health and survival—for drinking, for bathing and sanitation, and for food production. According to the World Bank, the minimum amount of water one human needs to remain alive and healthy is 100 to 200 liters per day, or 36 to 72 cubic meters per year.[14] But this represents only a fraction of total need: agriculture, industry, and energy production all require additional quantities of water for a variety of critical processes. Together, these uses bring the minimum human water requirement to approximately 1,000 cubic meters (265,000 gallons) per person per year.[15]

By far the greatest need for water—beyond that needed for basic human survival—is for the irrigation of essential food crops. Irrigation not only allows for the production of food in areas that receive little rainfall (as is the case in most of North Africa, Southwest Asia, and the American Southwest) but also permits double-cropping in temperate climates and the use of high-yield crops. Irrigated farming has led to a vast increase in food production over the past fifty years, thus making possible a steady increase in the human population. Today, about 70 percent of all fresh water appropriated by humans from the world's rivers, lakes, and aquifers is used for agricultural purposes.[16]

Clearly, any further increase in world population will produce a corresponding surge in the demand for water. With most of the planet's arable, rain-fed land already under cultivation, any future expansion in grain and vegetable production will require the conversion of currently barren land into productive use through irrigation, along with the more efficient and intensive use of existing fields. While it may prove possible to reduce the amounts of water needed to raise any given crop through the use of hybrid seeds and more efficient water-distribution systems, the task of feeding a global population of eight billion people—the number expected in the year 2020—will necessitate diverting additional supplies of fresh water to irrigated croplands.[17]

Can the world supply all of this fresh water? Although the planet is brimming with salt water—which covers about 70 percent of the earth's surface—the global supply of fresh water is relatively limited. Less than 3 percent of the world's total water supply is fresh water and, of this amount, approximately two-thirds is locked up in glaciers and the polar ice caps; much of the rest, moreover, is sequestered in the soil and deep underground aquifers. As a result, less than 1 percent of the world's freshwater supply—or about 0.01 percent of all water on earth—is accessible to the human population.[18]

This tiny fraction of the earth's total water supply is made available through precipitation on land. Every year, some 110,000 cubic kilometers (km^3) of fresh water falls on dry land in the form of rain and snow. About two-thirds of this amount, or 70,000 km^3, is returned to the atmosphere through evaporation and transpiration (the natural release of moisture by plants). This leaves about 40,000 km^3 of water per year as runoff—the flow of fresh water back to the oceans through rivers, streams, and underground aquifers.[19] About half of this runoff is lost each year through seasonal flooding (even more would be lost except for the dams built to retain flood water), and another fifth is carried off by rivers in Siberia and other remote

locations. The remaining fresh water—about 12,500 km³ per year—
is the amount actually accessible to humans on a renewable basis for
drinking, irrigation, and other basic uses.[20]

An additional source of fresh water is found in so-called fossil
aquifers, large underground reservoirs that have formed over long
periods of time. Some of these sources, like the vast Ogallala aquifer
of the American Southwest, lie close enough to the surface to be
accessible to humans. Indeed, aquifers of this sort are an important
source of fresh water for farmers and urban populations in many
areas, including Israel and the West Bank, northwest India, northern
China, and Saudi Arabia. Once their waters have been fully tapped,
however, these reservoirs will not fill up again for many thousands of
years and so, like fossil fuels, must be considered *nonrenewable* resources.[21]

If divided evenly, the 12,500 km³ of renewable fresh water available each year would be more than sufficient to satisfy the basic needs
of world's existing human population. Indeed, scientists estimate that
only about half of the total renewable worldwide supply is currently
being used. With each spurt in population, however, the amount of
water available per person grows smaller. As societies become more
affluent and developed, moreover, they tend to use more water, because of the wider availability of indoor plumbing, the use of dish-
washers and other appliances, the consumption of meat (which
requires the increased production of grain), and so on. Thus, while
world population doubled between 1950 and 1990, global water use
grew by 300 percent. If this rate of increase persists, we will soon be
using 100 percent of the world's available supply. A large increase in
the desalination of seawater or in the reclamation of urban waste
water could significantly augment that supply, but existing processes
are too costly to make this practical in the near-term future.[22]

If the world's supply of fresh water was distributed evenly, shortages would begin to affect everyone at about the same time—perhaps
two or three decades from now. But water is *not* distributed evenly:
certain areas are blessed with relatively abundant supplies, while others are forced to make do with much less. The Amazon River, for
example, accounts for approximately 16 percent of the earth's total

annual runoff; by contrast, the world's arid and semiarid regions—which together constitute approximately 40 percent of the earth's landmass and house perhaps one-fifth of its total population—receive only 2 percent of the global water runoff.[23] Because of these variations in the distribution of water, some areas of the world are *already* experiencing significant scarcity.

The emergence of severe water scarcities is most evident in the Middle East and Southwest Asia. According to the World Bank, the average annual runoff in these areas in 1995 was 1,250 cubic meters per person, or just enough to satisfy basic human needs. Within these areas, moreover, the bank found eleven countries—Algeria, Egypt, Israel, Jordan, Libya, Morocco, Saudi Arabia, Syria, Tunisia, the United Arab Emirates, and Yemen—with annual per capita supplies at or below 1,000 cubic meters, the minimum amount considered necessary for healthy human life. These countries have been able to supplement their meager rain-fed supplies with desalinated seawater and/or water drawn from fossil aquifers; most, however, are encountering great difficulty in meeting the basic needs of their growing populations.[24] (See Table 6.1.)

What makes this situation so precarious from a security point of view is the fact that many of the key sources of water in these areas are shared by two or more countries. Typically, these sources are large river systems like the Nile and the Euphrates that arise in one country and then pass through several others before exiting to the sea. The Nile, for instance, is shared by no fewer than nine countries, while the Tigris-Euphrates system is shared by four, and the Jordan by three (along with those areas of the West Bank controlled by the Palestinian Authority). Under ideal conditions, the states involved in these river systems would work out a formula for the equitable distribution of the annual water flow, irrespective of their location on the river's path from headwaters to final outlet. Unfortunately, this has rarely occurred; rather, the stronger states in the system have tended to appropriate a disproportionate share of the total supply, causing hardship and resentment in the other countries involved.

A recent study by scientists at Oregon State University indicates the magnitude of this problem. Using sophisticated topographical

Table 6.1: Annual per Capita Water Availability in Selected States of North Africa, the Middle East, and Southwest Asia		
	Per Capita Water Availability (cubic meters per person per year)	
Country	1990	2025
Algeria	750	380
Burundi	660	280
Egypt	1,070	620
Ethiopia	2,360	980
Iran	2,080	960
Israel	470	310
Jordan	260	80
Kenya	590	190
Lebanon	1,600	960
Libya	160	60
Morocco	1,200	680
Oman	1,330	470
Rwanda	880	350
Saudi Arabia	160	50
Tunisia	530	330
United Arab Emirates	190	110
Yemen	240	80

Source: Peter H. Gleick, "Water and Conflict," *International Security*, summer 1993, p. 101. The change between 1990 and 2025 is due solely to projected increases in population.

data systems to map the world's major river basins, they discovered that 261 such basins extend over two or more international boundaries. These basins cover approximately 45 percent of the earth's land area, excluding Antarctica. No less than 145 nations depend on shared river systems for at least some portion of their freshwater supply, and a good number of these are almost wholly dependent on such systems.[25] Many important underground aquifers, such as the vital "Mountain aquifer" lying beneath Israel and the West Bank, are also shared in this manner.[26]

The distribution of water in shared rivers is a chronic source of tension even under the best of circumstances, when the flow of water is relatively copious and the states involved enjoy good relations with one another. When the flow of water subsides and the political environment deteriorates, these tensions often reach the breaking point. If a member of the system should attempt to increase its share of the dwindling supply, the other members are likely to respond forcefully. Likewise, any effort by upstream countries to dam the river or otherwise control its onward flow is likely to produce concern and hostility among the downstream states.[27]

Conflict over water can also arise *within* countries. In the 1920s, for instance, farmers in the Owens Valley of eastern California regularly sabotaged the aqueduct built by state authorities to transport their water supply to distant Los Angeles.[28] More recently, a struggle has erupted in southern India, as farmers in the states of Karnataka and Tamil Nadu battle over irrigation rights to the Cauvery River.[29] Another form of conflict can break out when developing countries attempt to privatize their water supply in order to attract foreign investment. In April 2000, five people died and hundreds were injured in Bolivia during violent protests against water-supply privatization and the imposition of charges on drinking water in Cochabamba, the country's third-largest city.[30] Further upheavals are likely in other developing nations as governments move to privatize their publicly owned (and subsidized) water systems.[31]

Although domestic conflicts of this sort may become more widespread in the years ahead, it is interstate conflict over shared water sources that is of greatest concern. The major shared systems of the Middle East and Southwest Asia—the Nile, the Jordan, the Tigris-Euphrates, and the Indus—have been the sites of conflict throughout human history; indeed, many of the earliest recorded wars occurred along their banks.[32] Although, in recent times, efforts have been made to negotiate equitable water-sharing arrangements among the states dependent on these rivers, disagreement over the distribution of their flow persists. Unless more progress is made in negotiating cooperative arrangements, growing scarcity combined with rising population will produce an increasingly unstable environment.

As in the case of oil, the best way to appreciate the dynamics of future water conflict is to examine the intersection of political, economic, and military factors in the major arenas of likely combat.

THE NILE RIVER BASIN

Since very early times, the waters of the Nile River have sustained human habitation in what is now Egypt and Sudan. Every fall, raging floodwaters pour down from the Ethiopian highlands into the Nile and its tributaries, drenching the fertile lowlands of the river valley. Many centuries ago, farmers in the lower valley learned to trap the receding floodwaters in shallow basins, thus allowing an extended growing season and more intensive cultivation. The resulting abundance permitted a sharp rise in human population and, in time, the emergence of cities, states, and empires. The great civilizations of Egypt owed their durability and opulence to the life-giving properties of the Nile River, and so it is hardly surprising that their rulers took every precaution to ensure its continued flow—through the rigorous performance of religious ritual and, when deemed necessary, the use of military force.

Military force has been employed on a recurring basis in northeast Africa to provide Egypt with dominion over the upper reaches of the Nile River and its principal tributaries. Because all of the water of the Nile is supplied by areas lying outside of Egyptian territory and because Egypt possesses no other significant source of water, Egypt's rulers have consistently sought to control the river's headwaters in order to ensure that no foreign power tampered with its natural flow. Although the ancient Egyptians were not able to locate the ultimate source of the river, they did trace its path into present-day Sudan and mounted periodic campaigns to conquer the area. The British copied this behavior when they established a protectorate over Egypt in the mid–nineteenth century, and Egypt's modern leaders have continued the practice ever since.[33]

This strategy has enabled Egypt—which contributes nothing to the Nile's annual flow—to appropriate the great bulk of its waters for its exclusive use. Because the upstream riparians have lacked the capital or the capacity to build extensive dams and waterworks, Egypt has benefited enormously from its privileged position. Thus far, moreover, Egypt has always possessed sufficient military strength to deter its neighbors from proceeding in this direction. But the need for water is growing throughout the region, and so the temptation to draw from the Nile can only grow stronger. The likelihood of future conflict hinges, therefore, on the willingness of upstream powers to risk Egyptian ire by appropriating more of the Nile's flow, and on Cairo's determination to prevent that from happening.

To fully appreciate the mechanics of this equation, it is useful to map out the geography of the Nile River and to consider its past, present, and future use by human societies.

The River and Its Utilization

The Nile is the longest river in the world, stretching some 6,650 kilometers (4,130 miles) from its ultimate sources in equatorial Africa to its outlet into the Mediterranean Sea. As it travels northward, the Nile collects and disperses water in nine countries—Burundi, Congo, Egypt, Ethiopia, Kenya, Rwanda, Sudan, Tanzania, and Uganda. All told, the Nile basin encompasses 3,350,000 square kilometers, about one-tenth of the total land area of Africa. Within this vast area can be found an unusually diverse range of climates, including tropical rain forests, broad savannahs, extensive marshlands, and desert. Each of these areas, in its own way, contributes to the unique hydrology of the Nile.[34] (See map.)

The longest arm of the river, the White Nile, originates in the Great Lakes region of Central Africa. From the well-watered highlands of Burundi, Kenya, Rwanda, and Tanzania come a torrent of rivers and streams that empty into Lake Victoria, the largest of the equatorial lakes that drain into the Nile. Emerging from Lake Victoria's northern rim, the infant White Nile flows north to Lake Kyoga in Uganda, and then west to Lake Albert (also known as Lake Mobutu) in the Congo. Upon exiting from Lake Albert, the river descends to the savannahs of southern Sudan and empties into the vast marshlands known as the Sudd. Finally, after leaving the Sudd (where it collects the organic matter that provides its distinctive milky coloring), the White Nile proceeds north to Khartoum and its junction with the Blue Nile.

Although shorter in length than its sister stream, the darker-hued

Nile River Basin

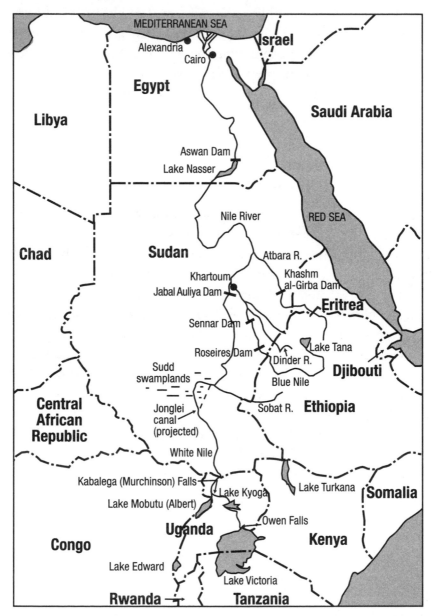

Blue Nile carries a greater volume of water. Originating at Lake Tana, high in the mountains of western Ethiopia, the river attracts a number of tributaries before plunging into eastern Sudan. After traveling some three hundred miles to Khartoum, the Blue Nile combines with the White Nile to form the Nile proper. Another major tributary, the Atbara (which, like the Blue Nile, originates in the highlands of Ethiopia) joins the river some two hundred miles north of Khartoum. Together, the Atbara and the Blue Nile contribute about 72 percent of the Nile's total flow. After its junction with the Atbara, the Nile proceeds north to the Egyptian border and Lake Nasser (the giant reservoir created by the Aswan High Dam) before completing its northward passage to the Mediterranean.[35]

As it enters Egypt, the Nile forms a long, narrow valley, approximately 475 miles long by 6 to 10 miles wide, within which most of Egypt's population lives and the bulk of its food is grown. Every summer, floodwater from the Blue Nile and the Atbara pour into the valley, providing the water and nutrients that have sustained intensive agriculture in this region for over seven thousand years. This is the famous Nile Valley of Egypt: the home of the ancient pharaohs and the great monuments at Giza and Luxor; it is also the location of modern-day Cairo, with an estimated population (in 1995) of ten million people. After passing through Cairo, the Nile breaks up into a number of branches that fan out toward the Mediterranean, forming the triangular region of the Nile Delta.

From the Egyptian perspective, control of the Nile and all of its headwaters is essential to the survival and well-being of the country. Egypt has thus been reluctant to condone the construction of any dams or other works on the upper Nile that might interfere with the normal flow of the river. However, when the complex hydrology of the Nile River was initially mapped out at the beginning of the twentieth century, water engineers began to speak of the need to view the entire region as an integrated hydrological system. In 1920, Sir Murdoch MacDonald—then the senior British engineer in Egypt—proposed a series of dams on the upper Nile that would permit the storage of water in times of plenty and its release in times of drought. Known as the "Century Storage Scheme," this plan would have assured Egypt of adequate water even in those desperate periods when rainfall declines in equatorial Africa. It would, however, have given the upper Nile riparians greater control over the flow of the river, and because of this it aroused considerable opposition in Egypt.[36]

Basinwide planning of the sort proposed by Sir MacDonald was conceivable during the early twentieth century because Great Britain and other European powers dominated the entire region. As the region was divided up into separate, independent states, however, integrated planning became increasingly difficult. Egypt became fully independent in 1922 and moved immediately to assert its "historic rights" to the bulk of the Nile's waters. Before signing an agreement with Great Britain over the utilization of the Nile's waters, Egyptian leaders secured from London a promise that no works would be constructed on the upper Nile or its tributaries (insofar as they were under British jurisdiction) without Cairo's prior approval. The resulting Nile Waters Agreement of 1929—the first of its kind in the region—thus served to discourage the development of a basinwide management system.[37]

The prospects for integrated development of the Nile became even less promising in the years following World War II, when first Sudan and then the British-controlled colonies of Central Africa became independent. Although quick to tout the benefits of regional development, the leaders of these new nations were reluctant to approve any schemes that might diminish their control over water resources located within their borders. Accordingly, all of these states declared that the 1929 Nile Waters Agreement was null and void with respect to their sovereign territory. At the same time Ethiopia—which had never signed the 1929 agreement and had repudiated all water-sharing accords made in its name by Italy (its former imperial overlord)—began to consider the use of Blue Nile waters in vast irrigation projects of its own.[38]

These developments naturally produced great anxiety in Cairo. For the first time facing serious competition for access to the Nile's precious flow, the Egyptians began speaking openly of water as a national security matter.[39] The government pressed ahead with construction of the Aswan High Dam, which, when completed in 1971, gave it an assured reserve of some 160 billion cubic meters of water. The Egyptians also sought to influence water developments in Sudan, particularly the construction of new dams and irrigation schemes. Although relying primarily on diplomacy and economic pressure to achieve its objectives, Egypt also threatened the use of force and, on one occasion, actually sent its troops into a disputed area on the Egyptian-Sudanese border.[40]

After enduring years of Egyptian bullying, the Sudanese signed a new Nile waters agreement with Cairo in 1959, replacing the 1929 agreement with Great Britain. Under this accord, the "Agreement for the Full Utilization of the Nile Waters," Egypt was given an annual allocation of 55.5 billion cubic meters (bcm) of water from the river, or about two-thirds of its estimated average annual flow of 84 bcm. Sudan was allocated 18.5 bcm per year, while the remaining flow, 10 bcm per year, was assumed to be lost through evaporation and seepage from Lake Nasser. By signing this accord, the two countries assured each other of unimpeded access to substantial quantities of Nile water and minimized the risk of water conflict between them (at least for the time being). But the agreement had one significant flaw: it awarded no Nile waters to the states lying farther upstream, several of which could be expected to seek substantial water resources for their own use.[41]

Fearing that Ethiopia and other upstream riparians would proceed with their own plans for increased utilization of the Nile and that Sudan would someday seek more than its 18.5 bcm allocation, Egypt continued to warn of dire action should any of this materialize. After signing a peace treaty with Israel, for instance, President Anwar el-Sadat declared, "The only matter that could take Egypt to war again is water."[42] Sadat also threatened to bomb water facilities in Ethiopia if its government implemented a plan to divert some of the Blue Nile's waters to domestic irrigation projects.[43] Equally threatening comments were made in the 1980s by Egypt's then minister of state for foreign affairs (later secretary-general of the United Nations), Boutros Boutros-Ghali: "The next war in our region will be over the waters of the Nile, not politics."[44]

Despite such posturing, Cairo's freedom of action in the water field was somewhat constrained by the exigencies of the Cold War era. Although the two superpowers were fully prepared to conduct "proxy" wars when they concluded that their own geostrategic interests were at stake, they generally discouraged their clients from initiating regional conflicts over what were seen in Washington and Moscow as secondary considerations. With the Cold War over, however, the restraining influence of the superpowers has dissipated, and so local powers like Egypt, Sudan, and Ethiopia have more room in which to pursue what they view as critical national interests—as so tragically illustrated by the disastrous war between Ethiopia and Eritrea in 1998–2000.

Fortunately for Egypt, the upstream riparians were in no position to proceed with ambitious plans for the diversion of Nile River waters during the 1990s. Ethiopia was paralyzed by an ongoing conflict with separatist forces in Eritrea, by incursions from Somalia, and later by the war with independent Eritrea. Sudan was torn by internal discord and a separatist conflict in the non-Muslim south; the equatorial states were wracked by ethnic and political strife. These perils consumed the attention (and the resources) of the governments involved, precluding any new investment in dams and irrigation projects. Apparently sensing advantage in this state of affairs, Egypt sought to perpetuate its privileged position on the Nile by aiding antigovernment forces in neighboring countries. This entailed support for Somali irredentists in the Ogaden region of Ethiopia and for the rebel Sudanese People's Liberation Army (SPLA) in southern Sudan.[45]

Prospects for Water Conflict in the Twenty-first Century

As the century drew to a close, the upstream riparians were still, for the most part, mired in internal conflict or border disputes.* It is

---

*Many of these conflicts also have significant resource components. The civil war in Sudan, for example, is driven in part by the government's efforts to retain control over the White Nile (which passes through rebel-dominated areas of southern Sudan) and newly developed oil fields in the country's central region.

reasonable to assume, however, that this picture will change in the years ahead as the violence subsides. Indeed, peace talks were under way in several conflict zones, and a cease-fire was in place in Ethiopia and Eritrea. It is likely, then, that at least some of these states will proceed with long-delayed plans for hydroelectric and irrigation schemes on the upper Nile. Ethiopia, for instance, has announced ambitious plans to divert water from the Blue Nile to new agricultural developments,[46] while Uganda is considering new hydroelectric projects.[47]

Sudan has also expressed its intention to draw more water from the Nile, although the country remains divided by the SPLA insurgency in the south. With assistance from Iran and Iraq, however, the government of President Omar Hassan Ahmad al-Bashir has been able to bolster its military capabilities and to acquire additional weaponry from China and the former Soviet Union. Defections from the SPLA and divisions within the ranks of opposition groups have also helped the al-Bashir regime strengthen its position.[48] Peace talks are now under way with several opposition groups, and the central government evidently believes it is in a position to proceed with extensive water projects, including a proposed new dam on the Nile at Dongola, north of Khartoum.[49]

All of this is deeply troubling to the Egyptians. To complicate matters, Egypt's annual water requirements are continually growing as its population expands and the country becomes increasingly urbanized. In 1922, when Egypt became independent, its population was approximately 13.5 million people; by 1960 it had grown to 30 million, and by 1998 to 66 million. If Egypt's population continues to expand at anticipated rates, it will reach 95 million people by 2025 and 115 million by the middle of the twenty-first century.[50] Providing all of these additional people with sufficient water for their everyday needs will be a daunting task in itself; feeding them will be an even greater challenge. With all of Egypt's existing fields already under cultivation, the only way to produce more food is to convert ever larger expanses of barren desert into irrigated cropland.

To expand food production while also relieving population

pressures in the crowded Nile Valley, Cairo is spending billions of dollars to develop virgin agricultural areas in the Western Desert. At the heart of the "New Valley" project is a $4 billion pumping station on Lake Nasser that will pour 5.5 billion cubic meters per year of Nile water into canals serving the communities. If all goes as planned, the scheme will provide water for 500,000 acres of land and permit the resettlement of up to seven million Egyptians in man-made oases.[51] Egypt is also seeking to resettle excess population in the "New Lands" being created on the margins of the Nile Delta.

These projects can succeed, the Egyptian government contends, without increasing the country's total consumption of Nile River waters. This, it is claimed, can be accomplished through the treatment and reuse of urban and industrial water in irrigating crops. Most experts believe, however, that any savings achieved through water conservation and reuse will inevitably be lost through population increase and continuing urbanization. With Egypt's population expected to grow by nearly 30 million people between 1998 and 2025, Egypt will be hard-pressed to freeze its appropriations from the Nile at the 55.5 bcm per year allowed under the 1959 agreement with Sudan. This being the case, Cairo is likely to prove even more antagonistic to any upstream projects that might have the effect of reducing Egypt's access to water.[52]

What makes this situation so potentially explosive is the fact that other states in the region are *also* facing very high levels of population growth, and so will need to increase their own withdrawals from the Nile. Indeed, population growth in this area is advancing by some of the highest rates found anywhere in the world—3.2 percent per year in Ethiopia, 2.6 percent in Uganda, and 2.2 percent in Kenya and Sudan (compared to the average worldwide rate of 0.8 percent). If this trend continues, Ethiopia's total population will rise from 62 million people in 1998 to an estimated 212 million in 2050, a net increase of 150 million people (equivalent to twice the total population of Egypt in 2000). Sudan will see its population expand from 29 to 60 million people over this period, while Kenya will grow from 29 to 66 million people and Uganda from 21 to 66 million. Counting these countries alone, this means that the total population of the Nile

Table 6.2:
Anticipated Population Growth for Selected Countries in the Nile River Basin

Country	Estimated Population (in millions)				Percent Increase, 1998–2050
	1950	1998	2025	2050	
Egypt	21.8	65.7	95.8	115.5	76
Ethiopia	18.4	62.1	136.3	212.7	243
Kenya	6.3	29.0	50.2	66.1	128
Sudan	9.2	28.5	46.9	59.9	110
Uganda	4.8	21.3	45.0	66.3	211
Total	60.5	206.6	374.2	520.5	152

Source: World Resources Institute, *World Resources 1998–99* (1998), p. 244.

River basin (including Egypt) will gain approximately 300 million people between 2000 and 2050.[53] (See Table 6.2.)

These extraordinary numbers suggest that competition for Nile River water can only grow more intense as the new century proceeds. It is hard to imagine how Ethiopia, Sudan, and Uganda will be able to feed an additional 225 million people without irrigating more land, and the only major source of water in this area is the Nile and its tributaries. Clearly, the leaders of these states will seek to proceed with long-delayed plans to build new dams and divert additional Nile water to domestic irrigation schemes. Even Sudan, which has long deferred to Egypt on major water-related issues, has announced plans to increase its annual withdrawals from the Nile.[54]

Competition among these states for access to the Nile's waters is also likely to be affected by global climate change. Although it is not possible to predict reliably the net effect of higher worldwide temperatures and changing rainfall patterns on the Nile region, it is probable that significant changes will occur. In some scenarios, the Nile will gain additional water in its upper reaches, from elevated levels of rainfall in the highlands of Central Africa and Ethiopia, but lose much or all of this due to higher rates of evaporation (caused by increased ground temperatures) in lower, drier areas. This would be good news for the upper Nile riparians but bad news for Egypt—a development that would undoubtedly intensify Cairo's opposition to any new water projects in these other countries.[55]

Until now, Egypt has been able to preserve its privileged position on the Nile through threat and intimidation. Whenever one of its neighbors has announced plans for a major new water project, Cairo has been quick to warn of dire consequences should it proceed with any such plans. Thus, when the Sudanese leadership suggested in 1995 that it might seek to amend the 1959 Nile Waters Agreement, President Muhammad Hosni Mubarak wasted no time in delivering the Egyptian riposte: "Any step taken to this end will force us into confrontation to defend our rights and life. Our response will be beyond anything they can imagine."[56] Mubarak's bluster worked on this particular occasion—the Sudanese immediately eschewed any intention of moving in this direction—and such threats will no doubt work again in the future. But the day may come when, in desperation, one or another of these states calls Cairo's bluff.

Given the risks inherent in any use of military force, the Egyptians are most likely to seek a solution short of war. Indeed, Egypt reportedly agreed in August 2000 to consider the adoption of a new compact governing the distribution of Nile River waters that would guarantee additional amounts to the upstream riparians. But it is unlikely that Cairo will ever acquiesce to a significant reduction in its own allocation, and any move by an upstream state to appropriate increased amounts for itself without Egyptian approval could provoke a military response.

When and if Cairo chooses to employ force in defense of its claim to Nile waters, the most likely Egyptian action would be an air campaign against the dams and other facilities seen as threatening to the river's unimpeded flow. This is what Egypt threatened in 1978, when Ethiopia announced plans to take water from the Blue Nile for a domestic irrigation scheme,[57] and presumably this would be the favored Egyptian tactic in any future confrontation of this sort. With assistance from the United States, Egypt has built up a formidable air force, organized around hundreds of late-model American and French combat planes. Although no match for Israel's powerful air armada, the Egyptian force is far superior to those of all other neighboring states.[58]

The only situation in which Egypt might employ its ground forces in a conflict over the Nile would be in response to an act of extreme defiance by Sudan, its neighbor to the south. In antiquity, and again during the colonial period, Egyptian forces invaded Sudan when vital interests were deemed at risk, so there is ample precedent for such a move. In 1994, moreover, Egypt sent its forces into the Halayeb district—a disputed border area on the Red Sea occupied by Sudan.[59] Were Khartoum to abrogate the 1959 agreement and push its annual withdrawals beyond the 18.5 billion cubic feet allowed by this accord, Egypt would almost certainly carry through on its threat to respond with overwhelming force. With 3,855 tanks at its disposal (including 555 of America's top-rated tank, the M-1A1 Abrams), along with thousands of armored personnel carriers, Egypt would no doubt rely on its superior armored capabilities to crush the much inferior Sudanese army.[60]

Other scenarios are also possible. Rather than fight each other, Egypt and Sudan could join forces to oppose any threatening moves by Ethiopia or another upstream riparian. Alternatively, Ethiopia and Sudan could establish an anti-Egyptian coalition of some sort. Even more likely, the Nile riparians would continue to support insurgent forces in the territories of their respective competitors, thus undermining these states' capacity to undertake major water projects. Various permutations of these can easily be imagined.

Ultimately, the only way to avert an outcome of this sort is for the countries of the region to establish a regionwide development plan—like the "Century Storage Scheme" developed by Sir Murdoch MacDonald in 1920—that would aim to maximize the water supplies of all parties concerned. Such a plan would entail the construction of additional dams and reservoirs on the upper reaches of the Nile, where evaporation rates would be lowest. Once completed, these upstream projects would make it possible to reduce the water level in Lake Nasser, saving billions of cubic meters of water that are lost each year to evaporation. Completion of the Jonglei canal in southern

Sudan—a project begun in 1978 and then abandoned in 1984 due to fighting in the area—would also save billions of bcms lost every year through evaporation. If pursued in a coordinated fashion, these works would increase the waters available for irrigation and provide additional reserves for times of drought.[61]

For any of this to occur, however, the states in the region would have to subordinate their own plans for the Nile to a regional scheme that would place the group interest over that of individual members. This would no doubt prove attractive to the upper riparians—most of which have yet to make significant use of the Nile—but would produce great anxiety in Cairo, which is loath to surrender any degree of control over the river's flow. Not surprisingly, the Egyptians have never agreed to any water-sharing scheme not under their direct control, and it is hard to imagine that they will do so in the future. The prospect, then, is for further military posturing over the Nile, with an ever-increasing risk of actual combat.

7

Water Conflict in the Jordan, Tigris-Euphrates, and Indus River Basins

In the Middle East and Southwest Asia, three prominent rivers have defined the ebb and flow of human civilization: the Jordan, the Tigris-Euphrates, and the Indus. All three of these rivers played a crucial role in the original development of irrigated agriculture, and later in the rise of urban settlements and stratified social systems. Like the Nile, these rivers have been a source of contention between competing kingdoms and empires, beginning with some of the earliest recorded episodes of organized warfare and extending well into the modern period. And, again like the Nile, these three systems are likely to witness continuing discord and strife in the twenty-first century.

The three river systems provide the only significant sources of water in an area that has known human habitation since the beginning of recorded history. Approximately 500 million people lived in the area in 1998, and this number is expected to double by 2050.[1] These inhabitants, like their ancestors, will depend on the rivers for drinking water and sanitation, and also for the bulk of their food: with natural precipitation so sparse in this largely arid region, and many local aquifers facing total depletion, irrigated agriculture is the only reliable means of producing sufficient food to support life. With all this at stake, it is hardly surprising that control of the rivers has long been viewed as a goal worth fighting for. (See Table 7.1.)

Since ancient times, this area has been inhabited by many distinct tribes and peoples—all of whom claim a legitimate right to draw on the water resources of the region. As particular groups have gained in strength and numbers, their need for water has grown, forcing others to fight for their continued survival. Many of the ancient texts of Mesopotamia record such contests in the Euphrates area, and much of the Book of Exodus in the Old Testament is devoted to accounts of battles between the Israelites and other tribes for control of the Jordan River Valley. Struggles of this sort have also arisen in more recent times, as the imperial powers of Europe penetrated the area and sought to impose their dominion over it.

As we enter the twenty-first century, the three river systems remain divided among competing political entities. The Jordan River basin flows through Israel, Jordan, Lebanon, Syria, and Palestinian territory; the Tigris-Euphrates system passes through Iran, Iraq, Syria, Turkey, and areas occupied by the Kurdish population; and the Indus is shared among Afghanistan, China, India, Pakistan, and Kashmir (some of whose inhabitants seek to become independent). These countries and regions are deeply divided along political, religious, ethnic, and ideological lines. Disputes over water are therefore likely to be intensified by historical grievances and animosities.

For many of these countries, disputes over water have taken on a deeply emotional or symbolic character, as matters of national (or regime) survival and identity. The Zionists who established the State of Israel were not interested solely in finding a sanctuary for European Jews; they also sought to resettle Jews *on the land,* in order to shed their urban, European identity and reestablish their ties with the ancient soil of Israel. This could only be achieved, they believed, by gaining access to the Jordan River and other sources of water for irrigation purposes, as the land in much of Israel is otherwise too dry for intensive agriculture.[2] Similarly, the leaders of modern Iraq and Syria rest much of their claim to legitimacy on their success in developing new agricultural zones in the Tigris-Euphrates basin. Any

Table 7.1:
Anticipated Population Growth in Selected Countries of the Jordan,
Tigris-Euphrates, and Indus River Basins

River Basin	Country	Estimated Population				Percent Increase, 1998–2050
		1950	1998	2025	2050	
Jordan	Israel*	1.3	5.9	8.0	9.1	54.2
	Jordan	1.2	6.0	11.9	16.7	178.3
	Lebanon	1.4	3.2	4.4	5.2	62.5
	Total	3.9	15.1	24.3	31.0	105.3
Tigris-Euphrates	Iraq	5.2	21.8	41.6	56.1	157.3
	Syria	3.5	15.3	26.3	34.5	125.5
	Turkey	20.8	63.8	85.8	97.9	53.4
	Total	29.5	100.9	153.7	188.5	86.8
Indus	India	357.6	975.8	1,330.2	1,532.7	57.1
	Pakistan	39.5	147.8	268.9	357.4	141.8
	Total	397.1	1,123.6	1,599.1	1,890.1	68.2

Source: World Resources Institute, *World Resources 1998–99* (1998), p. 244.
*Does not include population of the West Bank and Gaza.

threat to the survival of these endeavors is, therefore, likely to be met with unyielding resistance.

As in the Nile River basin, disputes over shared water supplies in the Jordan, Tigris-Euphrates, and Indus basins are likely to provoke high levels of tension along with periodic outbreaks of violent conflict. There are, however, some critical differences between the Nile area and the other systems. In the Nile region, no real effort has been made since the colonial period to establish a basinwide system for water management. Although Egypt and Sudan signed a bilateral water-sharing agreement in 1959, no plans exist for the distribution of water among all riparian states. In the other three systems, however, the riparians have tried to negotiate the allocation of water. Some of these efforts have failed or are in abeyance, but there is at least a history of resolving water disputes through nonmilitary means.[3] The question remains: will the negotiations make further strides in the years ahead, or will they fall victim to mounting population pressures and other obstacles to peace?

Table 7.2: **Military Capabilities of Selected Riparians** **in the Jordan, Tigris-Euphrates, and Indus River Basins**					
River Basin	Principal Riparian	Total Armed Forces	Tanks	Heavy Artillery	Combat Aircraft
Jordan	Israel	173,500	3,800	1,430	459
	Jordan	e. 104,000	1,200	521	93
	Lebanon	67,900	92	267	0
Tigris-Euphrates	Iran	545,600	e. 1,345	2,460	304
	Iraqª	e. 375,000	e. 2,200	e. 1,950	e. 310
	Syria	e. 316,000	4,650	1,930	589
	Turkey	e. 639,000	4,205	2,372	440
Indus	India	1,173,000	e. 3,314	e. 6,875	774
	Pakistan	587,000	2,320	1,830	389

Source: International Institute for Strategic Studies, *The Military Balance 1999–2000.*
ªFigures for Iraq are approximate, reflecting the uncertainties produced by the 1991 war in Kuwait.
e = estimated

The paramount difference between the Nile and the other three systems involves the distribution of military power. In the Nile area, Egypt is the only state with significant military strength and so has been able to deter challenges to its dominant position by other states in the region. In the other three basins, however, we find that many of the key players possess a potent military capacity, allowing them to threaten or to employ military force when negotiations fail and disputes over shared water supplies erupt. Indeed, as shown by Table 7.2, the nations of these three areas possess some of the largest and best-equipped armed forces in the developing world. Other parties to these disputes, such as the Palestinians and the Kurds, may lack regular armies but can bring other forms of pressure to bear— terrorism, guerrilla warfare, rioting, and civil disobedience.

The nations of the Jordan, Tigris-Euphrates, and Indus river basins face a critical race for time: will they be able to adopt practical and equitable water-sharing arrangements covering their common water supply before the forces of population growth and nationalism lead to war? At this point, nobody can predict the answer. While it is possible to see signs of hope in each of these areas, there are also many reasons for concern.

WATER CONFLICT IN THE JORDAN RIVER BASIN

The area occupied by Israel and Jordan, along with the West Bank (much of which is governed by the Palestinian Authority), is primarily arid or semiarid. Water is scarce in this region: according to the World Bank, Israel's renewable water supply in 1990 was 467 cubic meters per person, well below the healthy minimum of 1,000 cubic meters, and Jordan's was even smaller—a scant 224 cubic meters.[4] Both countries have attempted to supplement their meager supplies by drawing on underground aquifers and recycling waste water, but none of these measures has alleviated the scarcity. Both countries, therefore, have sought to maximize their utilization of the Jordan River, the only significant source of surface water in the region.

By world standards, the Jordan is not a particularly large or copious river. Its total average flow, about 1,200 million cubic meters (mcm) per year, represents only about 1 percent of the Congo's flow, or 2 percent of the Nile's.[5] The Jordan River also suffers from heavy salinity, especially at its southern end, where it empties into the Dead Sea. Nevertheless, the Jordan and its tributaries (including the Yarmuk) supply a large proportion of the water consumed by Israel and Jordan, and are essential to the elaborate irrigation projects undertaken by these countries. It is not surprising, then, that control over the Jordan River and its headwaters have been a contentious and often explosive issue since the establishment of Israel in 1948.[6]

The Jordan River originates in Lebanon, on the flanks of Mount Hermon. Towering some 2,800 meters (9,185 feet) above sea level, Mount Hermon collects substantial precipitation from the Mediterranean Sea and redistributes this through a number of streams and aquifers. Three of these sources combine to form the Jordan River: the Hasbani River, originating on the western side of the mountain in Lebanon; the Dan River, arising from the Dan spring in the northernmost corner of Israel; and the Baniyas River, originating on the southeastern flank of Mount Hermon in Syria. From the confluence of these three streams, about three miles into Israeli territory, the Jordan flows south some twenty-five miles to Lake Tiberias (also known as the Sea of Galilee and Lake Kinneret), Israel's main source of fresh water.[7] (See map.)

About six miles south of Lake Tiberias, the Jordan River is joined by its principal tributary, the Yarmuk. Arising in southern Syria, the Yarmuk travels some twenty-five miles along the Syrian-Jordanian border before entering Israel and merging with the Jordan. At this point, the Jordan River is at its peak level of flow; from here on in, it loses water to evaporation and becomes increasingly saline. Meandering wildly as it travels farther south, the river terminates at the Dead Sea.

As far back as the Mandate period, when the territories of Palestine and Transjordan were under British control, government officials have sought to exploit the Jordan River system for agricultural and industrial projects. In 1939, Michael Ionides (then director of development in the British-run Transjordan Administration) released a proposal for the construction of irrigation canals on both the east and west sides of the Jordan River to carry fresh water from Lake Tiberias and the southern Yarmuk. Another plan, prepared in 1944 by Walter Clay Lowdermilk, combined the irrigation scheme envisioned by Ionides with a canal to carry Jordan River water to the heavily populated coastal plain and the Negev Desert in the south. These plans were never implemented, but they did lay the groundwork for many of the proposals that emerged in the postwar era.[8]

After the establishment of the Hashemite Kingdom of Jordan (in 1946) and the State of Israel (in 1948), water engineers in the two new countries began to develop independent plans for the exploitation of the Jordan River's waters. Israel, under its All-Israel Plan of 1951, drained the Huleh swamp above Lake Tiberias and initiated planning for the diversion of Jordan River waters to populated areas on the coast. At about the same time, Jordan developed plans to divert waters from the Yarmuk River to a system of irrigation canals on the eastern terrace (or East Ghor) of the Jordan Valley. An agreement allowing for such diversion was signed with Syria in 1953, and

Jordan River Basin

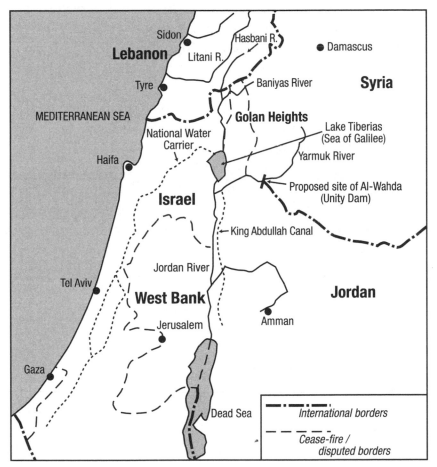

construction of the East Ghor Canal began shortly thereafter. Although these early efforts did not jeopardize the immediate water consumption of either Israel or Jordan, they did produce fears of future competition over what was, in fact, a very limited resource.[9]

Recognizing that conflict between Israel and its neighbors over shared water supplies could undermine U.S. efforts to combat the possible spread of Soviet influence in the Middle East, the administration of Dwight D. Eisenhower took a direct interest in the problem. For Secretary of State John Foster Dulles and other senior officials, promoting the cooperative development of the region's water resources was seen as a promising route to political accommodation. To facilitate such cooperation, Eisenhower appointed a special representative to the riparian states, Eric Johnston of the U.S. Technical Cooperation Agency, and gave him the task of negotiating a regional water-sharing agreement in the Jordan River basin.

Ambassador Johnston devoted two years to this diplomatic effort, traveling to the Middle East on four separate occasions between 1953 and 1955. Through painstaking negotiations, he succeeded in narrowing the differences between Israeli and Arab engineers and eventually secured agreement from them on the practical aspects of a water-sharing arrangement. Under this plan, Jordan would gain access to some of the water in Lake Tiberias and would control most of the Yarmuk; Israel would control the upper Jordan and obtain the right to divert water from Lake Tiberias to coastal areas and the Negev. But just when it seemed that a formal agreement was possible, political leaders on both sides balked at the plan: the Arabs were unwilling to sign anything that might be interpreted as conferring recognition to the State of Israel, and the Israelis were fearful of signing away any rights to Lake Tiberias and the upper Jordan.[10]

Once the Johnston effort collapsed, both Israel and Jordan turned to development of their own, independent water projects: Israel accelerated construction of its National Water Carrier (NWC)—a system of tunnels and canals intended to transport water from the Jordan River to coastal areas and the Negev—while Jordan intensified work on the East Ghor Canal and associated projects.[11] For a time, these efforts proceeded without major incident. However, when Israel moved closer to the completion of the NWC canal system, the atmosphere became increasingly tense. Viewing the NWC as an intolerable theft of shared Jordan River waters, Arab leaders began to consider measures for blocking the project. Finally, in 1960, they agreed on a bold and provocative move: damming the Hasbani River in Lebanon and the Baniyas in Syria, and diverting their waters (via the Yarmuk) to the East Ghor Canal in Jordan—thus bypassing the upper Jordan and Lake Tiberias, the main intake site for the Israeli canal system.[12]

Clearly, the Arab plan to divert the headwaters of the Jordan River represented a major threat to Israel. Without the 260 million cubic meters of water provided each year by the Hasbani and Baniyas Rivers, the NWC would be rendered useless, and accompanying plans to irrigate the Negev would have to be abandoned. After learning of the Arab League's decision in 1960, Israeli Foreign Minister Golda Meir warned that any move to divert the headwaters of the Jordan River would represent "an outright attack on one of Israel's means of livelihood" and would therefore be regarded as "a threat to peace."[13] Four years later, when Syria began to implement the diversion project, Premier Levi Eshkol warned the Arabs that "Israel would act to ensure that the waters continue to flow."[14]

By late 1964, with the NWC nearing completion and the Arab diversion project finally under way, events began to take a more violent turn. The first serious incident occurred in mid-November, when Israeli and Syrian forces clashed near the Dan spring. Further incidents were reported in the spring and summer of 1965, often accompanied by dogfights between Israeli and Syrian aircraft. A more serious incident occurred in July 1966, when Israeli planes struck the diversion works on the Baniyas-Yarmuk canal and Syrian planes attempted to drive them off. In yet another encounter, in August 1966, Israeli and Syrian planes fought over Lake Tiberias. As these events multiplied, tensions rose throughout the region and the various protagonists readied their forces for war.[15]

Water-related concerns were not, of course, the only issues that divided Israel and the Arab countries. The Arabs were highly critical of the Israelis' treatment of the Palestinians, while Israel was incensed at Jordanian and Syrian support for guerrilla activities by the Palestinian group Fatah. Nevertheless, the water issue was seen on both sides as a matter of national security, and so neither camp was prepared to back down on the Jordan River dispute. Both sides continued to bolster their forces along the various borders, and clashes along the upper Jordan River grew in intensity.[16]

On April 7, 1967, Israeli planes struck construction sites deep inside Syrian territory, provoking another major dogfight. This was followed by accusations and recriminations on each side, along with the further mobilization of forces. On May 18, Egypt expelled the

United Nations Emergency Force (UNEF) from the Sinai, where it had served as a buffer between Egyptian and Israeli forces, and closed the Gulf of Aqaba to Israeli ships. These steps prompted a series of moves and countermoves by Israel and Syria, leading to the outbreak of full-scale hostilities on June 5, 1967.

As a result of its stunning victories in the ensuing conflict—known since as the Six-Day War—Israel significantly enhanced its strategic position vis-à-vis the Arab states in the upper Jordan area. By occupying the Golan Heights of Syria, Israel gained direct control over the Baniyas River, thus eliminating any threat to the headwaters of the Jordan. Also, by seizing the West Bank, it gained access to the lower Jordan River and to the valuable aquifers located in the hills north of Jerusalem. The Jordanians, on the other hand, found themselves in a much weaker position: not only did they lose the West Bank, but they also gained an additional 300,000 Palestinian refugees who needed to be provided with food and water.[17]

Although the 1967 war significantly diminished the Arabs' capacity to impede Israel's plans for the Jordan, this did not prevent further conflict over water. From 1967 to 1969, the Palestine Liberation Organization (PLO) conducted a series of armed attacks on Israeli settlements in the Jordan Valley, in many cases targeting Israeli water installations. Israel responded by striking the East Ghor Canal in Jordan, asserting that the Jordanians were aiding the attackers and diverting more than their rightful share of Yarmuk waters. However, after high-level mediation by the United States, Israel agreed to suspend its attacks on the East Ghor Canal and Jordan agreed to expel the PLO from its territory.[18]

Water issues did not figure in the 1973 "October War" between Israel and the Arab states, and they remained in the background for most of the 1970s. In the 1980s, however, the water issue again provoked a crisis when Jordan and Syria revived plans to build a dam at Maqarin on the Yarmuk River. Long a goal of Jordanian water engineers, the proposed dam would store water from winter floods and make it available to farmers in the Jordan Valley via the East Ghor (now King Abdullah) Canal. Claiming that the project would consume water needed by Jewish settlements in the Golan Heights and adjacent areas, Israel threatened to block the dam through any means necessary—including military action. This time, threats proved effective in discouraging Jordan and its backers from going ahead with the plan.[19]

Since this incident, friction over water issues shifted from the Israeli-Jordanian relationship to Israel's relations with the Palestinians of the West Bank. Using its authority as the occupying power, Israel has prevented the West Bank Arabs from increasing their withdrawals from the abundant aquifers that underlie the region. At the same time, the Israelis have tapped into these supplies to satisfy a significant portion of their own water requirements and to supply Jewish settlements in the West Bank. By reserving most of the West Bank's underground water supply for its own use and that of the Jewish settlers, Israel has created a blatantly unequal situation in the area, with Jewish settlers receiving five to eight times more water per capita than the Palestinians. This, in turn, has stoked Palestinian resentment toward the occupying power and helped fuel the Palestinian *intifada,* or uprising, that began in 1987 and lasted for several years.[20]

As the 1990s commenced, little had changed since 1967 regarding the actual *distribution* of water in the West Bank and the Jordan River Valley. However, the various parties to these disputes began to consider a nonmilitary solution to the water problem as part of the Arab-Israeli peace process initiated in 1991 under U.S. auspices. In 1994, Israel and Jordan signed a peace treaty that covers a wide range of vital issues, including water. Under Article 6 of the treaty, and in an accompanying annex, Israel agreed to limit its annual withdrawals from the Yarmuk and to allow more water to flow into the King Abdullah Canal from the Jordan River proper. The two countries also agreed to cooperate in desalination projects in the Jordan River Valley and to consider other joint water-conservation efforts—although, as of early 2000, no such cooperation had taken place.[21]

Water issues have also figured in the negotiations between Israel and the PLO (now the Palestinian Authority) over the future status of the West Bank and the Gaza Strip. Under the "Interim Agreement" signed by the two sides in September 1995, Israel acknowledged that the Palestinians enjoyed certain "rights" to the underground water supply of the West Bank. It also gave the newly formed Palestinian Authority a partial role in the allocation of water supplies in the areas to be placed under its control. However, the Interim Agreement allowed Israel to retain control over all West Bank water supplies, while negotiations were held to determine the "final status" of the area— negotiations that have not yet occurred, as of this writing. With drought conditions affecting much of this area in 1999–2000, moreover, Palestinian resentment over Israeli water policies again boiled up.[22] Israel has also refused to concede any Palestinian rights to the water of the Jordan River itself, even though the West Bank (itself a reference to the Jordan) borders the river for much of its length.[23]

Finally, water issues are an important item on the agenda of the Israeli-Syrian peace talks that commenced in early 2000. As a precondition for any peace treaty between the two countries, Syria is demanding a complete Israeli withdrawal from the Golan Heights and, it is said, the land on the east bank of Lake Tiberias. This, however, would place Israeli access to the water of the Baniyas spring in jeopardy, and so Israel can be expected to insist on some form of control over this vital tributary of the Jordan. Israel is also likely to insist on full control over Lake Tiberias.[24] Although some preliminary discussions between the two sides were held in Shepherdstown, West Virginia, in January 2000, no progress was reported and the talks were suspended. The death of Syrian President Hafiz al-Assad in June of that year, as well as continued political uncertainty in Israel, has, at the time of this writing, prevented the resumption of talks.

These negotiations represent the best hope for a comprehensive settlement of the issues dividing Israel and its Arab neighbors, including the question of water. If all parties concerned reach agreement on fundamental issues and begin to cooperate in addressing common problems, it may prove possible to avert a water disaster in the area and to satisfy the basic needs of the region's inhabitants— Jew and Arab alike. But time is running out: the total population of the Jordan Valley area is expected to more than double between 1990 and 2020, from 9.6 to 21.2 million people, and to continue rising in the years that follow. If the nations of the area do not arrive at a common water strategy in the near-term future, population growth and other pressures will place an intolerable burden on the existing supply and lead to chronic instability throughout the region.

THE TIGRIS AND EUPHRATES

The Tigris-Euphrates system is much larger than the Jordan River Valley, encompassing an area approximately twenty times as great. Like the Jordan, however, the Tigris-Euphrates system is shared by several states and ethnic groups that distrust one another and rarely agree on water-related issues. In both cases, moreover, efforts to develop a basinwide management scheme have so far come to naught. Although some water agreements have been reached between individual pairs of countries, no plans yet exist for the overall distribution of system waters—allowing for continuing discord over the utilization of scarce resources. In both areas, moreover, rising population is a significant factor that bears heavily on the water-use equation.

The two main rivers in this system, the Tigris and Euphrates, originate in the same mountainous region of southeastern Turkey and eventually merge to form a single watercourse, the Shatt al-Arab (which eventually empties into the Persian Gulf). In between these points, however, the two streams swing far apart, with the Euphrates traveling in a southwesterly direction into north-central Syria, and the Tigris flowing in a southeasterly direction into northern Iraq. Although each river acquires additional water from tributaries that join them along their path to the Persian Gulf, both acquire the bulk of their flow from springs and streams in Turkey: the Euphrates obtains about 88 percent of its total volume in Turkey, while the Tigris obtains about 50 percent.[25] (See map.)

At their egress from Turkey, the Tigris and Euphrates lie about 250 miles apart. The Euphrates, the westernmost of the two, enters northern Syria and then flows in a southerly direction for about seventy miles before turning east toward the Iraqi border; along the way, it picks up two major tributaries, the Balikh and the Khabur, both of which also arise in southeastern Turkey. The Tigris, on the east, slides along the Syrian border for about fifty miles before plunging

Tigris-Euphrates River System

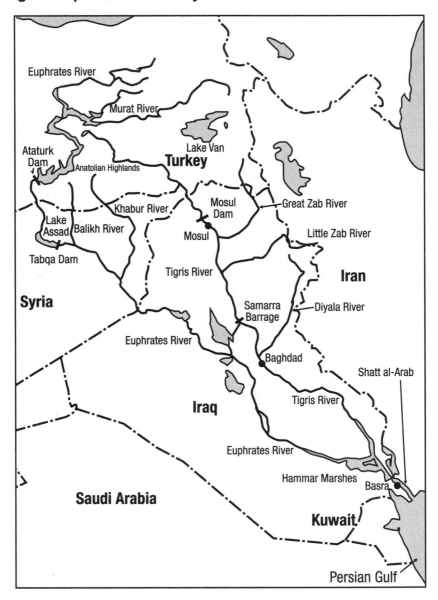

into northern Iraq. As it travels southward, the Tigris is joined by several key tributaries, including the Great Zab, the Little Zab, the Uzaym, and the Diyala. The first of these, the Great Zab, originates in Turkey, but the other three rise in the Zagros Mountains of western Iran.

After descending from the highlands of Turkey and Iraq, the Tigris and Euphrates enter the large alluvial plain of Mesopotamia— literally, "the land between the rivers." The Euphrates brackets this vast depression (approximately 500 miles long by 150 miles wide) on the south and west; the Tigris bounds it on the north and east. It is in this area that humanity first practiced irrigated agriculture, about 7,500 years ago, and it was here that the earliest human cities and kingdoms arose. The region fell into decay in late biblical times, when excessive irrigation led to the buildup of salts in the soil, but widespread irrigation was reintroduced in the nineteenth and twentieth centuries. Today, most of Iraq's population and croplands are concentrated in this area, along with much of its industry.[26]

At the southeastern edge of the Mesopotamian plain, the two rivers pass through huge swamps inhabited by the Madan, the "Marsh Arabs." Over the centuries, these hardy people have established a distinctive culture based on fishing and animal husbandry. Since the Gulf War of 1990–91, Iraq has attempted to drain the swamps— ostensibly to develop new lands for agriculture but also, it is suspected, to pacify an area that has long harbored Shiite opponents of the leadership in Baghdad.[27] After passing through this area, the Tigris and Euphrates finally come together at Al Qurnah to form the Shatt al-Arab; the combined stream then flows southward for a hundred or so miles before emptying into the Gulf.

Together, the Tigris and Euphrates Rivers are absolutely essential to the economies and domestic needs of Syria and Iraq. According to some estimates, Syria obtains about 85 percent of its total renewable water supply from the Euphrates, while Iraq obtains nearly 100 percent of its supply from the two rivers combined. Turkey is much less dependent on the Tigris-Euphrates system for its basic water requirements: at present, it derives about 30 percent of its supply from these rivers. However, the Turks have elaborate plans to irrigate new croplands in southeastern Anatolia, and so intend to increase their utilization of the Tigris and Euphrates.[28]

In recent years, all three of these countries have built dams on the Tigris and/or Euphrates for flood control, electrical power generation, and agricultural purposes. Turkey has been the most energetic in this regard, building three large dams on the Euphrates (the Keban, Karakaya, and Ataturk) and developing plans for several on the Tigris; Syria has built a large dam at Tabqa on the Euphrates, and is building another at Tishreen; Iraq has built several major dams on both rivers. These projects have given each country some degree of control over the seasonal flow of the rivers and permitted a substantial increase in irrigated agriculture. However, they have also given the upstream countries an ability to deny water to the downstream countries, and this has led to mounting tension throughout the region.

As in the case of the Jordan River system, the Tigris-Euphrates riparians are divided by more than water competition. Syria and Turkey have clashed over the disputed province of Hatay (ceded to Turkey by France in 1939 but originally part of Syria) and over Syria's aid to the separatist Kurdistan Workers' Party (PKK) in Turkey; Iraq and Syria have fought over the orientation and leadership of the Ba'ath Party (to which both countries claim allegiance) and other political matters; and Iraq and Turkey were adversaries during the Persian Gulf conflict of 1990–91. As in the Jordan Valley, however, water availability is considered essential to national security— especially in the two downstream states—and so tends to overshadow other issues when a threat of diminished supply arises.[29]

The first significant crisis of this sort occurred in 1975, when work on the Syrian dam at Tabqa on the Euphrates River was nearing completion. Built in part with Soviet assistance, the Tabqa Dam (later renamed the ath-Thawrah, or Revolution Dam) was intended to store 12 billion cubic meters of water and to irrigate some 640,000 hectares (259,000 acres) of farmland. As the reservoir behind the dam began to fill up, Iraq charged that the Euphrates's discharge into Iraq had fallen to a tiny fraction of its normal flow and that a year's worth of crops was facing ruin. The Syrians denied that there had been a significant drop in the river's flow, but relations between the two countries grew increasingly tense.[30] An emergency meeting of Arab League foreign ministers on May 1–3, 1975, in Jidda failed to produce a solution to the dispute, and subsequent mediation by Saudi Oil Minister Sheikh Ahmed Zaki al-Yamani produced only temporary relief. On July 8, Syria withdrew its military attachés from Baghdad and ordered the Iraqis to withdraw their own attachés from Damascus; each side then closed their airspace to aircraft belonging to the other, and both announced plans to reinforce their forces at the border.[31]

By August 1, the crisis was nearing the point of no return. Iraq had relocated many of its troops from the northeast (where they had been fighting Kurdish guerrillas) to the border with Syria, while Syria had redeployed some of its armored forces from the Golan Heights to the Tabqa Dam area and the border with Iraq. Each side also accused the other of conducting illicit military overflights and of mounting periodic border incursions.[32] Finally, on August 12, Saudi Crown Prince Fahd arrived in Damascus for a last-minute attempt at mediation. After wresting from the Syrians a promise to release additional water into the Euphrates, Prince Fahd persuaded Baghdad to call down its forces and resolve the matter through peaceful negotiations.[33]

In the wake of the Tabqa Dam crisis, representatives of the two sides met on several occasions to discuss a permanent resolution to the Euphrates dispute. However, no such agreement was adopted at that time, and Damascus and Baghdad continued to spar over the allocation of the Euphrates's waters. It was not until April 1990—when a far more serious crisis broke out over the Ataturk Dam in Turkey—that Syria and Iraq agreed on a formula for dividing the water of the Euphrates. Under this agreement, Syria pledged to deliver no less than 58 percent of all Euphrates waters it received from Turkey to the Iraqis.[34]

The impetus for the sudden rapprochement between Syria and Iraq was the decision by Turkey to cut off the flow of the Euphrates *entirely* for one month, from January 13 to February 12, 1990, in order to fill up the reservoir behind the Ataturk Dam. Because this occurred in winter (before the onset of the regular growing season) and because Turkey poured higher-than-normal water supplies into the river in the months that followed, the closure had little effect in practical terms. By demonstrating Turkey's ability to control the flow of the river, however, it aroused considerable resentment in both Syria and Iraq. This reaction was particularly strong because the cut-off was seen in both countries as a foretaste of worse to come, as Turkey proceeded with an elaborate scheme to harness the Tigris and Euphrates and use their waters for domestic irrigation projects.[35]

This scheme is known in Turkey as the Southeast Anatolian Project, or Güneydogu Anadolu Projesi (GAP). Originally launched in the 1960s, GAP is a mammoth, $30 billion project to spur development in Turkey's impoverished southeast, generate electricity, and increase the nation's supply of food. When complete, the project will include twenty-two high dams on the Tigris and Euphrates (and their tributaries), nineteen hydroelectric power stations, and numerous irrigation schemes spread over two million hectares of land. The entire landscape of southern Turkey will be transformed by this effort: desert valleys will be filled by reservoirs, canals will traverse the countryside, and formerly unproductive fields will blossom with valuable produce. All told, Ankara hopes to create three million new jobs through the project—many of which are intended for the Kurdish villagers who reside in this area and who in the past have shown sympathy for the separatist aspirations of the PKK.[36]

As the vast scope of the GAP effort became increasingly evident, leaders of both Syria and Iraq expressed concern about the future security of their nations' water supplies. In response, Turkish officials insisted that they would take no action to jeopardize the basic water requirements of either country. To demonstrate its goodwill, Turkey signed a protocol with Syria in 1987 under which it promised to maintain the river's flow into Syria at an average rate of 500 cubic meters per second, or 15.7 billion cubic meters per year. In return, Damascus pledged to tighten security on the Syrian-Turkish border and to discontinue its clandestine support for the PKK. However, Syria failed to satisfy Turkish demands for a crackdown on the PKK, and in October 1989 President Turgut Özal warned the Syrians that he would cut off the flow of the Euphrates if they did not terminate their support for the rebel group; Özal later retracted the threat, but the aura of menace remained.[37]

Tensions came to a head in January 1990 when Turkey cut off the flow of the Euphrates while filling up the reservoir behind the Ataturk Dam. Once again, as in 1975, both sides issued threatening statements, and talk of war filled the air. Syria and Iraq also chose this occasion to patch up their differences and establish a common front against Turkey on water issues. As it happened, Turkey restored the flow of the Euphrates River into Syria before these initiatives could lead to actual hostilities; the end result, however, was a deepening of Syrian hostility toward Turkey.[38]

Given the imbalance in military power between the two countries—Turkey's army is about twice the size of Syria's and (through its ties to NATO) much better equipped—Syria was in no position to contemplate an attack on Turkey. Indeed, the Turks openly bragged of their superiority, declaring that they were fully prepared to resist an attack on the Ataturk Dam or other GAP installations by Syria or Iraq: "I do not believe in worrying about threats of war resulting from development projects in Turkey," then Prime Minister Süleyman Demirel declared at the time. "If there is a threat we will repel it. Turkey has deterrence, [and] we will have more deterrence in the coming period."[39] But Syria did have one card to play in this contest, and it did not hesitate to do so. By aiding the PKK and providing sanctuary for its forces, Damascus was able to stimulate chronic instability in southeastern Anatolia, where GAP projects are concentrated and most Turkish Kurds reside.[40]

The fighting between the Turks and the PKK reached a crescendo in the mid-1990s, when the Turkish army was deployed in the region and hundreds of thousands of Kurds were driven from their homes by the government's scorched-earth strategy. At least 30,000 people died in this conflict, and many more were wounded, tortured, jailed, or uprooted. The war also witnessed significant and widespread human rights abuses by the Turkish military, along with numerous acts of terrorism by the PKK.[41] And while the conflict never deterred Turkey from proceeding with the GAP-related water projects, it did dissuade Turkish and foreign firms from relocating in the area and slowed the pace of dam construction.[42]

In 1998, Turkey decided to eradicate the PKK insurgency by going after its bases of support in Syria. Claiming that Syrian backing for the guerrillas represented an "undeclared war" against Turkey, Ankara warned of military action unless the PKK's training camps were closed and its leader, Abdullah Ocalan, was expelled from the country.[43] To back up its threat, Ankara placed its forces on high alert and deployed thousands of troops along the Syrian border.[44]

For several weeks, it appeared as if a full-scale conflict was inevitable. Turkish newspapers were full of speculation regarding the military's forthcoming offensive; typically, these spoke of an air assault against Syrian military installations, followed by a ground invasion.[45] Fearful of a significant regional conflagration, leaders of several countries in the area, including Egyptian President Muhammad Hosni Mubarak, flew to Ankara and Damascus in an effort to defuse the crisis.[46] Eventually, Turkish pressure achieved its principal objectives: fearing defeat in any head-on clash with Turkey, Syria agreed to terminate its support for the PKK. Under an agreement signed on October 21, 1998, Damascus pledged to close PKK training bases, cease providing it with financial aid, and expel Ocalan.[47] (Ocalan subsequently fled to Italy and then to Africa, where he was captured by Turkish agents and brought to Ankara for trial.)

The October 1998 agreement cooled tensions on the Syria-Turkey border and temporarily reduced the threat of bloodshed. But it addressed only one aspect of the antagonism between Damascus and Ankara: the issue of Syrian support for the PKK. Left untouched was the issue of the Euphrates. Indeed, concern in Syria over the threat posed by Turkish water projects peaked again in the summer of 1999, when a severe drought gripped the region and Turkey began construction of its fourth large dam on the Euphrates, at Birecik. No military crisis erupted on this occasion, but tensions rose throughout the region.[48]

As the new century commenced, water politics in the Tigris-Euphrates basin were more contentious than ever. The most worrisome factor, as before, was the construction of new dams and irrigation schemes in southeastern Turkey. With Ocalan in jail and the PKK in retreat, Ankara was ready to move ahead with projects that had been stalled for several years. Under current plans, Turkey intends to expand the area under irrigation along the Euphrates tenfold during the first decade of the twenty-first century—a step that would significantly reduce the flow of water into Syria (by as much as half, in some estimates) and contaminate what is left with increased levels of pesticides and fertilizer.[49]

On top of this, Ankara announced plans in 1999 to extend the GAP project to the headwaters of the Tigris River. Turkey will build a dam at Ilisu, in a Kurdish-populated area about forty miles north of the Syrian border. Once this and other dams on the Tigris are completed, Turkey plans to irrigate some 600,000 hectares (240,000 acres) of land with water from the river, reducing its annual flow by 5 to 7 billion cubic meters—or about one-third of its total natural flow into Syria and Iraq.[50] Because the Tigris is the only practical alternative to the Euphrates as a source of water for these two countries, any diminution in its flow would be a serious threat to their food supply and general well-being.[51]

As in the Nile River basin, the net demand for water is rising throughout the Tigris-Euphrates region. All three of the riparian states plan to increase their domestic food production through new irrigation schemes, and all seek to use more water for urban and industrial purposes. Even more worrisome, all three states are experiencing high rates of population growth: according to the World Resources Institute, Turkey's population is expected to climb from 64 million people in 1998 to 98 million in 2050, Iraq's from 22 million to 56 million, and Syria's from 15 million to 35 million. All told, the region is expected to gain 88 million people over the next fifty years—more than three times the combined population of these countries in 1950.[52]

The stage is being set, therefore, for a series of recurring crises over water supplies in the Tigris-Euphrates basin. Each time a new dam is completed or the flow of water into one or the other of the two rivers is diminished, resentment will flare up in the downstream countries. And while all previous crises of this sort have ended without the eruption of violence, there is no guarantee that this will continue to be the case in the future. Clearly, the only sure way of averting a regional conflagration is for the three states involved to agree on an equitable, basinwide plan for the distribution of Tigris and Euphrates waters.[53] No such plan has yet been developed, however, and there is no indication that these countries are ready to embrace such a scheme.[54]

THE INDUS RIVER

As in the Nile and Tigris-Euphrates regions, the Indus River basin has been the site of recurring conflict between its major riparians, India and Pakistan. For the most part, these encounters have been over political and territorial concerns—notably the status of Kashmir—rather than over water. Following an initial clash in 1948, the two countries have generally managed to resolve their differences over the Indus through peaceful means. However, tensions between India and Pakistan have increased in recent years, and there is a very real danger that water issues will prove a flashpoint for future confrontations.

The Indus follows a tortuous path as it travels from original source to final exit, passing through the jurisdictions of several states in the process. Its initial stream arises on the north slope of the Kailas Range in western Tibet, and then flows in a northwesterly direction through China to Ladakh in Indian-controlled Kashmir. At this point, the river turns south and passes into Pakistan. While still in northern Pakistan, it is joined by the Kabul River, which, as its name suggests, arises in Afghanistan. Farther south, five great rivers—the Jhelum, the Chenab, the Ravi, the Beas, and the Sutlej—combine to form the Panjnad, which joins the Indus proper at Chachran, about four hundred miles north of its outlet into the Arabian Sea.[55] (See map.)

For thousands of years, the Indus Plain has been occupied by human settlements. As in Egypt and Mesopotamia, the introduction of irrigated agriculture about five thousand years ago led to the emergence of great empires and civilizations. One after another, waves of

Indus River Basin

invaders from less fortunate regions—Aryans, Bactrians, Parthians, Huns, Persians, Mongols, and others—poured into this area and superimposed their culture on top of those laid down by earlier occupants. The British were the last to arrive, penetrating the region in the eighteenth century and gaining control over the Indus basin by the middle of the nineteenth century.

Among their many imperial ambitions in India, the British set out to harness the Indus and its tributaries for massive water projects. In doing so, they were able to exploit their dominant position in the region to incorporate the river's many tributaries into an integrated, basinwide management system—the first of its kind in the world. Large canals were built from one branch of the river to another, allowing for the safe release of floodwaters and the irrigation of interlying areas. The first such canals were built in 1859, and by 1915 the entire Punjab region was crisscrossed by an elaborate network of canals. At the moment of partition, the Indus Valley possessed approximately 26 million acres of irrigated farmland—3 million more than existed in the United States at that time.[56]

The partition of India into two sovereign states on August 15, 1947, produced havoc in the Indus River basin. Not only was the region itself bisected into separate, antagonistic nations, but the British-designed canal system—the very foundation of the region's economy—was broken up into separate networks. Sir Cyril Radcliffe, who was given the unwelcome job of dividing up the Indus basin, awarded most of the canals and irrigated land to Pakistan. However, the new border left the headwaters of all five of the Panjnad's tributaries in India, along with the upper reaches of the Indus itself. Hence, India became the "upstream" riparian with respect to Pakistan, with all the complications that this implied.[57]

The significance of this division soon became apparent. On March 31, 1948, when the "Standstill Agreement" governing the temporary management of the canal system expired, the authorities in East Punjab (India) cut off the flow of water to several key canals in West Punjab (Pakistan). The loss of water destroyed crops on more than one million acres of irrigated farmland in Pakistan, producing widespread famine. Many Pakistanis viewed this act as a calculated effort by India to undermine their new state and called for a military response; the Indians, on the other hand, treated the incident as a minor misunderstanding. By May, water was again flowing through the canals and the two countries adopted an interim agreement on the distribution of Indus waters. Nevertheless, tensions remained high and both countries rejected any intention of reintegrating their severed water systems.[58]

For the next several years, India and Pakistan argued incessantly over the terms of the May 1948 interim agreement and related aspects of the water issue. Both countries also began to build new canals and waterworks so as to diminish their dependence on shared resources and infrastructure. The risk of a violent encounter was further reduced when the World Bank (then known by its more formal title, the International Bank for Reconstruction and Development) offered to mediate the dispute over the Indus and its tributaries. For eight years, from 1952 to 1960, bank officials conducted intense and often acrimonious negotiations between the two sides.[59] Finally, in September 1960, the leaders of India and Pakistan signed an agreement known as the Indus Waters Treaty.

It had been the oft-expressed hope of the World Bank's American negotiators that India and Pakistan would agree to the integrated development of the Indus River basin through some form of joint management system. However, neither side was willing to entrust its vital water interests to a mixed governing body. In the end, the 1960 treaty called for the permanent division of the river network into two separate systems: India would receive exclusive control over the waters of the Ravi, the Beas, and the Sutlej (representing about one-fifth of the combined Indus flow), while Pakistan would control the waters of the Indus proper plus the Jhelum and the Chenab (representing four-fifths of the total flow). In addition, India agreed to continue supplying water from the three rivers it controlled to Pakistan for a specified period of time, while the Pakistanis built new dams and waterworks on their tributaries to compensate for the eventual loss of the eastern rivers. To make all of this palatable to the two countries, the World Bank and several Western countries agreed to finance the necessary Pakistani works, along with new irrigation canals in India.[60]

The Indus Waters Treaty has been viewed by many experts as a model for the peaceful resolution of international water disputes. It should be noted, however, that the treaty does not allow for the joint development of the Indus basin; nor does it eliminate the grounds for conflict over water distribution between India and Pakistan. Rather, it is a plan for the *separate* development of the basin, with

India receiving a smaller share of the total water supply but retaining control of several key Indus tributaries.[61] This means that the Indians can argue in the future that they were denied an equitable share of the combined resources of the river; and, at the same time, India's position as the upstream riparian gives it the capacity to impede the flow of water to Pakistan.

Indian leaders have rejected such action in the past, choosing instead to focus on the more pressing issue of Kashmir. With the introduction of "Green Revolution" grain seeds, moreover, both India and Pakistan have been able to achieve a significant increase in food production in their own sectors of the basin.[62] But it cannot be assumed that these conditions will prevail indefinitely. The water supply in Punjab, Rajasthan, and other major grain-producing areas of India has contracted significantly due to serious aquifer depletion, placing a greater burden on the Indus River system. With population growth continuing unabated, New Delhi could feel compelled to violate or abrogate the 1960 treaty.

At present, the most unstable factor in the Indo-Pakistani relationship is the status of Kashmir. Once a semiautonomous "princely state" within British-controlled India, Kashmir was given the option in 1947 of joining India or Pakistan or becoming independent. When pro-Pakistani Muslims staged a revolt against the Kashmiri government, the reigning maharaja, Hari Singh, opted for accession to India. A war then broke out between India and Pakistan, resulting in the partition of Kashmir into Pakistan-controlled Azad ("Free") Kashmir in the north and west, and the Indian-controlled state of Jammu and Kashmir in the south and east. Another war, in 1965, left the situation relatively unchanged, with Pakistani and Indian forces arrayed on either side of the so-called Line of Control (LoC). Since then, Islamabad has continued to press for the incorporation of Indian-controlled Kashmir (which has a Muslim majority) into Pakistan, while New Delhi has adamantly refused to consider this option.

The conflict in Kashmir simmered throughout the Cold War period but reached a new level of intensity in 1990, when pro-independence forces launched a guerrilla campaign in Indian-controlled Kashmir and pro-Pakistani Islamic militants initiated a rebellion of their own. India responded by pouring 250,000 troops into Kashmir and imposing martial law. On several occasions, tensions in Kashmir led to the massing of Indian and Pakistani forces along the border—and, it is believed, the transfer of nuclear weapons (normally kept in secret government installations) to the air forces of the two sides.[63] Conditions became even more volatile in the summer of 1999, when Pakistani forces crossed into Jammu and Kashmir and occupied a strategic mountainside at Kargil on the Indian side of the LoC. Only a last-minute decision by then Prime Minister Nawaz Sharif to withdraw the forces averted a major Indo-Pakistani conflict.[64] (Partly as a result of this decision, Sharif was overthrown by army officers who had backed the incursion into Kashmir.[65])

Kashmir plays a pivotal role in the India-Pakistan rivalry for several reasons. First, it is a manifestation of the religious politics that divide the two countries: as a Muslim-majority area, it is thought by most Pakistanis to belong in their country; for Indian leaders, it is a symbol of nationalism and of India's claim to constitute a multiethnic state. Kashmir is also a rallying cry for the ultranationalist movements that have come to prominence in both countries: the Bharatiya Janata Party (BJP) in India and the Jamaat Islami (and similar groups) in Pakistan. For military leaders on both sides, moreover, Kashmir is seen as a likely battleground in the war between them that most believe will eventually occur.[66]

The political and military dimensions of the Kashmir dispute are well known. But Kashmir also figures in the *water* politics of the Indus basin: the Indus River itself passes through Kashmir on its journey from China to Pakistan, and several of its key tributaries, including the Jhelum, the Chenab, and the Ravi, arise in this area. If India were to give up control of Kashmir—whether to Pakistan or an independent regime of some sort—it would lose its status as an upstream riparian and, therefore, much of its clout in determining the river's future use. Although secondary to other issues in the Kashmir dispute, competition over water will rise in significance as aquifers are depleted and both sides seek to increase their appropriations from the Indus and its tributaries.

Also bearing on the calculations of Indian and Pakistani leaders is the question of population growth and food production. In 1950, shortly after partition, the population of India stood at 358 million people and that of Pakistan at 40 million; by 1998, India's population had jumped to 976 million and Pakistan's to 148 million. Assuming that current predictions prove accurate, the population of India will rise to approximately 1.3 billion people in 2025 and to 1.5 billion in 2050; that of Pakistan will climb to 270 million and 357 million, respectively.[67] These numbers must give pause to anyone who seeks to plot the course of future events. With three times the population it had when it signed the Indus Waters Treaty in 1960, in 2025 India could well conclude that it was not bound by an agreement that gives Pakistan control over four-fifths of the Indus waters.

Environmental decline and greenhouse warming could also affect this equation. India has already overdrawn many key aquifers in the states of Andhra Pradesh, Karnataka, Maharashtra, and Tamil Nadu, and soil salination is increasing in many irrigated areas, including the Punjab.[68] Agricultural productivity in irrigated fields is also threatened by extensive deforestation in upland areas, which produces higher rates of erosion and the silting up of canals and reservoirs. Some experts believe, moreover, that the Green Revolution has exhausted its potential for increased crop yields, precluding any future spurts in grain production.[69] On top of all this, it is likely that global warming will have profound effects on the region's climate, producing drought in some areas and persistent flooding in others.[70]

The steady rise in population and the accompanying decline in environmental conditions must be viewed against a backdrop of continuing political upheaval in India and Pakistan. Both countries have witnessed the rise of ultranationalist political movements and increased levels of ethnic antagonism. In Pakistan, opposition to Prime Minister Nawaz Sharif culminated, in late 1999, in a military coup—the fourth in Pakistan's fifty-two-year history. India, for its part, faces widespread corruption and social disorder in many parts of the country. While economic reform has produced small pockets of affluence in both societies, growing numbers of people live in grinding poverty. Under these circumstances, it is not hard to imagine how future food shortages, combined with popular unrest and xenophobic politics, could lead to a head-on clash over the Indus River system.

THE GROWING RISK OF CONFLICT

Clearly, each of the three river systems described above harbors a significant risk of violent conflict. This risk stems from the fact that the demand for water is growing while the supply is not, and from the failure of the riparians in these systems to establish an integrated, basinwide regime for the equitable distribution of the shared resources. As population grows, and the need for water and food rises in tandem, each of the riparians will seek to maximize its utilization of the available supply. When the actions of any one of these states results in a declining supply for any of the others, the conditions are set for an intrabasin clash over the distribution of water.

Greatly contributing to the risk of conflict is the close relationship between internal and external security. The leaders of these countries are expected to provide the basic necessities of human life, especially water and food; if they fail in this, they lose their mandate to rule and can expect rising political unrest. In such circumstances, leaders usually respond in one of two ways: they attempt to stifle internal dissent through repressive measures, or they try to channel the discontent against external enemies, who are held responsible for the deprivation. The first approach can lead to civil war; the second, to interstate conflict.

8

Fighting for the Riches of the Earth: Internal Wars over Minerals and Timber

Oil and water—because of their critical roles in sustaining human life and economic activity—are the resources that are most likely to ignite full-scale combat between the armies of established nation-states. But certain other resources are sufficiently valuable and sought after to provoke conflict *within* states, usually between ethnic and political factions that are already divided over a variety of issues. Gold, diamonds, valuable minerals, and old-growth timber are in high demand around the world, and so their possession can be a source of considerable revenue. Internal warfare over such resources has, in fact, proved to be one of the most prominent and disturbing features of the current political epoch.

Typically, conflicts of this sort are interwoven with long-standing ethnic, political, and regional antagonisms. In many cases, a sought-after resource is concentrated in an area that is occupied by—or coveted by—an ethnic or religious group that seeks to increase its political power or to break away from the existing state. Such contests are regularly described in the international press as ethnic and sectarian conflicts. But while combatants often stir up and exploit ethnic and religious animosities in order to obtain new recruits, it is a desire to reap the financial benefits of resource exploitation that most often sustains the fighting.[1]

Angola provides a conspicuous and bloody example of this phenomenon. Fighting between the government, headed by the Popular Movement for the Liberation of Angola (MPLA, by its initials in Portuguese), and the rebel National Union for the Total Independence of Angola (UNITA) has been going on for more than twenty-five years, causing the loss of over one million lives and the internal displacement of several times that number. In the beginning, this war was being fought over ideology and power—at one point, Cuba and the Soviet Union were supporting the MPLA while the United States was supporting UNITA—but by the 1990s both sides were fighting largely for control over the country's valuable oil and diamond supplies. Reports by the United Nations and nongovernmental organizations have shown that leaders of both sides were siphoning off many millions of dollars from the sale of oil and diamonds for their private use, while telling their followers that the money was being used to purchase arms and other vital supplies.[2]

The fighting in Sierra Leone follows a similar pattern. As many as 50,000 people have been killed there since 1991, and hundreds of thousands have been forced to abandon their homes. The leading opposition group, the Revolutionary United Front (RUF), claims to be fighting on behalf of Sierra Leone's impoverished and unrepresented masses. But it appears that the group's major objective is to retain control over the country's valuable diamond fields. Even though the RUF's leader, Foday Sankoh, signed a U.N.-brokered peace agreement in 1999 and promised to disband his military forces, RUF elements continue to occupy the major diamond-producing areas and to oversee the flow of gems to international markets.[3]

In both Angola and Sierra Leone—and in similar conflicts occurring elsewhere—there is evidence that major resource conglomerates are contributing to the persistence of violence by purchasing diamonds, minerals, timber, and other commodities from the combatants. UNITA, for example, is said to have sold diamonds to buyers working for De Beers, the South African conglomerate that controls about two-thirds of the world diamond market.[4] The RUF, in collaboration with friendly groups in Liberia, has also been able to sell its diamonds to major dealers in Europe.[5] Another set of companies, also based in Europe, are believed to have purchased old-growth lumber from rebel-held areas of Liberia.[6] Such transactions provide the cash with which opposing forces pay for black-market weapons; alternately, the proceeds go into the private bank accounts of government and rebel commanders, increasing their personal power and authority. With arms and cash coming into their hands on a regular basis, the leaders of ethnic and insurgent factions have no incentive to sue for peace or to reach a compromise at the bargaining table—rather, their interests are best served by prolonging the conflict.[7]

Although modest when compared to the annual profits of the major oil corporations, the monies accumulated in these conflicts can be quite substantial. The illicit diamond trade in Angola, for instance, is believed to generate as much as $700 million per year; illicit diamond sales from Sierra Leone are thought to be worth at least half as much.[8] In Congo, royalties from copper and uranium mining are thought to have netted long-term dictator Mobutu Sese Seko and his close associates several hundred million dollars per year.[9] And a single large teak tree from Cambodia can be sold for as much as $25,000.[10]

With so much at stake, and so few other sources of wealth available in these countries, it is not surprising that ruthless and enterprising factions are prepared to provoke civil war or otherwise employ violence in the pursuit of valuable resources. In developed countries and in developing nations with strong central governments, competition for valuable resources is normally resolved through the operation of the marketplace and mediation of the state (in the form of civil courts and regulatory bodies). The terms of contracts are generally enforceable, and the systems of adjudicating disputes are viewed as legitimate and fair. In developing societies, matters are often more haphazard and conflict correspondingly more common. Fighting tends to occur when certain conditions are present, such as when the central government is weak and divided, or widely viewed as corrupt. In addition, conflict is more likely to persist if the larger community of nations refuses to in tervene to halt the fighting, and the belligerents in these contests are able to sell their products on the international market.

These conditions prevail in much of Africa and in other sectors of the developing world. Particularly vulnerable are once-colonized areas where the occupying power destroyed local institutions, plundered the countryside of its human and material resources, and departed without laying the groundwork for effective, self-financing national governments. Frequently, the governments that have sprung up amid this wreckage are autocratic regimes with close ties to the military and/or a particular ethnic constituency. When minority groups are denied access to political power, or when the economy is controlled by the ruling faction or family, opponents of the regime—or those who simply wish to break the elite's monopoly over profitable economic activity—often see no option but to engage in armed rebellion.

Once a rebellion has erupted, the fighting often evolves into resource conflict. To pay their troops and obtain money for arms and ammunition, rebel commanders naturally seek to gain control over territories containing valuable resources. Once in possession of such resources, they can continue fighting indefinitely, even if defeated in battles conducted elsewhere in the country. Over time, many of these leaders acquire the status of warlords—local despots who dominate a particular region by terrorizing the population and selling off the resources they control.[11] The government, for its part, is just as likely to fight for these resources, both to pay its bills and to ensure the continued loyalty of prominent cliques and families. The resulting warfare can persist for years or even decades, as in the case of Angola.

A similar pattern has developed in nations where important sources of valuable resources are located in areas occupied by indigenous peoples or ethnic minorities, as in Brazil and Indonesia. Many of the world's remaining stands of tropical hardwoods, for example, are in remote areas inhabited by indigenous groups. As the monetary value of the world's remaining old-growth timber rises, or when valuable minerals are found within the bounds of the forest, the governments of these countries often award valuable concessions to timber and mining companies—typically, companies with close ties to the the ruling clique or family. Clashes may erupt between the government and the indigenous groups that occupy these areas.[12]

Although not unknown during the Cold War era, separatist conflicts over resources were normally suppressed by Washington and Moscow. To reduce the threat of insurgency and separatism, both superpowers regularly provided their respective allies in the developing world with substantial military and economic assistance. The United States, for example, twice helped President Mobutu crush separatist drives in Congo's mineral-rich Katanga (now Shaba) province, while the Soviet Union helped Mengistu Haile Mariam of Ethiopia quell similar drives in Eritrea and the Ogaden region.[13] With the end of the Cold War, however, this type of assistance largely disappeared, and so the former recipients of such aid—Mobutu and Mengistu among them— found themselves far more vulnerable to internal challenges.

The end of superpower involvement in resource contests has not been followed by the adoption of new systems of international conflict management. Although the United Nations has attempted to resolve many of the internal struggles now under way, it has generally lacked the capacity and know-how to succeed at these efforts. The U.N.'s effectiveness has been further hampered by the unwillingness of the major powers—especially the United States—to provide troops, funds, and equipment for international peacekeeping operations. As a result, fighting has continued in Angola, Sierra Leone, and Somalia despite a series of U.N.-sponsored interventions.

The increasing vigor of globalization has also contributed to the persistence of resource contests in the developing world. With industrialization spreading to more countries than ever before, the worldwide demand for many basic materials—including minerals, gems, and timber—is growing rapidly, thereby increasing the monetary value of many once-neglected sources of supply. In 1995, for example, the World Resources Institute estimated the value of the world's untapped reserves of iron ore at $2 trillion, those of copper at $732 billion, and of bauxite (the ore used to produce aluminum) at $537 billion.[14] Rising commodity prices give greater incentive for separatist and insurgent groups to gain control over these materials, and for besieged governments to resist such efforts. Globalization has also expanded the roster of corporations with both the means and the incentive to procure resources from remote and undeveloped areas—even if this means dealing with warlords and/or transporting valuable commodities through areas of conflict.[15]

The growing presence of transnational resource firms in areas of conflict is responsible for another distinctive feature of such contests: the prominent role performed by private military companies (PMCs) like Executive Outcomes and Sandline International. These firms, often composed of soldiers demobilized at the end of the Cold War, provide protection for large oil and mining operations and, in some cases, assist governments in their efforts to suppress rebel movements.[16] The MPLA of Angola, for instance, once hired Executive Outcomes to spearhead a government drive into UNITA-controlled diamond fields in the interior.[17] Needless to say, such companies do not seek a resolution of conflict; rather, their interests are best served by allowing the fighting to continue as long as possible.

These multiple factors—the violent pursuit of resource wealth in poor and divided countries, the lack of an effective international response, the willingness of many resource firms to traffic with warlords and rebels, and the prominent role of PMCs—have combined to increase the intensity, lethality, and duration of many of the internal conflicts of the post–Cold War era. To appreciate how these factors tend to reinforce one another, it is useful to examine a number of case studies: a conflict over minerals (the Bougainville rebellion), a conflict over diamonds (the war in Sierra Leone), and a conflict over timber (the fighting in Borneo).

THE BOUGAINVILLE REBELLION

Bougainville is a mountainous, tropical island in the Southwest Pacific claimed by the state of Papua New Guinea (or, as it is widely known, PNG). Geologically a part of the Solomon Islands chain, Bougainville was ceded to British control under an Anglo-German agreement signed in 1898 and thereafter governed from the PNG capital of Port

Bougainville and Papua New Guinea

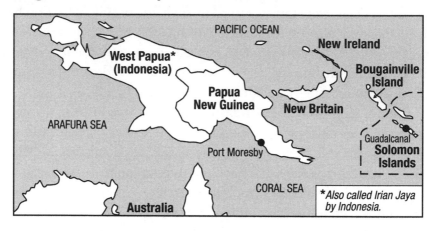

Moresby. After World War II, PNG and Bougainville were administered as a single unit by Australia under a U.N. trusteeship. In 1975, despite protests from its inhabitants, Bougainville was ceded to Papua New Guinea when that territory was granted independence. Thirteen years later, in 1988, the people of Bougainville commenced a war of secession from PNG. (See map.)

At the heart of the Bougainville-PNG dispute is the social and environmental damage wrought by large-scale copper mining. While still under Australian control, the PNG administration in Port Moresby granted London-based Rio Tinto Zinc (RTZ) a concession to copper-bearing areas at Panguna in central Bougainville. RTZ and its Australian affiliate, Conzinc Rio Tinto Australia, formed Bougainville Copper Ltd. (BCL) to exploit the Panguna concession. In time, BCL established the world's largest open-pit copper mine on Bougainville Island: a gaping chasm three-quarters of a mile deep, two and a half miles wide, and three and a half miles long.[18] At the time of peak production, in the mid-1980s, the Panguna mine was producing $500 million worth of copper, gold, and silver every year—most of which went to RTZ (80 percent) and the PNG government in Port Moresby (20 percent); the Bougainvilleans received next to nothing.[19]

By the late 1980s, local opposition to the Panguna concession had reached the boiling point. Not only had the area's residents been denied adequate compensation for their confiscated properties, but the mine itself had produced severe environmental damage. Each year, vast quantities of poisonous "tailings"—mine refuse—were dumped into the local river system, killing fish and contaminating the island's drinking water.[20] When repeated efforts to gain compensation from BCL for all of this damage came to naught, a group of islanders formed the Bougainville Revolutionary Army (BRA) and seized control of the mine, which they then shut down. Two years later, in 1990, leaders of the BRA established the Bougainville Interim Government and declared their independence from Papua New Guinea.[21]

The BRA revolt presented the PNG government with an acute dilemma: although the Papuan elites who governed the state had few ethnic or political ties to Bougainville, they relied on royalties from the Panguna mine for a large share of government income. With the mine in rebel hands, government spending plummeted and the nation experienced widespread political and social unrest. Rather than attempt to resolve the dispute with Bougainville through peaceful negotiations, the PNG government chose to reestablish control over the island through military action. The national army, known as the Papua New Guinea Defense Force (PNGDF), was ordered to invade Bougainville and reestablish PNG control over the copper-producing area. But while successful in gaining a beachhead on the island, the PNGDF was never able to occupy central Bougainville and the Panguna mine complex.[22]

Frustrated in its efforts to recapture Panguna through military means, in 1995 the PNG government reluctantly agreed to participate in peace negotiations with representatives of the BRA. Although neither side made any significant concessions, the two sides refrained from attacking each other. In 1996, however, the newly elected PNG prime minister, Sir Julius Chan, decided to renew military operations against the BRA. Once again, PNGDF forces attempted to seize the Panguna mine, and, once again, they failed. Chan then took another tack: with funds provided by the World Bank (supposedly for development purposes), he offered a British PMC, Sandline International, $36 million to organize a new invasion of Bougainville.[23]

Sandline personnel arrived in Port Moresby in February 1997 and immediately began preparations for a major military offensive against the BRA. To bolster its ranks, Sandline hired experienced combat personnel from another private military firm, Executive Outcomes of South Africa.[24] Sandline also contracted with a firm in Belarus to provide $7 million in Soviet-era military hardware, including four assault helicopters, six 57mm rocket launchers, and five hundred cases of ammunition.[25] As news of these preparations swept the country, however, a new problem arose: senior PNGDF officers, incensed that $36 million had been promised to an outside firm at a time when their own funds were being cut, turned on Chan and demanded his resignation. After several days of rioting, Chan stepped aside as prime minister and canceled the Sandline contract.[26]

Although Chan was later exonerated of any wrongdoing in the Sandline affair, his party was rebuffed in national elections in late 1997. The new government, headed by Bill Skate, eschewed any intention of reoccupying Bougainville through force. A cease-fire was signed between PNG and the BRA, and in 1998 a small U.N. peacekeeping force was deployed on Bougainville to monitor the agreement. Talks have also begun in New Zealand on a final resolution of the dispute. However, neither side has as yet conceded any of its main demands, so it is not clear how the dispute will be resolved.[27]

The Bougainville conflict, although still unresolved, is revealing on a number of accounts. To begin with, it exposes the close relationships that often develop between postcolonial governments and the multinational resource firms that frequently provide much of their income. It also shows how far these governments are often prepared to go in defending that relationship against armed opposition forces. (Similar arrangements can be found elsewhere. In Irian Jaya—the Indonesian-controlled sector of New Guinea—the government has teamed up with the Freeport McMoRan Copper and Gold Company of New Orleans to protect the giant Grasberg mine against attacks by Papuan separatists.[28]) Lastly, the Bougainville case exhibits the growing involvement of private military companies in resource conflicts.

West Africa Region

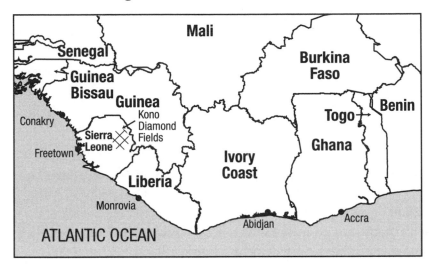

THE WAR IN SIERRA LEONE

Like the island of Bougainville, Sierra Leone possesses valuable mineral supplies that have long been exploited by foreign mining companies with little benefit to the local population. Although very poor by world standards—the GNP per capita was a mere $180 in 1995—the country harbors substantial reserves of rutile (titanium ore), bauxite, and diamonds. Prior to the outbreak of fighting in 1991, Sierra Leone exported diamonds worth as much as $300 million per year, while bauxite and rutile exports generated another $75 to $100 million. The national government, which received only a small share of the income from domestic mining operations, was largely dependent on external aid for the upkeep of most essential services.[29] (See map.)

From 1968 to 1985, Sierra Leone was ruled by Dr. Siaka Stevens. Like Mobutu in Zaire, Stevens siphoned much of the nation's wealth into his own pockets and rewarded loyal supporters by giving them control over some of the country's lucrative mining areas. Stevens's handpicked successor, General Joseph Momah, sought to establish control over the diamond fields, but his forces often refused to fight the local diamond barons (many of whom had formed their own private militias). By 1991, few government services were functioning, and corruption was rife.[30]

This situation proved irresistible to Charles Taylor, the Liberian insurgent leader whose forces controlled the territory adjoining Sierra Leone to the east. Taylor had invaded Liberia in late 1989 with the aim of ousting President Samuel Doe and assuming control of the country. When frustrated in this endeavor by the arrival of a peacekeeping force organized by the Economic Community of West African States (ECO-WAS), he set out to control the countryside and gradually starve the capital, Monrovia, into submission.[31] To finance his growing army and achieve his long-term objectives, Taylor sold off as much of Liberia's timber and mineral wealth as he could get his hands on.[32] And, when still more funds were needed to equip his forces, Taylor sought to gain control over the diamond trade in Sierra Leone.[33]

To spearhead his penetration into Sierra Leone, Taylor turned to the Revolutionary United Front (RUF), a small insurgent force made up of disgruntled Sierra Leonean officials and led by a former army corporal, Foday Sankoh. With strong support from Taylor's rebel army, the RUF invaded southeastern Sierra Leone in 1991 and proceeded to seize control of the Kono diamond fields. Resistance by the government army, the Republic of Sierra Leone Military Force (RSLMF), was scattered or nonexistent; in addition, many of the local diamond barons chose to collaborate with the RUF (and, by extension, with Taylor) rather than side with the Sierra Leonean government. By 1995, following a series of unsuccessful RSLMF counteroffensives, the RUF controlled much of the countryside and was poised to attack the capital, Freetown.[34]

At this point, the government—now headed by Valentine Strasser, a former RSLMF officer—sought outside help to protect the capital and drive off the RUF. Strasser initially employed Gurkha Security Guards (GSG), a private firm made up of Nepalese Gurkha fighters who had been dismissed from the British army. But when GSG personnel refused to conduct offensive operations against the RUF, Strasser turned in desperation to Executive Outcomes (E.O.), the same firm that was later to figure in the Bougainville conflict. E.O. operatives arrived in Freetown in April 1995 and quickly organized a successful campaign to drive the RUF away from the capital; three months later, E.O.-led units of the RSLMF regained control of the Kono diamond region and, by the end of the year, had recaptured the Rutile Sierra mine at Gbangbatok.[35]

The defeat of rebel forces in 1995 produced a welcome degree of stability in the country. Although Strasser was deposed by another senior officer in February 1996, multiparty elections for a new civilian government were held in March and, following what was generally considered a free and fair election, Ahmed Tejan Kabbah of the Sierra Leone People's Party was chosen as president. Believing that conditions in the country had been stabilized, Kabbah terminated the government's contract with Executive Outcomes in January 1997.

Unfortunately, Kabbah's optimism proved to be premature: within weeks of E.O.'s departure, a loose coalition of disgruntled RSLMF officers and surviving RUF insurgents took control of Freetown.[36] Once again, the government—now operating from exile in Guinea—sought outside help to oust the rebels. In July 1997, Kabbah signed a $10 million contract with Sandline International to wage a counteroffensive.[37] Nigeria also stepped in at this time, supplying troops for an ECOWAS peacekeeping mission. Together, the Sandline-led national army and the ECOWAS peacekeeping force regained control of Freetown and, in March 1998, reinstated Kabbah as president. The pro-government forces then fanned out into the countryside, driving the rebels out of many towns and villages.

Although successful in some parts of the country, the 1998 campaign did not eradicate the rebel threat. Remnants of the RUF held out in many remote areas, terrorizing the population and recruiting new soldiers—often using threats of execution or mutilation to overcome resistance from villagers.[38] After rebuilding their strength, RUF forces launched a fresh offensive in January 1999. This time, President Kabbah concluded that it would be better to strike a deal with the RUF than to risk another all-out conflict. With U.N. support, talks were convened in Lomé, Togo, and in July 1999 a peace agreement was signed between the Kabbah government and the RUF.[39]

Under the 1999 Lomé agreement, RUF forces were to be integrated into the national army and the rebel leader, Foday Sankoh, was named vice president and chairman of the Strategic Resources Commission—essentially giving him control over the disposition of the country's diamond and mineral wealth.[40] The elevation of Sankoh to the vice presidency was seen by many Sierra Leoneans as the price they would have to pay for a measure of peace in the country. However, it soon became evident that even this form of tribute was insufficient to satisfy Sankoh's appetite. With new arms and ammunition obtained through the sale of diamonds, the RUF commenced a fresh offensive in early 2000, overpowering a weak U.N. peacekeeping force and occupying much of the countryside.[41]

This new round of fighting had one unexpected but revealing sidelight: during the RUF advance on Freetown, opponents of the rebel group invaded the house occupied by Foday Sankoh while he was serving as vice president and seized a cache of documents concerning his involvement in the illicit diamond trade. The documents, which were later described in *The New York Times,* indicated that Sankoh personally supervised the export of diamonds from rebel-held areas of Sierra Leone to markets in Europe. During the last six months of 1999, for example, Sankoh received over two thousand stones from his confederates in the field. The documents also revealed that he ordered his forces to go on the offensive against U.N. peacekeeping forces when he learned that the peacekeepers' leader, General Vijay Kumar Jetley, was preparing to send his troops into the Kono diamond region.[42] Rarely has the link between resource exploitation and internal conflict been made more visible and concrete.

THE FIGHTING IN BORNEO

Aside from Amazonia and Central Africa, the world's largest surviving tropical forests are found on the islands of the Southwest Pacific, mostly on Borneo and New Guinea. Borneo, the world's fourth-largest island, is divided between Indonesia, Malaysia, and the Sultanate of Brunei. Indonesia calls its portion of the island Kalimantan;

the Malaysian portion is divided between the states of Sarawak (in the northwest) and Sabah (in the northeast), with Brunei in the middle. For over twenty years, the forests of Sarawak and Kalimantan have been the sites of recurring conflict between indigenous peoples and those who seek to harvest the original trees or replace them with palm-oil plantations. (See map.)

Until recently, what little development occurred in Borneo was confined to a few coastal enclaves that were connected to one another only by boat and plane. Beginning in the 1960s, however, the governments of Malaysia and Indonesia opened up vast areas of the interior to commercial logging—in many cases awarding the largest and most lucrative concessions to members of their political and business elites. As the global demand for timber expanded, these concessionaires began to strip their holdings of all marketable trees. The pace of timber harvesting has been extraordinary: by 1985, approximately one-third of Sarawak's forests had been logged over, and another 700,000 acres (about 5 percent of the total forest cover) were being cleared every year.[43] A similar pattern prevailed in Kalimantan, where 12 percent of the total forest cover disappeared between 1982 and 1990.[44]

As a result of intensive logging in Borneo, Malaysia and Indonesia have become the world's leading exporters of tropical logs and timber products. Malaysia now leads the world in the overseas sale of logs and sawn lumber; Indonesia, which has emphasized the sale of "value-added" wood products, is the world's leading exporter of plywood.[45] Although some of these products come from the more developed parts of Malaysia and Indonesia, the greatest yields have come from the forests of Borneo.

The production of logs and wood products in Sarawak and Kalimantan has generated enormous wealth for the privileged elites who control the principal concession areas.[46] In Sarawak, the chief minister grants the concessions; in many cases, these prized assets have been awarded to the friends, political associates, and family members of the current officeholder. In 1987, for example, the former chief minister, Tun Abdul Rahman Yakub, was reported to possess (or to have given to friends) concessions covering some three million acres of

The Island of Borneo

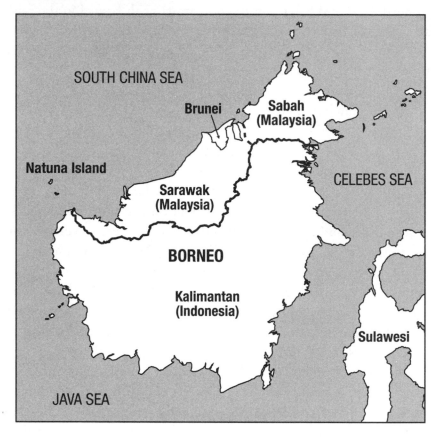

forest, worth an estimated $9 to $22 billion; his successor, Datuk Patinggi Hagi Abdul Taib Mahmud, was said to control another four million acres.[47] (Together, these holdings represented about one-third of Sarawak's total forested area.) Similarly, in Kalimantan, vast concessions were awarded to business associates of the Suharto family and to senior military officers.[48]

To obtain profit from these vast holdings, the concessionaires must strip the forests of all marketable timber. This has enormous environmental consequences, both in terms of loss of biodiversity—the forests of Borneo are home to many species of animals and plants that are not found elsewhere—and soil degradation. Even more worrisome, logging on this scale poses a direct threat to the indigenous people who live in Borneo's forests and depend on them for their food, shelter, clothing, and medicine. These communities are composed of many different ethnic groups, but all share a strong sense of identification with the living forest and its resident species. Like the inhabitants of Amazonia, the forest peoples of Borneo view the plants and animals of the forest as sacred, as the embodiment of powerful spirits and deities. Ever since outsiders have come to log or clear the forests, the natives have attempted to protect their ancestral lands by whatever means available.[49]

In Sarawak, conflict between the Dayak (the collective name for the indigenous peoples of Borneo) and government-backed logging companies has continued since 1987. For years, the Dayak had petitioned local authorities to stop the destruction of their traditional lands, only to be rebuffed on every occasion.[50] Then, on February 13, 1987, the Penan people (one of the subgroups of the Dayak) issued an ultimatum to the authorities:

> We, the Penan people of the Tutoh, Limbang, and Patah rivers region, declare: Stop destroying the forest or we will be forced to protect it. The forest is our livelihood. We have lived here before any of you outsiders came. We fished in clean rivers and hunted in the jungle. . . . Now the logging companies turn rivers into muddy streams and the jungle into devastation. . . . By your doings you take away our livelihood and threaten our very lives. . . . We want our ancestral land, the land we live off, back. . . . If you decide not to heed our request, we will protect our livelihood. We are a peace-loving people, but when our very lives are in danger, we will fight back.[51]

Like all prior communications from the Dayak, this message was ignored by local officials. This time, however, the Penan turned to direct action: armed solely with traditional blowpipes, small groups of men and women established blockades across logging roads and stopped the transportation of timber. Soon other indigenous groups, including the Kayan and Kelabit, erected obstacles of their own. By October 1987, blockades had been established at twenty-three sites, halting logging operations in much of Sarawak.[52]

Faced with a significant loss of income, the logging companies pressed the government to take decisive action. As a result, paramilitary police were deployed throughout the region and large numbers of Dayak were arrested. In November 1987, the state government adopted Amendment S90B of the Forest Ordinance, making it a major offense for any person to obstruct the flow of traffic along any logging road in Sarawak. Large numbers of protestors were arrested under this law, forcing the Penan and their allies to abandon many of the blockades. By early 1989, however, new blockades had been established at many sites, and clashes between the Dayak and government forces had become a regular occurrence.[53]

The intensity of these clashes have ebbed and flowed over the years, but the Dayak have steadily lost ground to the loggers. More and more of Sarawak's forests have been cleared, and the indigenous people have been forced to resettle in government encampments or to move deeper into what remains of the original forest. Even the special parks and "biospheres" established by the Malaysian government to house the Penan have been invaded by the logging companies. Meanwhile, the protests continue.[54] In 1997, for example, forty-two Dayak were arrested in one incident and three were shot (one fatally) in another.[55]

In neighboring Kalimantan, the Dayaks have faced a similar challenge: in a bid to increase agricultural productivity, the Indonesian government is attempting to convert many forested areas into commercial rubber and palm-oil plantations. In West Kalimantan alone, the government has set aside 5.7 million acres of forests—much of it occupied by indigenous groups—for such plantations. To provide labor for these endeavors, the central government in Jakarta has also subsidized the relocation in Kalimantan (or "transmigration," to use the government's term) of unemployed laborers from other parts of Indonesia, especially the highly populated islands of Java and Madura. As employees of the plantation firms, these settlers have been forced to participate in the clearing of original forests—placing them, as it were, on the front lines of conflict with the Dayak population. As a result, clashes between indigenous groups and the settlers (especially the Madurese) have become increasingly frequent and violent.[56]

By February 1997, these clashes had escalated into a low-level insurgency. Army troops were deployed throughout western Kalimantan, and travel into the interior was banned. Although journalists were unable to visit the conflict zone, refugees spoke of scattered encounters between armed Dayak gangs and elite army commandos—the former armed with spears and machetes, the latter with modern weapons. Hundreds of people were killed in these encounters, and thousands more were forced to relocate in government-run refugee camps.[57]

As the conflict intensified, the belligerents on each side resorted to one of the oldest and most terrifying weapons of all: fire. To clear the concession lands of both flora and fauna (including humans), plantation workers—many of them transmigrants from Java and Madura—have set fires throughout Kalimantan, destroying millions of acres of forest and forcing more of the Dayak into refugee camps. In retaliation, the Dayak have periodically set fire to the settlers' communities. Because of especially dry conditions in the late 1990s (caused, in part, by the El Niño effect), these fires have often burned out of control, filling the air with soot and smoke and producing an environmental disaster of vast proportions.[58]

Government intervention succeeded in arresting the violence in 1998, but fighting between the Dayaks and the Madurese erupted with renewed intensity in early 1999. Allied on this occasion with native Malays, the insurgent Dayak tore through Madurese communities, burning houses and killing anyone who stood in their way. "The roads and fields swarm with men carrying swords, crossbows, and home-made shotguns," *The Economist* reported in March. In some areas, "severed heads are displayed openly on the roadside."[59] Within days, 185 people were killed and thousands driven from their homes. Once again, the Indonesian government sent troops to quell the fighting, but, as before, this brought only a temporary calm—not an end to the conflict.[60] As the twenty-first century commenced, hostility between the indigenous people of Borneo and the various settler communities was as powerful as ever.

Like the rebellion in Bougainville, the violence in Sarawak and Kalimantan revolves around efforts by governments—usually in league with local business interests—to ensure access to valuable resource supplies despite determined resistance by local residents. Because the invaders of these lands are often of a different racial or religious background than the inhabitants, the fighting is often experienced by belligerents on both sides as an ethnic conflict, and is usually described as such by the international media. But as these encounters demonstrate, it is not racial animosity between the Penan and Malays or the Dayaks and Madurese that is primarily responsible for the bloodshed, but rather the relentless pursuit of resource wealth by powerful government factions.

OTHER CONFLICTS OVER MINERALS AND TIMBER

The conflicts in Bougainville, Sierra Leone, and Borneo are characteristic of an assortment of disputes over valuable supplies of gems, minerals, and timber that are now occurring in various parts of the world. Other such hostilities are under way in Angola, Brazil, Burma, Cambodia, Colombia, Congo, Indonesia, Liberia, and the Philippines. In all of these countries, warlords and local elites—some with government support, some without—seek to dominate a particular mining or logging region and garner whatever revenues can be derived from its exploitation. Very often, this means driving off the people who have long inhabited the area or depriving them of any benefits from the appropriation of their traditional lands.

The fighting over diamond-producing areas of Angola and Liberia, involving rebel groups and warlordism, has already been mentioned. In Brazil and Indonesia, the fighting has been of a somewhat different nature. In these cases, private mining and timber interests have invaded the territory of indigenous peoples, taking their land (usually without compensation) and ravaging the environment. While lacking the skills and numbers to pose a really serious challenge to such invasions, these peoples have in some instances chosen to fight back. In response, the invaders have usually been able to call on government forces—which often enjoy economic links to foreign corporations—or have formed their own private armies. Most often, the original inhabitants are forced to give way in the face of superior numbers and strength; however, resistance may continue long after the mining has begun.[61]

One example of such resistance is the struggle of the Amungme people against the Grasberg gold and copper mine in Irian Jaya. Believed to harbor the richest gold deposit on earth, worth an estimated $50 billion, the mine has been operated by Freeport McMoRan since 1967. As in Bougainville, tailings from the mine have caused severe environmental damage to the surrounding rivers and forests, threatening the livelihoods of the Amungme and other indigenous groups who inhabit the area. Periodic protests by these groups have been brutally suppressed by Indonesian troops (a battalion of which is stationed at the mine at company expense) and private security forces.[62] In frustration, many of the Amungme have joined the separatist Free Papua Movement (OPM) and are fighting for the creation of an independent state of West Papua.[63]

Most conflicts that fit this pattern are largely domestic in nature, with outside forces limited to U.N. peacekeepers and the private armies of major resource firms. However, in a possible harbinger of what is to come, the conflict in Congo has taken on a more international character. The country has been wracked by violence over resources since the 1880s, when King Leopold II of Belgium colonized the region and commenced the systematic exploitation of its natural wealth.[64] Mobutu, who seized control over Congo in 1965, appropriated much of the country's vast timber and mineral wealth for his own and his closest friends' benefit, periodically using military force to silence internal dissent and suppress separatist movements in outlying areas.[65] Finally, in 1997, a revolt led by Laurent Kabila succeeded in overthrowing Mobutu (whose private wealth, at the time of his flight to France, was estimated at over $4 billion).

Kabila promised to root out the economic cronyism that had prevailed under his predecessor, but dissatisfaction with his performance led to the outbreak of a new insurgency in 1998. Unable to suppress the revolt on his own, Kabila asked friendly leaders in the region, including those of Angola and Zimbabwe, to bolster his forces. By agreeing to provide such support, these leaders sought to promote their own national interests (the Angolans, for example, hoped to enlist Kabila's aid in joint operations against UNITA, which has long used Congo as a base of operations) while gaining access to Congo's enormous mineral and timber wealth.[66] The Zimbabweans, in particular, are thought to be fighting to protect mining and timber concessions in Congo acquired by high government officials and their associates.[67] The United Nations has attempted to negotiate a general settlement of this conflict, but, as of this writing, its efforts had failed to result in the withdrawal of foreign forces from the Congo.

SPOTLIGHTING THE LINKS BETWEEN RESOURCES AND WAR

Protracted warfare over valuable resources, involving combat between government forces, warlords, insurgents, and various private interests, has become a conspicuous feature of the post–Cold War landscape. These contests have produced an enormous toll in human life, accompanied in many cases by severe environmental damage. Typically, wars of this type have erupted in poor and undeveloped areas, where the ownership (or control) of major sources of minerals or timber is a pivotal factor in domestic power struggles. The conditions that give rise to these conflicts—high external demand for resources combined with unrepresentative governments and ruthless political factions—are likely to persist in the years ahead.

Experts on internal warfare have long been aware of the connection between resource exploitation and the financing of civil conflicts. It was only in the year 2000, however, that this connection came to the attention of the larger world. Two events were responsible for this development. The first was the release of a United Nations report on illicit diamond trafficking and arms procurement by UNITA in Angola. Prepared by Ambassador Robert K. Fowler of Canada, the study accused a number of African governments and companies of helping UNITA exchange its diamonds for arms, fuel, and other military commodities.[68] "Diamond revenues constitute the essential component of UNITA's capacity to wage war," Fowler told the U.N. Security Council.[69] The second key event was the publication of a study by Paul Collier of the World Bank on the relationship between "natural resource predation" and the incidence of civil war. On the basis of extensive statistical analysis of all major internal conflicts between 1960 and 1995, Collier determined that the greatest risk factor for civil war was not ethnic antagonism but the availability of easily procured, "lootable" resources.[70]

The release of these two documents, both of which received widespread media attention, spurred government officials and nongovernmental organizations (NGOs) to call for measures to break the link between resource exploitation and war. On March 17, 2000, the Diamond High Council of Belgium (an industry group in Antwerp, the world's premier diamond market) announced that it had reached agreement with the Angolan government on procedures for verifying the origin of uncut stones, so as to exclude any supplied by UNITA.[71] Two weeks later, the U.N. Security Council announced that it would impose economic sanctions on any country that allowed itself to be used by UNITA as a way station for the shipment of diamonds to overseas markets.[72] On July 5, the Security Council voted to ban diamond sales by rebel factions in Sierra Leone.[73] Taken together, these steps represented a significant effort by the international community to starve UNITA and the RUF of funds, thus impeding their ability to fight and, it was hoped, encouraging them to sue for peace.

These measures may substantially alter the internal conflict dynamic in Angola and Sierra Leone, leading to the eventual termination of the fighting. (As of this writing, neither UNITA nor RUF had abandoned its military struggle.) It is doubtful, however, that piecemeal interventions will succeed by themselves in breaking the links between resource exploitation and war. The profits from the illicit traffic in diamonds are so great that it will not be easy to eradicate the trade entirely. Moreover, even the proceeds from the *legal* sale of resources can be used to finance guerrilla wars and counterinsurgencies. In June 2000, at the peak of concern over diamond smuggling, the Angolan government received approximately $1 billion from foreign oil companies for the right to drill in Angola's offshore waters—funds that were promptly used for the purchase of arms and other war-related items.[74]

Publication of the Fowler Report and the World Bank study on civil conflict gave the world its first detailed look at the connection between resource extraction and civil war. The subsequent actions by the U.N. Security Council and other organizations demonstrated that the international community is prepared to address this problem in a serious way. It is clear, however, that far more sweeping measures will be needed to sever the ties between resources and war. Developing such measures will prove to be a major challenge for international policy makers in the decades to come.

9

The New Geography of Conflict

The conflict scenarios discussed in this book—from the Persian Gulf and the Caspian Sea to Sierra Leone and Borneo—all possess distinctive characteristics, and so tend to be viewed by analysts and policy makers as isolated phenomena. But the resource wars of the post–Cold War era are not random or disconnected events. Rather, they are part of a larger, interconnected geopolitical system. Whereas international conflict was until recently governed by political and ideological considerations, the wars of the future will largely be fought over the possession and control of vital economic goods—especially resources needed for the functioning of modern industrial societies. Whatever their individual roots, each of the conflicts described in previous chapters is a manifestation of this global contest.

It is the central thesis of this book that resource wars will become, in the years ahead, the most distinctive feature of the global security environment. This is so for all of the reasons outlined in previous chapters: the priority accorded to economic considerations by national leaders, the ever-growing demand for a wide range of basic commodities, looming shortages of certain key materials, social and political instability in areas harboring major reserves of vital commodities, and the proliferation of disputes over the ownership of important sources of supply. As noted, some of these problems will be mitigated by market forces and the onward progress of technology; others, however, will be exacerbated by the corrosive side effects of globalization.

It is not possible, of course, to predict the date and locale of future resource wars. Some of the regions described above may escape outbreaks of violence while other areas, not discussed in this book, will experience protracted conflicts. But what we are seeing is the emergence of a new geography of conflict—a global landscape in which competition over vital resources is becoming the governing principle behind the disposition and use of military power.

The distinctive features of this new strategic geography look very different from those of the Cold War era, with its military blocs and confrontation zones. Regions that once occupied center stage, such as the east-west divide in Europe, will lose all strategic significance, while areas long neglected by the international community, such as the Caspian basin and the South China Sea, will acquire expanded significance. Attracting the greatest interest will be places that harbor particularly abundant supplies of vital materials—oil, water, diamonds, minerals, old-growth timber—along with the supply routes that connect these areas to major markets around the world. These regions will command attention from the media, dominate the deliberations of international policy makers, and invite the heaviest concentrations of military power.

To better appreciate the nature of this emerging landscape, imagine a map of the world on which the major deposits of vital materials are represented by different colors: black for oil and coal, blue for water, white for diamonds and gems, green for timber, and red for copper, iron, and other key minerals. Once the map is tinted in this fashion, our eyes will naturally jump to those areas with the greatest profusion and intensity of color: the Amazon region and Southeast Asia for green, the Persian Gulf for black, sub-Saharan Africa for white and red, and so on. The result is a new strategic geography in which resource concentrations rather than political boundaries are the major defining features.

Although every area of the world would possess fragments of color, the greatest concentration of hues on such a map would be found in a wide band of territory straddling the equator. Included in this band is the northern half of South America (including Amazonia), Central Africa (including the headwaters of the Nile), the Persian Gulf, South and Southeast Asia, Indonesia, and the islands of the western Pacific. Together, these areas encompass the world's principal sources of petroleum, many important supplies of minerals, all of its tropical timber, and several of its most important river systems. In contrast to resource deposits found elsewhere, moreover, the reserves located in this area are often found in contested territories or in countries suffering from ethnic conflict or political factionalism. Thus, while conflict over resources may occur in areas lying outside this zone, the heaviest fighting is likely to occur within its broad reaches.

Starting in the Western Hemisphere, the band incorporates the vast green expanse of the Amazon along with a large pool of black in Colombia and Venezuela. These two countries seem likely to experience conflict and political turmoil over resources in the coming years. Although both have a tradition of democratic rule, they also have histories of political violence. Venezuela appears to be headed for praetorian rule under President Hugo Chávez, a former paratrooper who led an abortive military coup in 1992.[1] Colombia, meanwhile, is riven by drug-related disorder and an ongoing guerrilla war. Both countries are also major sources of petroleum for the United States. It is not surprising, then, that Washington has begun to pay close attention to political developments in the two countries and, in the case of Colombia, has become a major supplier of arms and military assistance.[2] American aid is supposedly intended to help the Colombian government in its fight against the drug traffickers. But the aid will in all probability also be used to support army operations against guerrilla groups that regularly attack the nation's oil pipelines.[3]

The Amazon will also remain a major site of resource-related conflict. Despite repeated promises by the Brazilian government to restrict logging and mining in Amazonia and to protect the lands of indigenous peoples against outside invasion, illegal deforestation continues unabated. Some indigenous groups—backed by international NGOs—have won legal title to their traditional areas of settlement, but the government has lacked the will or the ability to prevent encroachment on these lands by miners, loggers, and ranchers. As a result, struggles over land—often involving periodic violence—persist throughout the region.[4]

Tracing the equatorial resource band across the Atlantic, we find concentrations of all major hues in sub-Saharan Africa: red, white, blue, and green in Congo, red in Guinea and Zambia, and various combinations in other countries. Included in this kaleidoscopic landscape are the tropical forests of Central Africa, the oil deposits in the Gulf of Guinea, the headwaters of the Nile, assorted mineral deposits, and the diamond beds of Angola and Congo. Indeed, the very profusion of colors in Africa is an indication of the region's growing strategic significance.

Farther north and east are the mammoth oil reserves of the Persian Gulf, the largest expanse of black on the map. Surrounding this area, moreover, are several major concentrations of blue—the fertile basins of the Nile, Jordan, Tigris, Euphrates, and Indus Rivers. Not far off, in Central Asia, lies the black of the Caspian and the blue of the Fergana Valley (stretching across Uzbekistan, Tajikistan, and Kyrgyzstan). All of these resource zones have experienced combat in the past, and most are likely to witness further contestation in the future.

Continuing eastward to Southeast Asia and the Pacific, we encounter large concentrations of forest green, particularly in Burma, Laos, Sumatra, Borneo, and New Guinea. The region also encompasses several large pools of black (notably in offshore areas of China, Indonesia, Vietnam, and Malaysia), along with significant patches of red (in Australia, New Guinea, and the islands of the western Pacific). This area, too, is rife with conflict over resources, of which several prominent examples—the South China Sea, Borneo, and Bougainville—are discussed in preceding chapters.

There is a high correlation between areas of conflict and concentrations of critical materials within this broad equatorial band. Even wars that are generally blamed on other factors—such as the fighting in Colombia, Timor, or Sudan—often possess, on closer inspection, a hidden resource-related element. It is the main thesis of this book that areas within this band will continue to suffer recurring resource conflict in the decades ahead. And nowhere, according to our imaginary map, is such conflict likely to be more protracted and bloody than in Africa.

RESOURCES AND CONFLICT IN AFRICA

Africa—especially sub-Saharan Africa—will acquire increased strategic importance in the decades ahead, because it houses vast reserves of untapped resources that are sought by a growing array of local and international interests. Africa is rich in four key resources: oil, minerals, gems, and timber. Although many of these assets have been fought over in the past—indeed, the colonization of Africa was driven by the quest for valuable commodities—they have become the object of intensified competition as the worldwide demand for resources has grown.

Africa possesses substantial reserves of some of the world's most important minerals, including bauxite, chromium, cobalt, copper, gold, manganese, phosphate rock, platinum, titanium, and uranium.[5] These reserves have long acted as a magnet for foreign mining companies, many of which have recently stepped up their efforts to exploit the region's mineral wealth. According to the Worldwatch Institute, spending by foreign mining companies on mineral exploration in Africa jumped by 54 percent between 1996 and 1997 alone.[6] Exports of minerals and gems are a major source of revenue for Angola, Botswana, Congo, Guinea, Namibia, South Africa, Zambia, and a number of other African countries.

Africa also houses substantial supplies of old-growth timber. The world's second-largest expanse of rain forest (after the Amazon) stretches across the continent's central region, covering much of Congo, Congo-Brazzaville, Gabon, Cameroon, and Equatorial Guinea.

These ancient woodlands, some over fifteen thousand years old, contain approximately one-fifth of the world's remaining tropical forest. Once neglected by timber companies in favor of more accessible supplies in Latin America and Asia, these forests are now being logged at a furious pace.[7] Valuable timber stands are also being harvested in Kenya, Malawi, Sierra Leone, Swaziland, Uganda, and Zambia. For many of these countries, timber sales represent 10 percent or more of their GNP or foreign trade.[8]

It is in the development of oil and gas reserves, however, that Africa is attracting the greatest attention from international resource firms. According to BP Amoco, African countries possess proven reserves of 75 billion barrels of oil, or about 7 percent of the total world supply; they also possess 8 percent of the world's natural gas reserves.[9] Although small in comparison to the hydrocarbon exports of the major Persian Gulf suppliers, the continent's petroleum output is expected to rise significantly in coming years. According to the U.S. Department of Energy, African production will grow from about 7.9 million barrels per day in 2000 to 12.1 million barrels in 2020, an increase of 53 percent. At that point, Africa will account for approximately 11 percent of total world production—as much as Iran and Iraq combined.[10]

Africa's hydrocarbon potential is attracting extraordinary interest from the world's oil companies. The ExxonMobil Corporation, for example, has acquired drilling rights to several large concession areas in offshore and onshore areas of Angola, Chad, Nigeria, and Congo-Brazzaville. In announcing its acquisition of these rights, Exxon officials have indicated that they expect to find major new deposits, including several in the "elephant" class (containing one billion or more barrels of crude petroleum). "Considering the discoveries we've already made [in these areas] and the potential for more," Exxon Vice President Harry Longwell remarked in 1999, "we expect that future operations in Africa will account for a significant portion of Exxon's worldwide production."[11]

In January 2000, Texaco reported that it had found a major deposit—possibly in the "elephant" class—in a concession area located some seventy miles off the coast of Nigeria. Texaco's find, known as the Agabami block, lies close to concession areas held by Royal Dutch/Shell, Elf TotalFina, Statoil, Chevron, and other prominent firms. Many analysts believe that this offshore area could house several billion barrels of oil.[12] "This is the hottest exploration play in the world right now," observed John J. O'Conner, Texaco's president for worldwide exploration and production.[13]

New producing areas are also being developed at several onshore sites, including southern Chad, central Sudan, and the interior of Nigeria. In Chad, Exxon has teamed up with Royal Dutch/Shell and Elf to develop the Doba basin in the country's southwestern corner. To bring this oil to market, these firms have teamed up with the World Bank to construct a 650-mile, $1.5 billion pipeline from southern Chad to Kribi in Cameroon, on the Gulf of Guinea.[14] (This pipeline has become the subject of considerable international controversy, in part because of concern for the fragile environment through which it will pass and in part because of the companies' and the bank's close association with the repressive government in Chad.)[15]

Although sub-Saharan Africa rarely attracted the interest of the major powers during the Cold War era, it is beginning to figure more prominently in the policy planning of the United States and the European countries. Washington's renewed interest in Africa was particularly evident during Bill Clinton's second term as president. The administration sent several high-ranking delegations to the area— including two headed by Mr. Clinton himself—and initiated a wide variety of cooperative efforts.* "We have substantially changed the way the U.S. Government is structured to deal with Africa," explained Susan E. Rice, the Assistant Secretary of State for African Affairs, in 1999. "There was a time not long ago when Africa was the exclusive domain of one understaffed bureau at Foggy Bottom [i.e., the U.S. Department of State]." But now "virtually every government agency is building the capacity to implement new programs that support our policy of comprehensive engagement with Africa."[16]

American officials have been very explicit about the nature of their

---

*Significantly, the second trip by Mr. Clinton, in August 2000, had a major focus on energy concerns. During a visit to Nigeria, the president appealed to Nigerian leaders to increase their production of oil in order to alleviate a worldwide shortage of petroleum.

growing interest in the region. We have "important strategic interests in Africa," Assistant Secretary Rice told the World Affairs Council of Seattle in November 1999. "Africa is the source of over 16 percent of our nation's imported oil," she said. "Within the next decade, oil imports from Africa are projected to surpass those from the Persian Gulf." Moreover, "the U.S. relies on Africa as a source of strategic minerals, including platinum, cobalt, bauxite, and manganese." Other political and economic interests enter into the equation, she noted, but "the natural resource sector" stands out because of its potential for "explosive" growth.[17]

Africa is attracting attention not only from American investors and diplomats but also from the U.S. military. The Department of Defense now provides training and/or military aid to thirty-three of the forty-eight sub-Saharan states and cooperates with them in a wide variety of training maneuvers. The United States is also involved in efforts to develop an African Crisis Response Force, a multinational contingent composed of troops from several countries that would be available for use in regional peacekeeping operations.[18] Although these efforts are relatively modest financially—costing approximately $120 million per year[19]—they nevertheless represent a significant expansion of American interest in the area. "Traditionally, the United States has not been a major player in the security environment of Sub-Saharan Africa," the head of the U.S. Army's Strategic Studies Institute, Douglas Lovelace, observed in 2000. "Today, it is appropriate to rethink this neglect. . . . A consistent and well-designed American strategy in the region could help tilt the scales in favor of security and stability."[20] To further demonstrate U.S. interest, Secretary of Defense William S. Cohen went on a weeklong "working visit" to Africa in February 2000, stopping in Morocco, Nigeria, and South Africa for extended talks with top military officials.[21]

The major western European powers, especially Britain and France, have also revived or expanded their links with the nations of sub-Saharan Africa. The British, for example, have deployed military advisory and training teams in Ghana and Zimbabwe, while the French have established their own, regionwide training program, called RECAMP.[22] China and Japan have also increased their presence in the area, principally through commercial investments and economic aid. Of particular note is the decision by the China National Petroleum Corporation to become a major partner in a joint effort by the Sudanese government and Canadian firms to develop promising oil reserves in southern Sudan—an area long contested by guerrillas of the Sudanese People's Liberation Army.[23]

If past experience is any guide, U.S. and European military aid deliveries and arms sales to Africa will be stepped up as a result of growing commercial engagement. Indeed, significant arms purchases have been announced or concluded by several countries in the region, including Angola, Botswana, Nigeria, South Africa, and Zimbabwe.[24]

Africa is also likely to witness greater resource conflict in the years ahead. All of the preconditions for recurring violence can be found here: large concentrations of vital materials, numerous territorial disputes in areas harboring valuable deposits, widespread political instability and factionalism, the presence of private armies and mercenaries, and a history of collaboration between foreign resource firms and local warlords. In the Democratic Republic of Congo, various coalitions of domestic, local, and regional interests have been formed to acquire control over the country's vast supplies of timber, gems, oil, and minerals. As we have seen, a similar pattern is evident in Sierra Leone.

At present, resource-related conflict in Africa is largely confined to internal strife or—as in Congo—to wars involving various combinations of local and regional actors. At some point, however, outside powers seem certain to increase their involvement. To some degree, of course, foreign powers are *already* involved in African conflicts, if only by supplying arms and military assistance to the forces engaged in regional disputes. Of the six countries that sent troops to Congo in 1999, four had received at least some military aid from the United States in the preceding period.[25] Whether the United States and its allies will also resort to direct military intervention (other than in U.N.-sanctioned peacekeeping operations) cannot be foreseen, but the stepped-up delivery of military assistance has often been followed by such involvement in the past.

WHAT PRICE RESOURCE PLENTY?

Most resource wars of the future will occur in the developing world—notably, in countries where the national government is weak or corrupt and where local and external actors are competing for political power. Armed combat will most likely be limited to periodic skirmishing between militias and other paramilitary formations. Typically, the civilians living in combat zones will suffer the greatest casualties, as has been the case in Angola, Congo, Liberia, and Sierra Leone. And while a handful of individuals may profit from the sale of diamonds and old-growth timber to foreign firms, most of the people living in these societies will remain entrapped in poverty and despair.

Future resource conflict also holds great peril for the major powers. Although interstate warfare over vital materials may be less common than internal wars, such fighting will often prove more intense and violent. Soldiers deployed by outside powers to protect supply sites in distant lands will be at risk both on the battlefield and, as targets of terrorism, away from it. Indeed, terrorism is likely to become a common feature of future resource wars. The presence of foreign troops in resource-producing regions will often stir up resentments among those living in the area, especially if they view these resources as part of their natural birthright. The American military deployment in Saudi Arabia, for example, has provoked widespread hostility among those Saudis who feel that the kingdom's oil wealth should be used solely for the advance of Islam. The 1996 bombing of the Khobar Towers in Dhahran is thought to be the work of local opponents of the Saudi government's close ties with the United States.[26]

A strategy based on the use of force to protect vital resources will prove very costly. As much as one-fourth of the U.S. defense budget—about $75 billion per year—is allocated to American forces in the Persian Gulf and to those units stationed elsewhere that are kept available for deployment to the Gulf. Similarly, Moscow has devoted a significant share of its military budget to the war in Chechnya and to the Russian presence in the Caspian area. China, Japan, the ASEAN countries, and a variety of other states have also increased their spending on forces used to protect major resource zones or transit routes.

Paradoxically, recurring conflict over resources will also squander vast quantities of critical materials—especially oil—and cause significant damage to key sources of supply.[27] During Operation Desert Storm, for example, the United States and its allies consumed an average of 19 million gallons of oil a day[28]—an amount equal to the daily petroleum consumption of a country the size of Argentina. Even more significant, sabotage committed by the Iraqis as they fled Kuwait resulted in the uncontrolled burning of an estimated 2 billion barrels of oil, equivalent to two and half years' worth of normal production by that country.[29]

ALTERNATIVES TO WAR

It seems reasonable to ask whether a resource-acquisition strategy based on global cooperation rather than recurring conflict might not prove more effective in guaranteeing access to critical supplies over the long run. Such a strategy would call for the equitable distribution of the world's existing resource stockpiles in times of acute scarcity, as well as an accelerated, global program of research on alternative energy sources and industrial processes. Coordinated international efforts would be inaugurated to conserve scarce commodities and employ material-saving technologies.

The key to making this strategy work effectively would be the establishment of robust international institutions that could address major resource problems while retaining the confidence of global leaders and the public. Such institutions would be needed to produce an accurate inventory of the world's supplies of critical commodities and to develop mechanisms for the global allocation of these materials in times of extreme scarcity or emergency. The scientific and technical expertise of participating nations could be pooled in the search for new materials and production techniques. In return for their support of these efforts, member states would be assured of emergency deliveries of vital materials and would be guaranteed access to any new technologies generated by the common research effort.

In the energy area, for example, a global authority could be formed to coordinate the world's search for alternative fuels and to allocate existing supplies in the event of crisis. The foundation for such an institution already exists with the International Energy Agency (IEA). Established in response to the 1974 Arab oil embargo, the IEA was intended to arrange for and supervise the sharing of oil by the Western countries in times of emergency.[30] An expanded version of the IEA, incorporating all regions, could bring suppliers and recipients together to find ways to alleviate future shortages.

A similar body is needed to protect the world's water resources. Although it may prove impractical to move large quantities of fresh water from one region to another (as can be done in the case of oil) it *is* possible to imagine a global water authority that could assist countries facing acute shortages. This authority could also help arrange for the equitable distribution of water among states dependent on a shared river or aquifer system and could lead the search for more economical methods of converting salt water into fresh water, or for irrigating crops with less water wastage.

We undeniably possess the ingenuity and capacity to develop such institutions. Existing organizations, such as the International Atomic Energy Agency, the United Nations Development Programme, and the World Health Organization, have demonstrated, over a considerable span of time, the capacity to address complex international problems in an effective and impartial fashion. As the world becomes more complex and interdependent, there is every reason to believe that new resource agencies could make a substantial contribution to reducing the likelihood of armed conflict.

New international procedures are also needed to reduce the incidence of fighting over gems and timber. Some progress has already been achieved in this area through the marking of diamonds and logs to indicate that they originated in "conflict-free" areas. Canadian diamond mines, for example, engrave a microscopic polar bear or maple leaf on their stones, so as to distinguish them from gems originating elsewhere.[31] Similarly, the De Beers diamond-trading firm has adopted measures to exclude stones coming from Angola and

Sierra Leone in its inventories.[32] Many timber companies, moreover, have agreed to certify that the logs they sell were not acquired from indigenous lands without the permission of local communities.[33] Once a comprehensive system of such controls is put in place, it should be possible to curtail the trade in illicit resources and thus limit the duration and severity of resource wars.

No one can guarantee that such a strategy will work in all situations, or that it will eliminate every cause of conflict. Any worldwide system of cooperation will attract some spoilers and cheats. The point is not to ask whether such a system can be made entirely foolproof but whether, even with its problems, it would prove more effective over the long run than the current system, which relies on the use of force to resolve resource disputes.

Seen from this perspective, a strategy based on cooperation has many distinct advantages. While the use of force by a particular state may result in the temporary alleviation of a resource shortage, it will only provoke resentments on the losing side, leading to further outbreaks of violence in the future. Furthermore, the daunting task of moving large amounts of oil or water from one region to another cannot be performed effectively in an environment of recurring violence—the risk of sabotage, accident, spills, and breakdowns is simply too great. And the use of force will consume resources that can more profitably be used for the public good.

By contrast, the repudiation of violence in favor of cooperative solutions is more likely to avert painful shortages. Cooperative solutions are also likely to prove more durable. By building trust in this manner, moreover, the partners to a cooperative scheme will be better positioned to cope with an emergency. The avoidance of military operations would also permit increased investment in new materials and technologies.

As we move deeper into the twenty-first century, the global human community faces a momentous choice: we can either proceed down the path of intensified resource competition, which will lead to recurring outbreaks of conflict throughout the world, or we can choose to manage global resource stockpiles in a cooperative fashion. Selecting the latter path will not prove easy: many states and private interests will resist the establishment of a system that gives international agencies a degree of control over the allocation of valuable materials in times of scarcity. But we must ask: Would it not be better to share resources equitably in times of need? Is it not in our long-term interest to make every effort to *avert* future shortages through collaborative research and action?

Natural resources are the building blocks of civilization and an essential requirement of daily existence. The inhabitants of planet Earth have been blessed with a vast supply of most basic materials. But we are placing increased pressure on these supplies, and in some cases we face, in our lifetimes, or those of our children, the prospect of severe resource depletion. If we rely on warfare to settle disputes over raw materials, the human toll will be great. To avoid this fate, and to ensure an adequate supply of essential materials, we must work now to establish a global system of resource conservation and collaboration.

APPENDIX:
TERRITORIAL DISPUTES IN AREAS CONTAINING OIL AND/OR NATURAL GAS

Disputed Area	Location	Rival Claimants	Comments
Middle East and Central Asia			
Warba and Bubiyan Islands; southern reach of Rumaila oil field	Northwestern corner of the Persian Gulf	Iraq, Kuwait	Kuwait's refusal to acknowledge Iraqi sovereignty over these areas was one of the reasons cited by Baghdad as a justification for its 1990 invasion. Iraq agreed to abandon these claims under pressure from the U.N. in 1994, but could reassert its sovereignty in the future.
Abu Musa; Greater Tunb and Lesser Tunb	Eastern corner of the Persian Gulf	Iran, United Arab Emirates (UAE)	Iran seized the Greater and Lesser Tunb islands from Ras al-Khaimah (part of the UAE) in 1971; Iran shared control of Abu Musa with Sharjah (also part of the UAE) until 1994, when it occupied the entire island. Iran now claims sovereignty over the islands and rejects adjudication of the dispute; since 1995, it has steadily expanded its military presence on Abu Musa.

Disputed Area	Location	Rival Claimants	Comments
Middle East and Central Asia (cont.)			
Hawar Island plus the Dibal and Jarada shoals	Persian Gulf	Bahrain, Qatar	The dispute over these features (which lie adjacent to major oil and gas fields) has been submitted to the ICJ for adjudication.
Border between Saudi Arabia and Yemen	Arabian Peninsula	Saudi Arabia, Yemen	Border clashes in late 1994 and early 1995 produced casualties on both sides; in June 2000, the two countries signed a treaty to finalize the location of their mutual border.
Border between Qatar and Saudi Arabia	Arabian Peninsula	Qatar, Saudi Arabia	Armed clash in 1992 at the border post of Khafus resulted in three fatalities (two Qatari and one Saudi); Qatar and Saudi Arabia have since agreed to settle the dispute, but final location of the border has yet to be resolved.
Border between Saudi Arabia and the United Arab Emirates	Arabian Peninsula	Saudi Arabia, United Arab Emirates (UAE)	In 1998, the Saudis began pumping oil from the vast Shaybah oil field, which straddles the undefined border between Saudi Arabia and the UAE, provoking protests from the latter and a demand to share in the production of the field.
Greater and Lesser Hanish Islands	Southeastern stretch of the Red Sea	Eritrea, Yemen	Clashes in 1995 and 1996 over control of the islands (which are thought to lie in an oil-rich area) produced casualties on each side; both countries then agreed to third-party arbitration of the dispute, which led, in 1999, to the award of the Hanish Islands to Yemen.
Halayeb Triangle	Egypt-Sudan border area on the Red Sea	Egypt, Sudan	After a brief clash in June 1995 that produced casualties on both sides, Egyptian forces entered the disputed area and drove out Sudanese police and officials. Earlier, Sudan had awarded a concession to a Canadian company for oil exploration in waters off the disputed area.

Disputed Area	Location	Rival Claimants	Comments
Middle East and Central Asia (cont.)			
Caspian Sea (offshore drilling rights)	Caspian Sea	Azerbaijan, Iran, Kazakhstan, Russia, Turkmenistan	Iran and Russia seek joint development of all offshore areas (beyond a narrow coastal strip) by all five littoral states; the others seek to divide the entire Caspian into five separate EEZs; negotiations between the parties on the ownership of offshore drilling rights are continuing.
Serdar/Kyapaz offshore oil and NG field	Caspian Sea	Azerbaijan, Turkmenistan	The disputed field (called Serdar by Turkmenistan and Kyapaz by Azerbaijan) lies midway between the two claimants, each of which insists it falls solely within its own EEZ; negotiations to resolve the dispute have so far proved inconclusive.
East and Southeast Asia			
Paracel Islands	Northwestern corner of South China Sea	China, Vietnam	Occupied by China since Vietnamese forces were driven from the area in 1974.
Spratly Islands	Scattered throughout the South China Sea	Brunei, China, Malaysia, Philippines, Taiwan, Vietnam	China and Taiwan each claim the entire chain of islands; the others claim those islands located in their offshore EEZs; all but Brunei have established military posts on one or more of the islands in their respective claim areas; armed clashes in the area have occurred on several occasions.
Natuna Sea (offshore drilling rights)	Southwestern corner of the South China Sea	China, Indonesia	Indonesia has given concessions to foreign energy firms for development of a large undersea NG field in this area, which is also claimed by China as part of its territorial waters.

Disputed Area	Location	Rival Claimants	Comments
East and Southeast Asia (cont.)			
Diaoyu/Senkaku Islands	East China Sea	China, Taiwan, Japan	These islands—called the Diaoyus by China and Taiwan and the Senkakus by Japan—have been the site of periodic clashes between ultra-nationalist groups and naval vessels from the various sides. (Although uninhabitable, they are thought to lie aside potentially valuable undersea oil and NG fields.)
Timor Sea (offshore drilling rights)	The body of water between Timor and Australia	Australia, East Timor, Indonesia	Under the 1989 Timor Gap Treaty, Indonesia and Australia divided the Timor Sea (which lies above a large oil and NG field) into Australian- and Indonesian-controlled areas plus a jointly held Zone of Cooperation. Indonesia declared the treaty void in 1999 when East Timor became independent; Australia now seeks to negotiate a new treaty with East Timor, but that nation has yet to install a functioning government.
Africa			
Bakassi Peninsula	Gulf of Guinea	Cameroon, Nigeria	In 1996, Nigerian army forces clashed with Cameroonian police in an effort to establish control over the region (which is believed to lie aside valuable offshore oil fields); the dispute has been submitted to the ICJ for adjudication.
Offshore tracts in the Gulf of Guinea	Gulf of Guinea	Equatorial Guinea, Nigeria	Nigeria insists that the Zafiro undersea oil field, claimed by Equatorial Guinea, extends into Nigeria's offshore territory; negotiations to resolve the dispute have so far proved fruitless.

Latin America			
Gulf of Paria	Southeastern corner of Caribbean Sea	Trinidad and Tobago, Venezuela	Venezuelan gunboats have boarded Trinidadian oil platforms and fired on Trinidadian vessels in an area claimed by both countries.
Offshore tracts in the Atlantic Ocean	Coastal areas of Guyana and Suriname	Guyana, Suriname	In June 2000, gunboats from Suriname evicted a Canadian-owned oil rig from disputed area; negotiations to resolve the dispute have so far proved fruitless.

Source: Compiled by the author on the basis of "country analysis briefs" provided by the U.S. Department of Energy and articles from *The Economist, The New York Times,* and other publications.
EEZ = Exclusive Economic Zone
ICJ = International Court of Justice, The Hague
NG = natural gas

NOTES

1: WEALTH, RESOURCES, AND POWER:
THE CHANGING PARAMETERS OF GLOBAL SECURITY

1. See U.S. Department of Defense, "Exercise Central Asian Battalion '97," news release, Washington, D.C., August 28, 1997, and U.S. Atlantic Command, "Exercise CENTRAZBAT '97," electronic communication posted at http://www. acom.mil, accessed September 23, 1997. See also R. Jeffrey Smith, "U.S. Leads Peacekeeping Drill in Kazakhstan," *Washington Post,* September 15, 1997; Smith, "U.S., Russian Paratroops Join in Central Asian Jump," *Washington Post,* September 16, 1997.

2. Quoted in Smith, "U.S., Russian Paratroops Join."

3. Quoted in Smith, "U.S. Leads Peacekeeping Drill."

4. U.S. Department of Energy (DoE), Energy Information Administration (EIA), "Caspian Sea Region," June 2000, electronic document accessed at http:// www.eia.doe.gov/emeu/cabs/caspian.html on July 12, 2000.

5. U.S. Department of State, *Caspian Region Energy Development Report,* Report to the House International Relations Committee Pursuant to H.R. 3610, April 15, 1997, p. 1.

6. Strobe Talbott, "A Farewell to Flashman: American Policy in the Caucasus and Central Asia," address at the Johns Hopkins School of Advanced International Studies, Washington, D.C., July 21, 1997, electronic document accessed at http:// www.state.gov/www/regions/nis/970721talbott.html on August 14, 1997.

7. "Visit of President Heydar Aliyev of Azerbaijan," statement by the press secretary, the White House, August 1, 1997, electronic document accessed at http://www.library.whitehouse.gov/ on March 2, 1998.

8. Jimmy Carter, State of the Union Address, January 23, 1980, as published in *The New York Times,* January 24, 1980.

9. For background, see the following press releases issued by the U.S. Atlantic Command, Norfolk, Va.: "Exercise CENTRAZBAT 98 Begins," "U.S. Forces Arrive in Central Asia," "Phase Two Begins in Kyrgyzstan," and "U.S. Forces Complete CENTRAZBAT 98." Electronic documents accessed at http://www.acom.mil/centraz.nsf/News on June 21, 1999.

10. Steven Lee Myers, "A Modern Caspian Model for U.S. War Games," *New York Times,* March 15, 1999.

11. Stephen Kinzer, "Azerbaijan Asks the U.S. to Establish Military Base," *New York Times,* January 31, 1999.

12. John C. Gannon, "A Global Perspective on Energy Security," address to the Energy Council Conference on Energy and the Environment, Keystone, Colo., December 6, 1996, electronic document accessed at http://www.odci.gov/cia/di/speeches/42842197.html on January 4, 1999.

13. For an analysis of Mahan's beliefs, see Philip A. Crowl, "Alfred Thayer Mahan: The Naval Historian," in Peter Paret, ed., *Makers of Modern Strategy* (Princeton: Princeton University Press, 1986), pp. 444–77.

14. This indebtedness to the ideas of Mahan was made explicit in Lt. Col. Reynolds B. Peele, "The Importance of Maritime Chokepoints," *Parameters* (U.S. Army War College), Summer 1997, pp. 61–74.

15. National Defense University (NDU), Institute for National Security Studies (INSS), *Strategic Assessment 1999* (Washington, D.C.: NDU/INSS, 1999), p. 30. For further discussion see Theodore H. Moran, *American Economic Policy and National Security* (New York: Council on Foreign Relations Press, 1993).

16. This speech was later published as "A New Covenant for American Security," *Harvard International Review,* Summer 1992, pp. 26–27.

17. Address to the World Affairs Council of Los Angeles, August 13, 1992, as published in *The New York Times,* August 14, 1992.

18. Warren Christopher, "Statement at Senate Confirmation Hearings," *U.S. Department of State Dispatch,* January 25, 1993, p. 46.

19. This statement appears in the 1999 version of the president's annual statement on national security strategy, and in previous editions of this document. See U.S. National Security Council, *A National Security Strategy for a New Century* (Washington, D.C.: White House, December 1999), p. 21.

20. Ibid.

21. Unofficial transcript of Hearing of the House National Security Committee on the FY 1999 Defense Budget, Washington, D.C., March 5, 1998, as recorded by the Federal News Service and provided in electronic form by the Congressional Information Service.

22. "The Russian Federation Military Doctrine," as approved by President Vladimir Putin on April 21, 2000. From the translation in *Arms Conrol Today,* May 2000, pp. 29–38.

23. Quoted in Ben Barber, "Beijing Eyes South China Sea with Sub Purchase," *Washington Times,* March 7, 1995.

24. "National Defense Program Outline in and After Fiscal Year 1996," electronic communication, Japanese Ministry of Foreign Affairs, accessed August 7, 1997.

25. See Steve Glain, "New Arms Race: Fearing China's Plans and a U.S. Departure, Asians Rebuild Forces," *Wall Street Journal,* November 13, 1997; Joris Janssen Lok, "ASEAN Navies Extend Their Regional Reach," *Jane's Defense Weekly,* November 27, 1996, pp. 25–28.

26. Quoted in Peter Gleick, "Water and Conflict," *International Security,* vol. 18, no. 1 (Summer 1993), p. 86.

27. Paul Collier and Anke Hoeffler, "Justice-Seeking and Loot-Seeking in War," unpublished paper, World Bank, Washington, D.C., February 17, 1999, p. 15.

28. Thomas L. Friedman, *The Lexus and the Olive Tree* (New York: Farrar, Straus, Giroux, 1999), p. xvii.

29. Samuel P. Huntington, "The Clash of Civilizations?" *Foreign Affairs,* vol. 72, no. 3 (Summer 1993), p. 22.

30. This thesis was first advanced in Robert D. Kaplan, "The Coming Anarchy," *Atlantic Monthly,* February 1994, pp. 44–75.

31. U.S. Department of State, *Caspian Region Energy Development Report,* p. 3.

32. Gary Gardner and Payal Sampat, *Mind over Matter: Recasting the Role of Materials in Our Lives,* Worldwatch Paper no. 144 (Washington, D.C.: Worldwatch Institute, December 1998), p. 15.

33. Lester R. Brown, Michael Renner, and Brian Halweil, *Vital Signs 2000* (New York: W. W. Norton and the Worldwatch Institute, 2000), p. 71. Hereinafter cited as WWI, *Vital Signs 2000.*

34. Ibid., p. 87.

35. For discussion, see Gardner and Sampat, *Mind over Matter.*

36. "Not Quite a Billion," *Economist,* January 2, 1999, p. 56.

37. U.S. Department of Energy, Energy Information Administration, *International Energy Outlook 2000* (Washington, D.C.: DoE/EIA, 2000), p. 169. Hereinafter cited as DoE/EIA, *IEO 2000.*

38. Allen R. Myerson, "U.S. Splurging on Energy After Falling off Its Diet," *New York Times,* October 22, 1998. See also Carlos Tejada and Patrick Barta, "Big Footprints: Hey, Baby Boomers Need Their Space, OK? Look at All Their Stuff," *Wall Street Journal,* January 7, 2000.

39. See the data provided in Albert Adriaanse, et al., *Resource Flows: The Material Basis of Industrial Economies* (Washington, D.C.: World Resources Institute, 1997).

40. World Resources Institute (WRI), *World Resources 1998–99* (Oxford and New York: Oxford University Press, 1998), pp. 141–45, 244–45. Hereinafter cited as WRI *World Resources 1998–99.*

41. U.S. National Intelligence Council (NIC), *Global Trends 2010* (Washington, D.C.: NIC, November 1997), p. 2.

42. World Wildlife Fund (WWF), *Living Planet Report 1998* (Gland, Switzerland: WWF, 1998).

43. BP Amoco, *Statistical Review of World Energy 2000* (London: BP Amoco, 2000), p. 4.

44. For discussion, see Colin J. Campbell and Jean H. Laherrère, "The End of Cheap Oil," *Scientific American,* March 1998, pp. 78–83, and James J. MacKenzie, "Heading Off the Permanent Oil Crisis," *Issues in Science and Technology,* Summer 1996, pp. 48–54.

45. See J. W. Maurits la Rivière, "Threats to the World's Water," *Scientific American,* September 1989, pp. 80–94.

46. WWF, *Living Planet Report 1998,* p. 6.

47. See Thomas F. Homer-Dixon, "On the Threshold: Environmental Changes as Causes of Acute Conflict," *International Security,* vol. 16, no. 2 (Fall 1991), pp. 76–116; Homer-Dixon, "Environmental Scarcities and Violent Conflict," *International Security,* vol. 19, no. 1 (Summer 1994), pp. 5–40.

48. See Lawrence Freedman and Efraim Karsh, *The Gulf Conflict, 1990–1991* (Princeton: Princeton University Press, 1993), pp. 48, 57, 59–60.

49. For discussion, see DoE, EIA, "World Oil Transit Chokepoints," May 1998, electronic document accessed at http://www.eia.doe.gov/emeu/cabs/choke.html on May 26, 1998.

50. For discussion, see Ian Fisher and Norimitsu Onishi, "Many Armies Ravage Rich Land in the 'First World War' of Africa," *New York Times,* February 6, 2000.

51. NDU/INSS, *Strategic Assessment 1999,* p. 29.

52. "Bolivia Calls an Emergency After Protest over Water," *New York Times,* April 9, 2000.

53. I first used this term in "Resource Wars," *Harper's,* January 1980, pp. 20–23. The term was also used at that time by General Alexander M. Haig Jr., former commander in chief of NATO, in testimony before the Mines and Mining Subcommittee of the House Committee on Interior and Insular Affairs. Suggesting that aggressive Soviet moves in Afghanistan, the Middle East, and Africa were designed to impede U.S. access to vital raw materials, Haig declared that "the era of 'resource wars' has arrived." Prepared statement (xerox copy), September 18, 1980.

2: OIL, GEOGRAPHY, AND WAR:
THE COMPETITIVE PURSUIT OF PETROLEUM PLENTY

1. For background on the decision to switch from coal to oil, see Geoffrey Jones, *The State and the Emergence of the British Oil Industry* (London: MacMillan, 1981), pp. 9–31.

2. For background and discussion, see ibid., pp. 129–76.

3. Ibid., p. 177. See also Daniel Yergin, *The Prize* (New York: Touchstone, Simon and Schuster, 1993), pp. 167–83.

4. This was said to a celebratory meeting of the Inter-Allied Petroleum Council in London on November 21, 1918. Cited in Yergin, *The Prize,* p. 183.

5. For background on this period, see Jones, *The State and the Emergence of the British Oil Industry,* pp. 208–44; Yergin, *The Prize,* pp. 184–206, 260–308.

6. See Yergin, *The Prize,* pp. 308–88.

7. For background on these endeavors, see David S. Painter, *Oil and the American Century* (Baltimore: Johns Hopkins University Press, 1986), and Michael B. Stoff, *Oil, War, and American Security* (New Haven: Yale University Press, 1980). On the Nixon Doctrine, see James H. Noyes, *The Clouded Lens* (Stanford, Calif.: Hoover Institution Press, 1979), and U.S. Congress, House, Committee on Foreign Affairs, Subcommittee on the Near East and South Asia, *New Perspectives on the Persian Gulf,* Hearings, 93rd Congress, 1st session (Washington, D.C.: Government Printing Office, 1973).

8. For background on these events, see Yergin, *The Prize,* pp. 588–632.

9. Interview in *Business Week,* January 13, 1975, p. 69.

10. From the transcript of Carter's address in *The New York Times,* January 24, 1980.

11. For background on this episode, see Anthony H. Cordesman and Abraham R. Wagner, *The Lessons of Modern War,* volume II, *The Iran-Iraq War* (Boulder: Westview Press, 1990), pp. 277–80, 295–302, 317, 329.

12. From the transcript of Bush's speech in *The New York Times,* August 8, 1997.

13. Alluding to Kissinger's earlier comments, Defense Secretary Richard Cheney told the Senate Armed Services Committee in September 1990 that Washington could not allow Saddam Hussein to acquire "a stranglehold on our economy." U.S. Congress, Senate, Committee on Armed Services, *Crisis in the Persian Gulf Region: U.S. Policy Options and Implications,* Hearings, 101st Congress, 2d Session (1990), pp. 10–11. These hearings represent one of the best sources for information on U.S. security thinking at the time.

14. U.S. Central Command (CENTCOM), *1997 Posture Statement* (MacDill Air Force Base, Fla.: CENTCOM, n.d.), p. 1.

15. U.S. Department of State, *Caspian Region Energy Development Report,* p. 3.

16. U.S. Department of Energy, Energy Information Administration, *Inter-*

national Energy Outlook 1999 (Washington, D.C.: DoE/EIA, 1999), Table A4, p. 145. Hereinafter cited as DOE/EIA, *IEO 1999.*

17. Edward L. Morse, "A New Political Economy of Oil?" *Journal of International Affairs,* vol. 53, no. 1 (Fall 1999), p. 2.

18. DoE/EIA, *IEO 1999,* Table A2, pp. 142–43.

19. Ibid.

20. Ibid., pp. 118, 216, 219, and Table E1, pp. 213–18.

21. DoE/EIA, *IEO 2000.* pp. 133–34.

22. American Petroleum Institute, "Facts About Oil," electronic communication accessed at http://www.api.org/factsoil.htm on August 6, 1999.

23. For data and analysis, see DoE/EIA, *IEO 1999,* pp. 19–35.

24. For discussion, see Barnaby J. Feder, "Digital Economy's Demand for Steady Power Strains Utilities," *New York Times,* July 3, 2000.

25. For discussion, see "The Future of Fuel Cells," a series of articles in *Scientific American,* July 1999, pp. 72–86.

26. See DoE/EIA, *IEO 2000,* pp. 133–55.

27. BP Amoco, *Statistical Review of World Energy 2000,* p. 4.

28. See DoE/EIA, *IEO 1999,* pp. 22–23. See also the discussion in Colin J. Campbell and Jean H. Laherrère, "The End of Cheap Oil," *Scientific American,* March 1998, pp. 78–83.

29. See DoE/EIA, *IEO 1999,* pp. 22–23. See also Sarah A. Emerson, "Resource Plenty," *Harvard International Review,* Summer 1997, pp. 12–15, 64–65.

30. See Campbell and Laherrère, "The End of Cheap Oil." See also James J. MacKenzie, "Heading Off the Permanent Oil Crisis," *Issues in Science and Technology,* Summer 1996, pp. 48–59.

31. For a similar assessment, see Joseph P. Riva Jr., *World Oil Production After Year 2000: Business as Usual or Crises?* Congressional Research Service (CRS) Report for Congress (Washington, D.C.: CRS, August 18, 1995), electronic version, accessed at http://www.cnie.org/nle/eng-3.html on November 24, 1997.

32. "In the early stages [of oil production], it is the large fields that are readily discovered," oil expert James J. MacKenzie wrote in 1996. "In the declining stages, geologists are much more likely to find small fields, and [so] oil companies must do a lot more drilling just to stay even." For this reason, he noted, "it's so much harder to maintain production in the declining stages than in the growing phase of the industry." MacKenzie, "Heading Off the Permanent Oil Crisis," p. 49.

33. For further articulation of this "pessimistic" assessment, see Campbell and Laherrère, "The End of Cheap Oil"; MacKenzie, "Heading Off the Permanent Oil Crisis."

34. For discussion of the pros and cons of relying on these materials, see Stever Fetter, *Climate Change and the Transformation of World Energy Supply* (Stanford, Calif.: Stanford University, Center for International Security and Cooperation, May

1999), pp. 58–63. See also Richard L. George, "Mining for Oil," *Scientific American,* March 1998, pp. 84–85.

35. For further articulation of this "optimistic" assessment, see Emerson, "Resource Plenty."

36. For a thorough articulation of this perspective, see C. J. Campbell, *The Coming Oil Crisis* (Brentwood, U.K.: Multi-Science Publishing Co. and Petroconsultants S.A., n.d.).

37. For further articulation of this assessment, see Riva, *World Oil Production After Year 2000.*

38. For further discussion of this point, see Edward R. Fried and Philip H. Trezise, *Oil Security: Retrospect and Prospect* (Washington, D.C.: Brookings Institution, 1993).

39. For discussion, see the essays in Gary G. Sick and Lawrence G. Potter, eds., *The Persian Gulf at the Millennium* (New York: St. Martin's Press, 1997).

40. U.S. National Security Council, *A National Security Strategy for a New Century* (Washington, D.C.: White House, October 1998), p. 32.

41. U.S. Department of Energy, Energy Information Administration, "World Oil Transit Chokepoints," electronic document accessed at http://www.eia.doe.gov/emeu/cabs/choke.html on August 10, 1999.

42. For discussion, see Richard N. Schofield, "Border Disputes in the Gulf: Past, Present, and Future," in Sick and Potter, *The Persian Gulf at the Millennium,* pp. 127–66.

43. BP Amoco, *Statistical Review of World Energy 1999,* pp. 4, 7.

3: OIL CONFLICT IN THE PERSIAN GULF

1. See, for example, William W. Keller, *Arm in Arm: The Political Economy of the Global Arms Trade* (New York: Basic Books, 1995), pp. 1–19.

2. "We know from experience that [hostile] leaders respect and are intimidated by military strength," General J. H. Binford Peay III, then the commander of all U.S. forces in the Gulf area, told Congress in 1997. "Consequently, we deter these individuals by continuing to organize, equip, and exercise premier joint and combined forces; positioning a credible mix of those forces forward in the region; maintaining the national will to use them; and communicating our resolve to our opponents." J. H. Binford Peay III, "Promoting Peace and Stability in the Central Region," Report to the House Appropriations Committee Subcommittee on National Security, March 17, 1997, electronic document accessed at http://www.centcom.mil/execsum.html on August 6, 1997.

3. BP Amoco, *World Energy Review 2000,* pp. 4, 7.

4. Ibid. For an assessment of Saudi Arabia's hydrocarbon potential, see U.S. Department of Energy, Energy Information Administration (DoE/EIA), *Saudi Arabia,* Country Analysis Brief, January 2000, electronic document accessed at http://www.eia.doe.gov/emeu/cabs/saudfull.html on January 14, 2000.

5. DoE/EIA, *IEO 2000,* Table D1, p. 229.

6. Ibid., Table 13, p. 38.

7. For a discussion of these and other scenarios for conflict over oil, see NDU/INSS, *Strategic Assessment 1999,* pp. 40–41.

8. On France's ties with Iraq, see Andrew J. Pierre, *The Global Politics of Arms Sales* (Princeton: Princeton University Press, 1982), pp. 84, 194–96. On China's ties with Iran, see Mamdouh G. Salameh, "China, Oil, and the Risk of Regional Conflict," *Survival,* vol. 37, no. 4 (Winter 1995–96), p. 141.

9. One U.S. analyst, Professor Kent E. Calder of Princeton University, has suggested that growing Chinese dependence on Persian Gulf oil could result in a Chinese-Iranian-Iraqi alliance counterposed to a U.S.-Saudi alliance, with "unsettling" implications. See Calder, "Asia's Empty Tank," *Foreign Affairs,* vol. 75, no. 2 (March–April 1996), pp. 55–68. Similar concerns are expressed in NDU/INSS, *Strategic Assessment 1999,* p. 41.

10. In January 1975, following the fourfold OPEC price rise of 1974 and the resulting outbreak of a global recession, Professor Robert W. Tucker of Johns Hopkins University proposed that U.S. forces occupy the area extending "from Kuwait down along the coastal region of Saudi Arabia to Qatar" in order to "break the present price structure [for oil] by breaking the core of the cartel politically and economically." See Tucker, "Oil: The Issue of American Intervention," *Commentary,* January 1975, pp. 21–31. Two months later, a prominent Washington military analyst using the pseudonym "Miles Ignotus" made a similar proposal in *Harper's* magazine. American power, he said, "must be used selectively to occupy large and concentrated oil reserves [in Saudi Arabia] in order to end the artificial scarcity of oil and thus cut the price." Ignotus, "Seizing Arab Oil," *Harper's,* March 1975, pp. 45–62.

11. General Anthony C. Zinni, Prepared Statement Before the Senate Committee on Armed Services, Washington, D.C., April 13, 1999, as released by the Federal Information Systems Corporation and distributed electronically by the Congressional Information Service via Lexis-Nexis.

12. For background on this effort, see Stoff, *Oil, War, and American Security,* pp. 34–88.

13. The text of NSDM-92 was never made public. However, an unclassified summary of the document can be found in the testimony of Deputy Assistant Secretary of Defense James H. Noyes in House Committee on Foreign Affairs, *New Perspectives on the Persian Gulf,* p. 39. For background on these events, see Michael Klare, *American Arms Supermarket* (Austin: University of Texas Press, 1985), pp. 112–15; James H. Noyes, *The Clouded Lens* (Stanford, Calif.: Hoover Institution Press, 1979), pp. 53–54.

14. House Comittee on Foreign Affairs, *New Perspectives on the Persian Gulf,* p. 6. For discussion, see Noyes, *The Clouded Lens,* pp. 54–55.

15. Gerry E. Studds, "U.S. Entangled in Iranian Web," *Boston Evening Globe,*

December 23, 1978. For further information and background on these arms transfers, see Klare, *American Arms Supermarket,* pp. 109–62.

16. For background on these initiatives, see Michael Klare, "The Brown Doctrine: Have R.D.F., Will Travel," *Nation,* March 8, 1980, pp. 63–66; Klare, "Is Exxon Worth Dying For? The Pentagon's Plans for Energy Wars," *Progressive,* July 1980, pp. 21–26.

17. For background on these developments, see H. Norman Schwarzkopf, *It Doesn't Take a Hero* (New York: Bantam Books, 1992), pp. 331–36.

18. For background on these developments, see Freedman and Karsh, *The Gulf Conflict, 1990–1991,* pp. 85–94; Michael Klare, *Rogue States and Nuclear Outlaws* (New York: Hill and Wang, 1985), pp. 35–41; Schwarzkopf, *It Doesn't Take a Hero,* pp. 337–57; Bob Woodward, *The Commanders* (New York: Simon and Schuster, 1991), pp. 247–89.

19. Department of Defense News Briefing, the Pentagon, Washington, D.C., May 17, 1995, electronic communication, accessed at http://www.defenselink.mil: 80/cgi-bin/ on September 3, 1997.

20. Prepared statement of General Zinni before the Senate Armed Services Committee, April 13, 1999.

21. For discussion of Saudi Arabia's reluctance to support these operations, see Steven Lee Myers, "U.S. Will Not Ask to Use Saudi Bases for a Raid on Iraq," *New York Times,* February 9, 1998.

22. "We've made it very clear by our force movements in the past and by our actions in the past that we're willing to use military force if necessary to contain Iraq from either attacking our forces, attacking neighboring countries, or from reconstituting its weapons of mass destruction," Assistant Secretary of Defense Kevin H. Bacon declared at a Pentagon news briefing on May 26, 1998. From the electronic text of his comments, as posted at http://www.defenselink.mil on May 26, 1998.

23. "With few forces stationed in the region," General Zinni explained in February 2000, "our vitally important power projection strategy is based on . . . rapidly deployable forces from the continental U.S. and other theaters with associated strategic and theater lift, and robust land- and sea-based prepositioning assets." Prepared statement of General Anthony C. Zinni before the Senate Armed Services Committee, Washington, D.C., February 29, 2000, as distributed electronically by the Congressional Information Service via Lexis-Nexis.

24. For details of these efforts, see Anthony H. Cordesman, *U.S. Forces in the Middle East: Resources and Capabilities* (Boulder, C.O.: Westview Press, 1997), pp. 39–81. See also U.S. Central Command (CENTCOM), *1997 Posture Statement* (MacDill Air Force Base, Fla.: CENTCOM, 1997), pp. 36–37.

25. U.S. National Defense University (NDU), Institute for National Security Studies (INSS), *Strategic Assessment 1998* (Washington, D.C.: NDU/INSS, 1998), electronic document accessed at http://www.ndu.edu/inss/sa98ch4.html on August 9, 1999.

26. Richard F. Grimmett, *Conventional Arms Transfers to Developing Nations, 1990–1997,* CRS Report to Congress (Washington, D.C.: Library of Congress, Congressional Research Service, July 31, 1998), pp. 46, 51. For background on U.S. arms sales to the Persian Gulf countries, see Cordesman, *U.S. Forces in the Middle East,* pp. 68–81; William D. Hartung, *And Weapons for All* (New York: HarperCollins, 1994), pp. 198–221.

27. See Wade Boese, "U.A.E. to Receive 80 F-16s with Features More Advanced Than Similar U.S. Jets," *Arms Control Today,* April 2000, p. 28.

28. See "UAE F-16 Sale Part of Larger U.S. Strategy: U.S. to Use New UAE Base for Pre-Positioning," *Arms Trade News,* Council for a Livable World, November 1999, electronic document accessed at http://www.clw.org/cat/atn11999.html on August 7, 2000.

29. Cited in Luke Warren, "More Than Meets the Eye: F-16 Sale Precursor to Establishing U.S. Bases in UAE," *Arms Trade Insider,* no. 29, March 29, 2000, electronic document accessed at http://www.clw.org/cat/insider29.html on August 7, 2000.

30. For an authoritative statement of the "dual containment" policy, see Anthony Lake, "Containing Backlash States," *Foreign Affairs,* vol. 73, no. 2 (March–April 1994), pp. 45–55. (Lake was then the assistant to the president for national security affairs.) For a more recent articulation of this policy, see Martin S. Indyk, "U.S. Policy Toward the Middle East," testimony before the House International Relations Committee, June 8, 1999, as published in *U.S. Department of State Dispatch,* July 1999, pp. 9–16.

31. Television address by President Clinton on December 16, 1998, as published in *New York Times,* December 17, 1998.

32. Remarks by Samuel Berger at the National Press Club, Washington, D.C., December 23, 1998, electronic document accessed at http://www.pub.whitehouse.gov on March 3, 1999. For analysis of U.S. policy toward Iraq, see Zalmay Khalilzad, "The United States and the Persian Gulf: Preventing Regional Hegemony," *Survival,* vol. 37, no. 2 (Summer 1995), pp. 95–120.

33. Peay, "Promoting Peace and Stability in the Central Region," March 17, 1997.

34. See "Iraq Weapons of Mass Destruction Programs," U.S. Government White Paper, February 13, 1998, electronic document accessed at http://www.state.gov/www/regions/nea/iraq_white_paper.html on August 3, 2000. See also the testimony of George J. Tenet, director of central intelligence, before the Senate Armed Services Committee, February 2, 1999, electronic document accessed at http://www.odci.gov/cia on February 11, 1999.

35. For background on these activities, see the congressional testimony of Generals Peay and Zinni, as cited above. See also Cordesman, *U.S. Forces in the Middle East.*

36. Zinni, statement before Senate Armed Services Committee, February 29, 2000.

37. See Steven Lee Myers, "U.S. Presses Air Attacks on Iraq in Low-Level War of Attrition,"*New York Times,* February 3, 1999; Myers, "In Intense but Little-Noticed Fight, Allies Have Bombed Iraq All Year," *New York Times,* August 13, 1999.

38. Berger, remarks at National Press Club, December 23, 1998.

39. Zinni, statement before Senate Armed Services Committee, April 13, 1999.

40. Myers, "Intense but Little-Noticed Fight."

41. "The final component of [the U.S.] military capability [in the Gulf] is having an operational plan for using all of these forces," then Secretary of Defense William Perry told the Council on Foreign Relations in 1995. "We do have such a plan, and it does not just sit on the shelf gathering dust. We war-game it, we exercise it, and we modify it to meet challenging circumstances." William J. Perry, "Working with Gulf Allies to Contain Iraq and Iran," remarks to the Council on Foreign Relations, New York City, May 18, 1995, electronic document accessed at http://www.defenselink.mil/speeches/1995/s1995051-perry.html on August 3, 2000. For background on U.S. exercises in the Gulf, see CENTCOM, *1997 Posture Statement,* pp. 6, 8, 34–36. See also Zinni, statement before Senate Armed Services Committee, February 29, 2000.

42. Zinni, statement before Senate Armed Services Committee, April 13, 1999.

43. Ibid. For a comprehensive assessment of Iranian military capabilities, see Anthony H. Cordesman, "Iranian Military Capabilities and 'Dual Containment,' " in Sick and Potter, eds., *The Persian Gulf at the Millennium,* pp. 189–230. See also Khalilzad, "The United States and the Persian Gulf," pp. 99–104.

44. DoE/EIA, "World Oil Transit Chokepoints," August 1999.

45. "Iranian military leaders have described Iran's strategy in the event of a U.S. attack as being to block shipping through the Strait of Hormuz. While it might seem irrational for Iran to impede shipping through a strait vital to itself, that is in fact exactly what it tried to do in the 'tanker war' of 1987–88, during the Iran-Iraq war." NDU/INSS, *Strategic Assessment 1998.*

46. U.S. Department of Energy, EIA, "Iran," Country Analysis Brief, April 22, 1997, electronic communication accessed at http://www.eia.doe.gov/emeu/cabs/iran.html on April 22, 1997. For background on this dispute, see Richard N. Schofield, "Border Disputes in the Gulf: Past, Present, and Future," in Sick and Potter, eds., *The Persian Gulf at the Millennium,* pp. 142–56.

47. For background and discussion, see James Bruce, "Choking the Strait," *Jane's Intelligence Review,* September 1996, pp. 411–14.

48. As noted by W. Seth Carus of the NDU, "The United States currently has sufficient military forces in the region to counter virtually any move taken by the Iranians." Moreover, with ongoing economic problems and a growing population that must be housed and fed, "Iran lacks the resources to acquire a modern military capable of competing with the United States" in the foreseeable future. See Carus, "Iran as a Military Threat," National Defense University, Institute of National Security Studies, Strategic Forum No. 113, May 1997.

49. See Cordesman, "Iranian Military Capabilities and 'Dual Containment,' " pp. 206–11; Khalilzad, "The United States and the Persian Gulf," pp. 104–06.

50. On Iran's nuclear capabilities, see Cordesman, "Iranian Military Capabilities and 'Dual Containment,' " pp. 211–15. See also Rodney W. Jones, et al., *Tracking Nuclear Proliferation* (Washington, D.C.: Carnegie Endowment for International Peace, 1998), pp. 169–86.

51. See, for example, Douglas Jehl, "On Trip to Mend Ties, Iran's President Meets Saudi Prince," *New York Times,* May 17, 1999; Alessandra Stanley, "Iran's Leader Welcomed in Italy; Main Topic Is Business," *New York Times,* March 10, 1999. For discussion, see Eric Hooglund, "Khatami's Iran," *Current History,* vol. 98, no. 625 (February 1999), pp. 59–64; Gary Sick, "Rethinking Dual Containment," *Survival,* vol. 40, no. 1 (Spring 1998), pp. 5–32.

52. Address at the Asia Society, New York City, June 17, 1998, as published in *U.S. Department of State Dispatch,* July 1998, p. 8.

53. Peay, "Promoting Peace and Stability in the Central Region," March 17, 1997.

54. This historic relationship was cited by Defense Secretary Richard Cheney in 1990 as a key factor in the U.S. decision to intervene in the Gulf: "We do, of course, have historic ties to governments in the region, that hark back with respect to Saudi Arabia to 1945, when President Roosevelt met with King Abdul-Aziz on the U.S.S. *Quincy,* toward the end of World War II, and affirmed at that time that the United States had a lasting and a continuing interest in the security of the Kingdom." There never has been any doubt, moreover, about the reasons for this commitment: "We obviously also have a significant interest because of the energy that is at stake in the Gulf," Cheney affirmed. "Within a couple of hundred miles of the border of Kuwait, in the eastern province of Saudi Arabia, reside . . . 24 or 25 percent of the world's known reserves." Senate, Armed Services Committee, *Crisis in the Persian Gulf Region,* p. 10.

55. For background and discussion, see U.S. Congress, House, Committee on International Relations, *U.S. Policy in the Persian Gulf,* Hearing, 104th Congress, 2nd session 1996. See especially the prepared statements by F. Gregory Gause III and Judith S. Yaphe. See also Khalilzad, "The United States and the Persian Gulf," pp. 109–11.

56. See Youssef M. Ibrahim, "Saudi Rebels Are Main Suspects in June Bombing of a U.S. Base," *New York Times,* August 15, 1996. For background and discussion, see Anthony H. Cordesman, *Transnational Threats from the Middle East: Crying Wolf or Crying Havoc?* (Carlisle, Pa.: U.S. Army War College, Strategic Studies Institute, 1999), chapter 5.

57. For discussion, see prepared statement by Judith S. Yaphe of the Institute for National Security Studies before the House Committee on International Relations in *U.S. Policy in the Persian Gulf,* pp. 58–72. See also Edward Cody, "Saudi Islamic Radicals Target U.S., Royal Family," *Washington Post,* August 15, 1986;

Douglas Jehl, "Saudis' Heartland Is Seething with Rage at Rulers and U.S.," *New York Times,* November 5, 1996.

58. See, for example, Youssef M. Ibrahim, "Saudis Crack Down on a Dissident Islamic Group," *New York Times,* May 14, 1993; Ibrahim, "Saudi Arabia Arrests 110 in a Crackdown on Muslim Militants," *New York Times,* September 28, 1994.

59. Opposition to the regime has also come from Saudi Arabia's Shiite minority, most of whose members live in the kingdom's oil-rich Eastern Province. Long subjected to discrimination by the Sunni rulers of Saudi Arabia, the Shiites have rebelled periodically against central government control. Following the recent outbreak, in 1996, the government arrested scores of dissidents said to be members of a little-known opposition group known as the Saudi Hezbollah. See Douglas Jehl, "Saudis Crack Down on an Obscure Shiite Militant Group," *New York Times,* October 31, 1996.

60. Quoted in Jehl, "Saudis' Heartland Is Seething with Rage."

61. For discussion of these points, see the prepared statement by Judith S. Yaphe in *U.S. Policy in the Persian Gulf.* See also F. Gregory Gause III, "The Political Economy of National Security in the GCC States," in Sick and Potter, eds., *The Persian Gulf at the Millennium,* pp. 61–84; Andrew Rathmell, "Saudi Arabia Faces More Turbulent Times," *Jane's Intelligence Review,* April 1996, pp. 163–66.

62. CENTCOM, *1997 Posture Statement,* pp. 15–16.

63. For background and discussion, see Hartung, *And Weapons for All,* pp. 213–15.

64. ACA, "ACA Register of U.S. Arms Transfers," May 1997.

65. A key task of CENTCOM personnel is to establish cooperative intelligence-sharing arrangements with Saudi Arabia and other GCC countries. "The Command has implemented intelligence-sharing agreements with key partners in the region. These agreements enhance mutual security through exploitation of unique capabilities to gather, analyze, and disseminate timely intelligence. The Command's access to national [intelligence] resources, including space-based platforms, can augment human intelligence sources available to our partners to provide appropriate indications and warnings of attack." CENTCOM, *1997 Posture Statement,* p. 23.

66. See Seymour Hersh, "The Missiles of August," *The New Yorker,* October 12, 1998, pp. 34–41. See also Tim Weiner and James Risen, "Decision to Strike Factory in Sudan Based on Surmise," *New York Times,* September 21, 1998.

67. From a White House press conference on October 1, 1981, as published in *New York Times,* October 2, 1981.

68. For background, see Munira A. Fakhro, "The Uprising in Bahrain: An Assessment," in Sick and Potter, eds., *The Persian Gulf at the Millennium,* pp. 167–88. See also Andrew Rathmell, "Threats to the Gulf, Part II," *Jane's Intelligence Review,* April 1995, p. 182.

69. See "On Dubious Trial," *Economist,* March 8, 1997, pp. 48–49.

70. See Rathmell, "Threats to the Gulf, Part II," pp. 182–83.

71. For a summary of these, see Schofield, "Border Disputes in the Gulf," pp. 127–66.

72. For discussion, see Andrew Rathmell, "Threats to the Gulf, Part I," *Jane's Intelligence Review,* March 1995, pp. 129–31.

73. See Schofield, "Border Disputes in the Gulf," pp. 141–42.

74. Peay, "Promoting Peace and Stability in the Central Region," March 17, 1997.

4: ENERGY CONFLICT IN THE CASPIAN SEA BASIN

1. See "Chaos in the Caucasus," *Economist,* October 9, 1999, pp. 23–26; Stephen Kinzer, "Islamic Militants with Japanese Hostages Hold Kyrgyz at Bay," *New York Times,* October 18, 1999; Hugh Pope, "Central Asian Crisis Forges Tenuous Cooperation," *Wall Street Journal,* September 8, 1999.

2. See "Central Asia: Border Trouble," *Economist,* February 19, 2000, p. 43.

3. See Pope, "Central Asian Crisis Forges Tenuous Cooperation"; Stephen Kinzer, "A New Big-Power Race Starts on a Sea of Crude," *New York Times,* January 24, 1999; "Racing for Arms," *Economist,* June 5, 1999, p. 50; "Wooed but Not Wowed," *Economist,* April 22, 2000, p. 38.

4. Daniel Yergin and Thane Gustafson, "Evolution of an Oil Rush," *New York Times,* August 6, 1997.

5. De Charrette visited Baku in October 1996 to sign a multibillion dollar agreement for oil exploration and production by French companies in Azerbaijan's offshore waters. See "Elf Signs Oil Exploration Deal with Azerbaijan," Reuters, January 14, 1997, electronic communication accessed at http://beta.individual.com/1stbin on March 12, 1997.

6. For background and discussion, see Rosemarie Forsythe, *The Politics of Oil in the Caucasus and Central Asia,* Adelphi Paper no. 300 (Oxford: Oxford University Press and the International Institute for Strategic Studies, 1996).

7. Ibid., pp. 13–21. See also Kinzer, "A New Big-Power Race." For the perspective of American officials on this rivalry, see U.S. Senate, Committee on Foreign Relations, Subcommittee on International Economic Policy, Export and Trade Promotion, *U.S. Economic and Strategic Interests in the Caspian Sea Region: Policies and Implications,* Hearing, 105th Congress, 1st session, October 23, 1997 (Washington, D.C.: U.S. Government Printing Office, 1998). (Hereinafter cited as SFRC, *U.S. Economic and Strategic Interests in the Caspian Sea Region.*) For a Russian perspective, see Andrei Y. Urnov, "Russian and Caspian Energy Prospects," Address at Central Asia–Caucasus Institute, Johns Hopkins University, Washington, D.C., May 17, 2000, electronic document accessed at http://www.cacianalyst.org/ForumSummaries/May 17Urnov.htm on August 7, 2000.

8. For background and discussion, see Svante E. Cornell, "The Unruly Caucasus," *Current History,* October 1997, pp. 341–47; Gail W. Lapidus, "Conflict

Resolution in the Caucasus," in Aspen Institute, *U.S. Relations with the Former Soviet States,* 23rd Conference, April 17–21, 1998 (Washington, D.C.: Aspen Institute, 1998), pp. 23–30; Pope, "Central Asian Crisis Forges Tenuous Cooperation"; Rajan Menon, "In the Shadow of the Bear," *International Security,* vol. 20, no. 1 (Summer 1995), pp. 149–81; Diane L. Smith, *Breaking Away from the Bear* (Carlisle, Pa.: U.S. Army War College, 1998).

9. For background and discussion, see Martha Brill Olcott, "The Caspian's False Promise," *Foreign Policy,* Summer 1998, pp. 95–113; Forsythe, *The Politics of Oil,* pp. 21–28, 32–36; Lapidus, "Conflict Resolution in the Caucasus"; Menon, "In the Shadow of the Bear."

10. From his testimony before the Senate Foreign Relations Committee, in SFRC, *U.S. Economic and Strategic Interests in the Caspian Sea Region,* p. 13.

11. Olcott, "The Caspian's False Promise," p. 96.

12. U.S. Department of State, *Caspian Region Energy Development Report,* p. 1.

13. U.S. Department of Energy, Energy Information Administration (DoE/EIA), "Caspian Sea Region," June 2000, electronic document accessed at http://www.eia.doe.gov/emeu/cabs/caspfull.html on August 7, 2000. (Hereinafter cited as DoE/EIA, "Caspian Sea Region, 2000.")

14. For a less optimistic appraisal of the Caspian's reserves, see Hugh Pope, "Scramble for Oil in Central Asia Hits Roadblocks," *Wall Street Journal,* March 13, 1998. See also Christopher Cooper and Hugh Pope, "Dry Wells Belie Hope for Big Caspian Reserves," *Wall Street Journal,* October 12, 1998.

15. SFRC, *U.S. Economic and Strategic Interests in the Caspian Sea Region,* p. 13.

16. DoE/EIA, "Caspian Sea Region," December 1998, electronic document accessed at http://www.eia.doe.gov/emeu/cabs/caspian.html on January 4, 1999.

17. DoE/EIA, *IEO 1999,* Table D1, p. 201.

18. DoE/EIA, "Caspian Sea Region, 2000."

19. For discussion and details, see Frank C. Alexander Jr., "Caspian Reserves Luring Operators," *Oil and Gas Journal,* July 21, 1997, electronic document accessed at http://www.ogjonline.com on November 20, 1997. See also DoE/EIA, "Caspian Sea Region, 2000"; Forsythe, *The Politics of Oil,* pp. 37–43.

20. For background on the Tengiz project and CPC, see U.S. Department of Energy, Energy Information Agency (DoE/EIA), "Kazakhstan," Country Analysis Brief, April 2000, electronic document accessed at http://www.eia.doe.gov/emeu/cabs/kazakfull.html on April 19, 2000. (Hereinafter cited as DoE/EIA, "Kazakhstan 2000.") See also Forsythe, *The Politics of Oil,* pp. 37–39, 49–52; Michael R. Gordon, "Oil Pipeline Agreed on for Caspian Area," *New York Times,* November 25, 1998; Dan Morgan and David B. Ottaway, "Vast Kazakh Field Stirs U.S.-Russian Rivalry," *Washington Post,* October 6, 1998.

21. See U.S. Department of Energy, Energy Information Administration (DoE/EIA), "Azerbaijan," Country Analysis Brief, May 2000, electronic document accessed at http://www.eia.doe.gov/emeu/cabs/azerbjan.html on May 8, 2000.

(Hereinafter cited as DoE/EIA, "Azerbaijan 2000.") See also: DoE/EIA, "Caspian Region 2000"; Forsythe, *The Politics of Oil,* pp. 39–41; Morgan and Ottaway, "Americans Moved Early."

22. DoE/EIA, "Azerbaijan 2000." On the Kashagan field and OKIOC, see DoE/EIA, "Kazakhstan 2000"; David B. Ottaway, "Vast Caspian Oil Field Found," *Washington Post,* May 16, 2000.

23. For discussion, see Forsythe, *The Politics of Oil,* pp. 34–36; Nancy Lubin, "Pipe Dreams," *Harvard International Review,* Winter–Spring 2000, pp. 66–69; Tyler Marshall, "The New Oil Rush: Tapping Into This Fortune Isn't for the Fainthearted," *Los Angeles Times,* February 25, 1998. See also DoE/EIA, "Caspian Sea Region 2000."

24. For an American perspective on this contest, see the testimony and discussion in SFRC, *U.S. Economic and Strategic Interests in the Caspian Sea Region.* For a Russian perspective, see Sergo A. Mikoyan, "Russia, the U.S., and Regional Conflict in Eurasia," *Survival,* vol. 40, no. 3 (Autumn 1998), pp. 112–26; Urnov, "Russian and Caspian Energy Export Prospects."

25. See Forsythe, *The Politics of Oil,* p. 6; Pope, "Great Game II." See also P. Pavilionis and R. Giragosian, "The Great Game: Pipeline Politics in Central Asia," *Harvard International Review,* Winter 1996–97, pp. 24–27, 62–65.

26. Pope, "Great Game II."

27. Quoted in "Yeltsin Asserts Rights in Caucasus," *Washington Times,* August 21, 1997.

28. Urnov, "Russian and Caspian Energy Prospects."

29. As quoted in Dan Morgan and David Ottaway, "Drilling for Influence in Russia's Back Yard," *Washington Post,* September 22, 1997. Heslin was testifying before a Senate investigation of political donations to the 1996 Democratic presidential campaign, in this case focused on contributions by oil finacier Roger Tamraz. In separate testimony, Tamraz admitted that he gave $300,000 to Democratic causes in order to gain access to the White House so as to promote his plan for a pipeline to carry Caspian oil through Azerbaijan and Turkey.

30. For discussion of Russian objectives in the Caspian area, see Pavel Baev, *Russia's Policies in the Caucasus* (London: Royal Institute of International Affairs, 1997), pp. 30–36; Forsythe, *The Politics of Oil,* pp. 13–17; Menon, "In the Shadow of the Bear," pp. 156–61; Urnov, "Russian and Caspian Energy Export Prospects"; Irina Zviagelskaia, *The Russian Policy Debate on Central Asia* (London: Royal Institute of International Affairs, 1995), pp. 22–28.

31. For discussion of American objectives in the Caspian area, see Forsythe, *The Politics of Oil,* pp. 17–21. See also Stephen J. Blank, *U.S. Military Engagement with Transcaucasia and Central Asia* (Carlisle, Pa.: U.S. Army War College, 2000). For a more recent statement of U.S. policy, see the statement of John S. Wolf, special adviser to the president and secretary of state for Caspian basin energy diplomacy, before the Senate Foreign Relations Committee on April 12, 2000,

electronic text accessed at http://usinfo.state.gov/regional/nea/mena/casp0412.htm on August 4, 2000.

32. Quoted in Stephen Kinzer, "On Piping Out Caspian Oil, U.S. Insists the Cheaper, Shorter Way Isn't Better," *New York Times,* November 8, 1998.

33. For discussion, see Jonathan Cohen, "Peace Postponed," *Transitions,* July 1998, pp. 66–73; Robert D. Kaplan, "Why Russia Risks All in Dagestan," *New York Times,* August 17, 1999; Stephen Kinzer, "A Defiant Satellite, Georgia Finds Paternalistic Russia's Orbit Inescapable," *New York Times,* May 3, 1998.

34. See Peter Baker, "Clinton Courts Head of Oil-Rich Azerbaijan," *Washington Post,* August 2, 1997; David B. Ottaway and Dan Morgan, "Drilling for Influence in Russia's Back Yard," *Washington Post,* September 22, 1997; Hugh Pope, "U.S. Shows Support for Caspian Sea Oil Projects," *Wall Street Journal,* May 28, 1998; David E. Sanger, "Oilfields in Mind, White House Woos Turkmenistan's Chief," *New York Times,* April 24, 1998.

35. Urnov, "Russian and Caspian Energy Export Prospects."

36. International Institute for Strategic Studies (IISS), *The Military Balance 1999–2000* (London: IISS and Oxford University Press, 1999), pp. 112–88.

37. For example, the North Caucasus M.D. has been given priority in the establishment of "permanent readiness units," that is, formations with at least 80 percent of their full troop strength and 100 percent of their weapons and equipment. Ibid., p. 105.

38. See Celestine Bohlen, "New Russian Premier Has Plan to Quell Rebellion," *New York Times,* August 11, 1999; Bohlen, "In a Busy Start, New Russian Leader Goes to Chechnya," *New York Times,* January 2, 2000.

39. IISS, *The Military Balance 1999–2000,* pp. 108, 117. Under the terms of a revision of the CFE signed in November 1999, under the auspices of the Organization for Security and Cooperation in Europe (OSCE), Russia will close two of its bases in Georgia by 2001 and reduce its total troop strength there. See Michael R. Gordon, "Russia to Cut Its Military Forces in Georgia," *New York Times,* November 24, 1999.

40. For discussion, see Pavel K. Baev, *Challenges and Options in the Caucasus and Central Asia* (Carlisle, Pa.: U.S. Army War College, Strategic Studies Institute, April 22, 1997), pp. 6–8; Baev, *Russia's Policies in the Caucasus,* pp. 23–29; Smith, *Breaking Away from the Bear;* Jed D. Snyder, "Russian Security Interests on the Southern Periphery," *Jane's Intelligence Review,* December 1994, pp. 548–51; Zviagelskaia, *The Russian Policy Debate on Central Asia,* pp. 29–34.

41. See Menon, "In the Shadow of the Bear," p. 174; Smith, *Breaking Away from the Bear,* pp. 28–33.

42. See Steve Liesman, "Kazakhstan Agrees to Combine Its Army in Part with Russia's," *Wall Street Journal,* January 25, 1995; Smith, *Breaking Away from the Bear,* pp. 19–28; Richard Woff, "Kazakh-Russian Relations—an Update," *Jane's Intelligence Review,* December 1995, pp. 567–68.

43. Richard Woff, "Russia Strengthens Ties with Georgia and Armenia," *Jane's Intelligence Review,* July 1995, p. 294.

44. IISS, *The Military Balance 1999–2000,* p. 108.

45. Ibid., p. 106.

46. Ibid., p. 115.

47. Ibid., pp. 158, 168. Additional data from 1998–1999 edition.

48. "We have been very successful in encouraging high-level visits to and from the region," Under Secretary Eizenstat told Congress in October 1997. "Georgian President Shevardnadze, Azerbaijani President Aliyev, and Kyrgyz President Akayev visited Washington this summer [and] Kazakhstani President Nazarbayev will visit Washington in November. . . . The First Lady will visit Kazakhstan, Kyrgyzstan, and Uzebekistan in November; our new Ambassador-at-Large to the NIS [newly independent states] Steve Sestanovich will be traveling to Central Asia and the Caucasus next week; Energy Secretary Frederico Pena hopes to travel to Baku and Ashgabat in early November." Prepared statement of Eizenstat in SFRC, *U.S. Economic and Strategic Interests in the Caspian Sea Region,* p. 16. On Vice President Gore's ties to Caspian leaders, see Laurie Lande, "Gore Gets a Mouthful of Foreign-Policy Expertise with Turkmenistan, Kazakhstan and Azerbaijan," *Wall Street Journal,* April 22, 1998.

49. The White House, Office of the Press Secretary, "Joint Statement on U.S.-Kazakhstan Relations," November 18, 1997, electronic document accessed at http://www.whitehouse.gov on November 28, 1997.

50. During a 1999 meeting with senior military officials of Georgia, for instance, U.S. Secretary of Defense William S. Cohen discussed U.S. efforts to help the Georgians "reorient their armed forces towards more mobile militaries." U.S. Department of Defense (DoD), "Secdef's Trip to Asia, Ukraine, and Georgia," background briefing, July 21, 1999, electronic document accessed at http://www. defenselink.mil/news on July 26, 1999.

51. U.S. Department of State, *Congressional Presentation for Foreign Operations, Fiscal Year 2000* (Washington, D.C.: Department of State, 1999). (Hereinafter cited as DoS, *CPD-FY2000.*)

52. Ibid., pp. 656–59.

53. See U.S. Department of Defense, "DoD News Briefing," Joint Press Conference with Secretary of Defense William S. Cohen and Georgian President Eduard Shevardnadze, Tbilisi, Georgia, August 1, 1999, electronic document accessed at http://www.defenselink.mil/news on November 18, 1999.

54. As cited in ibid.

55. See sections on these countries in DoS, *CPD-FY2000,* pp. 649–51, 660–64. See also Blank, *U.S. Military Engagement with Transcaucasia and Central Asia,* pp. 23–26.

56. The Azeri blockade was imposed in retaliation for Armenian support for Armenian separatists in Nagorno-Karabakh, a largely Armenian enclave in Azer-

baijan that declared its independence in 1991. The U.S. ban on aid to Azerbaijan is incorporated into Section 907 of the Freedom Support Act. The Clinton administration has waged a vigorous lobbying effort to persuade Congress to repeal this section. See testimony by Under Secretary of State Stuart Eizenstat in SFRC, *U.S. Economic and Strategic Interests in the Caspian Sea Region,* pp. 12, 16, 19.

57. See U.S. Department of Defense, "U.S. and the Republic of Azerbaijan Sign WMD Counterproliferation Agreement," news release, October 6, 1999, electronic document accessed at http://www.defenselink.mil/news on November 18, 1999. See also U.S. Department of Defense, "Exercise CENTRAZBAT '98: Soldiers from the 10th Mountain Division Intermingle with Their Foreign Counterparts," news photo, electronic document accessed at http://www.defenselink.mil:80/news on November 18, 1999.

58. See Cornell, "The Unruly Caucasus," p. 343.

59. U.S. Department of Defense, "U.S., Kazakhstan Increase Military Ties," news article, November 1997, electronic document accessed at http://www.defenselink.mil/news on November 18, 1999. On the *Dauntless,* see IISS, *The Military Balance 1999–2000,* p. 158.

60. See Clive Schofield and Martin Pratt, "Claims to the Caspian Sea," *Jane's Intelligence Review,* February 1996, pp. 75–79; DoE/EIA, "Caspian Sea Region 2000."

61. For background and discussion, see Forsythe, *The Politics of Oil,* pp. 29–31; Elaine Holoboff, "Russia and Oil Politics in the Caspian." *Jane's Intelligence Review,* February 1996, pp. 80–84.

62. See Elaine Sciolino, "It's a Sea! It's a Lake! No. It's a Pool of Oil," *New York Times,* June 21, 1998.

63. Recently, there have been some signs of Russian flexibility on this issue; see DoE/EIA, "Caspian Sea Region 2000."

64. See U.S. Department of Energy, Energy Information Administration, "Turkmenistan," Country Analysis Brief, September 1999, electronic document accessed at http://www.eia.doe.gov/emeu/cabs/turkmen.html on November 8, 1999.

65. Ibid.

66. For a comprehensive survey of these impediments, see John Roberts, *Caspian Pipelines* (London: Royal Institute of International Affairs, 1996). See also Forsythe, *The Politics of Oil,* pp. 44–54; Pavilionis and Giragosian, "The Great Game."

67. DoE/EIA, "Caspian Sea Region 2000"; Ottaway and Morgan, "U.S. Backs Non-Iranian, 'Eurasian' Corridor." U.S. opposition to a pipeline across Iran was reiterated by John S. Wolf in his statement to the Senate Foreign Relations Committee of April 12, 2000. (See note 31.)

68. For discussion, see Kaplan, "Why Russia Risks All in Dagestan"; Jean Radvanyi, "Moscow's Designs on Chechnya," *Le Monde Diplomatique,* November 1999, English-language edition, accessed at http://www.monde-diplomatique.fr/en on November 15, 1999; Roberts, *Caspian Pipelines,* pp. 8–9, 20–32; Michael Wines,

"In Remote Dagestan, Moscow Wages a High-Stakes War," *New York Times,* September 19, 1999.

69. For discussion, see Cohen, "Peace Postponed"; Lapidus, "Conflict Resolution in the Caucasus."

70. Energy Secretary Bill Richardson, press briefing on Caspian basin policy, Istanbul, Turkey, November 18, 1999, electronic document accessed at http://usinfo.state.gov/regional/nea/mena/caspia19.htm on August 4, 2000.

71. For background, see Ambassador Richard Morningstar, special adviser to the president and secretary of state for Caspian basin energy diplomacy, Address to the CERA Conference, Washington, D.C., December 7, 1998, electronic document accessed at http://www.state.gov/www/policy_remarks/1998/981207_mrngstar_ceraconf.html on August 4, 2000. See also "Fact Sheet: Caspian Energy Pipelines," White House Fact Sheet, November 17, 1999, electronic document accessed at http://usinfo.state.gov/regional/nea/mena/caspia 18.htm on August 4, 2000.

72. Richardson, press briefing on Caspian basin policy, November 18, 1999. See also Stephen Kinzer, "Caspian Lands Back a Pipeline Pushed by West," *New York Times,* November 19, 1999.

73. See Stephen Kinzer, "Oil Pipelines from Caspian Lack Money from Backers," *New York Times,* November 28, 1998; Kinzer, "U.S. Bid to Build Caspian Pipeline Appears to Fail," *New York Times,* October 11, 1998; "Oil out of Troubled Waters," *Economist,* November 28, 1998, p. 50.

74. See Stephen Kinzer, "Crackdown on Rebels Renews Fears of War and Terror in Turkey's Kurdish Region," *New York Times,* February 25, 2000.

75. Hugh Pope, "Unocal Group Plans Central Asian Pipeline," *Wall Street Journal,* October 27, 1997.

76. DoE/EIA, "Turkmenistan," September 1999.

77. See "China Fears for Its Wild West," *Economist,* November 15, 1997, p. 40; Liz Sly, "China's 'Chechnya': A Powder Keg of Mistrust, Hatred," *Boston Globe,* October 19, 1999.

78. See DoE/EIA, "Caspian Sea Region," December 1998; DoE/EIA, "Kazakhstan," January 1999; "Pipeline Poker," *Economist,* Central Asian Survey, February 7, 1998, pp. 7–11.

79. For background and discussion, see Cornell, "The Unruly Caucasus"; Forsythe, *The Politics of Oil,* pp. 32–33; Lapidus, "Conflict Resolution in the Caucasus"; Rajan Menon, "American Interests in Central Asia," in Aspen Institute, *U.S. Relations with the Former Soviet States,* 1998, pp. 31–36.

80. This term was used by Central Asian expert Shirin Akiner in a reference to the government of Kazakhstan. Quoted in Hugh Pope, "Kazakhstan Weathers Worst of Turmoil," *Wall Street Journal,* January 8, 1999.

81. Most of these regimes "practice a repressive, autocratic style of political rule with symbolic elections, few true political parties, and no succession mechanisms. With some variations, these are leader-dominated systems with few oppor-

tunities for citizen voices to be heard and little tolerance for opposition or political critics." Sylvia Babus and Judith Yaphe, "U.S.–Central Asian Security," *Strategic Forum,* National Defense University, Institute for National Security Studies, no. 153, January 1999, p. 1. For background on the 1998–99 elections in Azerbaijan and Kazakhstan, see "After the Landslide," *Economist,* January 16, 1999; "Aliev and Son," *Economist,* March 6, 1999; Nair Aliev and Shahin Abbasov, "Little Choice, Little Change," *Transitions,* August 1998, pp. 57–61; Pope, "Kazakhstan Weathers Worst of Turmoil."

82. For discussion, see Anthony Hyman, "The Feeble Breath of Democracy," *Transitions,* September 1998, pp. 78–81; Stephen Kinzer, "In Post-Soviet Era, the Old Style Works," *New York Times,* September 21, 1997; Steve LeVine, "Democracy? Sure, Sure. But Now Buy Our Oil," *New York Times,* January 3, 1999; Menon, "American Interests in Central Asia"; Hugh Pope, "Autocracy Is Spreading in Former Soviet States," *Wall Street Journal,* October 14, 1998.

83. For discussion, see "The Crusade Against the Wahhabis," *Economist,* July 4, 1998, pp. 36–37; Olcott, "The Caspian's False Promise," pp. 102–10; Menon, "American Interests in Central Asia," pp. 34–35; Menon, "In the Shadow of the Bear," pp. 162–68.

84. See "Bombs Kill 13 at Uzbekistan Government Offices," *New York Times,* February, 1999; "Chaos in the Caucasus"; "Emergency Declared in Kyrgyzstan," BBC World News, August 26, 1999, electronic document accessed at http://news.bbc.co.uk/hi/english/world on August 26, 1999; Michael R. Gordon, "Caucasus Rebels Press Offensive, Seizing Six Villages," *New York Times,* September 7, 1999; "Worries About Islam," *Economist,* February 21, 1998, p. 40.

85. For discussion, see Cornell, "The Unruly Caucasus"; Lapidus, "Conflict Resolution in the Caucasus"; Menon, "In the Shadow of the Bear," pp. 150–56.

86. "In all four [major separatist] conflicts [in the Caucasus] the current cease-fires are largely the result of the exhaustion of the combatants rather than of successful mediation efforts; the conflicts remain essentially frozen, without any political resolution, and could well flare up again in the future." Lapidus, "Conflict Resolution in the Caucasus," p. 26.

87. For discussion, see Stephen Kinzer, "Riches May Roil Caspian Nations," *New York Times,* February 17, 1998; Steve LeVine, "Instability by the Barrelful?" *New York Times,* February 17, 1998; "Ruinous Riches?" *Economist,* Central Asian Survey, February 7, 1998, p. 3.

88. Olcott, "The Caspian's False Promise," p. 107.

5: OIL WARS IN THE SOUTH CHINA SEA

1. For background data and analysis, see U.S. Department of Energy, Energy Information Administration (DoE/EIA), "East Asia: The Energy Situation," July 1998, electronic document accessed at http://www.eia.doe.gov/emeu/cabs/eastasia.html on August 4, 1998. (Hereinafter cited as DoE/EIA, "East Asia Energy 1998.") See also the updated version of this document, DoE/EIA, "East Asia: The

Energy Situation," August 1999, electronic document accessed at http://www.
eia.doe.gov/emeu/cabs/eastasia.html on August 27, 1999. (Hereinafter cited as
DoE/EIA, "East Asia Energy 1999.") For additional economic analysis, see Ed-
uardo Lachica, "Pacific Rim Appears on Way to Recovery," *Wall Street Journal,*
July 9, 1999; "Asia's Economies: On Their Feet Again?" *Economist,* August 21,
1999, pp. 16–18.

2. DoE/EIA, "East Asia Energy 1998."

3. DoE/EIA, *IEO 2000,* Table A1, p. 169.

4. Ibid., Tables A4, A5, pp. 173–74.

5. Ibid., Tables A4, D1, pp. 169, 229.

6. The connection between Asia's growing energy needs and the struggle for
control of the South China Sea is addressed in a number of important books and
articles, including: Kent E. Calder, *Pacific Defense* (New York: William Morrow,
1996); Calder, "Asia's Empty Tank"; Calder, "Fueling the Rising Sun," *Harvard
International Review,* Summer 1997, pp. 24–27, 68; Michael Leifer, "Chinese Economic Reform and Security Policy: The South China Sea Connection," *Survival,*
vol. 37, no. 2 (Summer 1995), pp. 44–59; Mark J. Valencia, *China and the South
China Sea Disputes,* Adelphi Paper no. 298 (Oxford: Oxford University Press and
International Institute for Strategic Studies, 1995); and Valencia, "Energy and Insecurity in Asia," *Survival,* vol. 39, no. 3 (Autumn 1997), pp. 85–106.

7. See U.S. Department of Energy, Energy Information Administration,
"South China Sea Region," January 2000, electronic document accessed at http://
www.eia.doe.gov/emeu/cabs/schinafull.html on January 31, 2000. (Hereinafter
cited as DoE/EIA, "South China Sea 2000.")

8. DoE/EIA, *IEO 2000,* Table A1, p. 169.

9. BP Amoco, *Statistical Review of World Energy 2000,* p. 30.

10. U.S. Department of Energy, Energy Information Administration, "China:
An Energy Sector Overview," October 1997, electronic document accessed at http:
//www.eia.doe.gov/emeu/cabs/china/china97.html on April 3, 1998.

11. DoE/EIA, *IEO 2000,* Table A10, p. 179.

12. See "Dirt Poor," *Economist,* March 21, 1998, Development and the Environment Survey, p. 5.

13. According to the China Institute of Aeronautic Systems, increased air
travel in China will generate a requirement for an additional 1,134 jet transports
and 371 turboprop airliners over the next twenty years alone. See "China Demand
Looks Strong," *Aviation Week and Space Technology,* March 16, 1998, p. 13.

14. For discussion, see Calder, "Asia's Empty Tank," pp. 56–58.

15. DoE/EIA, *IEO 2000,* pp. 173–74.

16. BP Amoco, *Statistical Review of World Energy 2000,* pp. 7, 10.

17. DoE/EIA, *IEO 2000,* pp. 173, 229.

18. U.S. Department of Energy, Energy Information Administration, "China,"
Country Analysis Brief, June 1999, electronic document accessed at http://
www.eia.doe.gov/emeu/cabs/china.html on June 2, 1999.

19. Ibid.

20. For a profile of Japan's energy situation, see U.S. Department of Energy, Energy Information Administration, "Japan," Country Analysis Brief, May 2000, electronic communication accessed at http://www.eia.doe.gov/emeu/cabs/japan.html on July 22, 2000.

21. Ibid.

22. U.S. Department of Energy, Energy Information Administration, "Persian Gulf Oil Export Fact Sheet," June 2000, electronic communication accessed at http://www.eia.doe.gov/emeu/cabs/pgulf.html on June 5, 2000.

23. For background and discussion, see John H. Noer, *Chokepoints* (Washington, D.C.: National Defense University Press, 1996), pp. 7–30.

24. BP Amoco, *Statistical Review of World Energy 2000*, p. 10.

25. From the May 1989 issue of the *China Geology Newspaper*, as cited in Leifer, "China's Economic Reform and Security Policy," p. 44.

26. For discussion of the South China Sea's hydrocarbon potential, see DoE/EIA, "South China Sea 2000"; Valencia, *China and the South China Sea Disputes*, pp. 8–11. See also Bruce and Jean Blanche, "Oil and Regional Stability in the South China Sea," *Jane's Intelligence Review*, November 1995, pp. 511–14; Leifer, "Chinese Economic Reform and Security Policy," pp. 44–49.

27. For discussion, see U.S. Institute of Peace (USIP), *The South China Sea Dispute: Prospects for Preventive Diplomacy*, Special Report (Washington, D.C.: USIP, August 1996), pp. 5–9.

28. For discussion of these overlapping claims, see DoE/EIA, "South China Sea 2000"; Valencia, "Energy and Insecurity in Asia," pp. 92–98. See also Henry J. Kenny, "The South China Sea: A Dangerous Ground," *Naval War College Review*, vol. 49, no. 3 (Summer 1996), pp. 96–108.

29. See DoE/EIA, "South China Sea 2000"; Valencia, "Energy and Insecurity in Asia," pp. 92–98.

30. See Michael G. Gallagher, "China's Illusory Threat to the South China Sea," *International Security*, vol. 19, no. 1 (Summer 1994), pp. 171–73.

31. This law empowered China to "adopt all necessary measures to prevent and stop the harmful passage of vessels through its territorial waters," including the South China Sea, and to "order the eviction of foreign military vessels or vessels of foreign governments that violate China's laws in the area." From the *South China Morning Post* of March 8, 1992, as cited in Leszek Buszynski, "ASEAN Security Dilemmas," *Survival*, vol. 34, no. 4 (Winter 1992–93), p. 92.

32. See Mark J. Valencia, "Troubled Waters," *Bulletin of the Atomic Scientists*, January-February 1997, pp. 49–54.

33. Leifer, "Chinese Economic Reform and Security Policy," pp. 51–55. See also USIP, *The South China Sea Disputes*, pp. 7–8.

34. For background, see Kenny, "The South China Sea," pp. 100–01; Valencia, *China and the South China Sea Disputes*, pp. 30–39.

35. See Valencia, *China and the South China Sea Disputes*, pp. 39–42.

36. Ibid., pp. 10–11, 44–48.

37. Ibid., pp. 4–5, 42–44.

38. For background, see DoE/EIA, "South China Sea 2000"; "Treacherous Shoals," *Far Eastern Economic Review,* August 13, 1992, p. 15; Valencia, *China and the South China Sea Disputes,* pp. 8–24.

39. In an earlier clash, occurring in January 1974, China and Vietnam fought for control of the Paracel Islands, a small archipelago in the northwestern quadrant of the South China Sea. In this incident, forty-eight South Vietnamese soldiers plus one American military adviser were captured by the Chinese. Since then, China has established a major military facility on Woody Island, one of the larger features in the group. See "Treacherous Shoals"; Salameh, "China, Oil, and the Risk of Regional Conflict," pp. 143–44.

40. "Treacherous Shoals," p. 15.

41. See Nicholas D. Kristof, "China Signs U.S. Oil Deal for Disputed Waters," *New York Times,* June 18, 1992.

42. Quoted in ibid.

43. Philip Shenon, "China Sends Warships to Vietnam Oil Site," *New York Times,* July 21, 1994. See also Leifer, "Chinese Economic Reform and Security Policy," pp. 51–52; Valencia, "Energy and Insecurity in Asia," pp. 96–97.

44. For discussion, see Valencia, *China and the South China Sea Disputes,* pp. 30–33.

45. For background on the Mischief Reef incident, see Ian Storey, "Manila Looks to USA for Help over Spratlys," *Jane's Intelligence Review,* August 1999, pp. 46–50; Valencia, *China and the South China Sea Disputes,* pp. 44–48. See also William Branigin, "China Takes Over Philippine-Claimed Area of Disputed Island Group," *Washington Post,* February 11, 1995.

46. See Valencia, *China and the South China Sea Disputes,* pp. 29, 44–45.

47. See ibid., pp. 29–30, 45–48. See also Philip Shenon, "Rivals Edgy over Islands on Asia's Rim," *New York Times,* April 5, 1995; Abby Tan, "Spratlys Tussle Eases as China Starts to Talk," *Christian Science Monitor,* August 16, 1995. China reaffirmed its rights to the Spratlys in 1998, saying that Chinese sovereignty is "indisputable." From a foreign ministry statement quoted in "China Says Spratlys Sovereignty 'Indisputable,' " Reuters, August 5, 1998.

48. See "Scraply Islands," *Economist,* May 24, 1997, pp. 39–40; "Reef-Stricken," *Economist,* May 29, 1999, p. 36; Ian Storey, "Manila Looks to USA for Help."

49. See "Scraply Islands."

50. For discussion of China's views regarding the use of force, see Robert A. Manning and James J. Przystup, "China's Syndrome: Ambiguity," *Washington Post,* March 19, 1995. See also USIP, *The South China Sea Dispute,* pp. 7–9.

51. IISS, *The Military Balance 1999–2000,* p. 302.

52. For discussion, see John Downing, "Maritime Ambition: China's Naval

Modernisation," *Jane's Navy International,* April 1998, pp. 10–17; Michael D. Swaine, "Chinese Military Modernization and Asia-Pacific Security," in Aspen Institute, *Congressional Program on U.S.-China Relations,* 2nd conference, March 30–April 4, 1999 (Washington, D.C.: Aspen Institute, 1999), pp. 35–41.

53. See USIP, *The South China Sea Dispute,* pp. 9–15; Valencia, *China and the South China Sea Disputes,* pp. 50–67.

54. For discussion of such a scenario, see Valencia, "Troubled Waters," p. 52.

55. The author first discussed this phenomenon in "The Next Great Arms Race," *Foreign Affairs,* vol. 72, no. 1 (Summer 1993), pp. 136–52. See also "Asia's Arms Race," *Economist,* February 20, 1993, pp. 19–22; Steve Glain, "New Arms Race: Fearing China's Plans and a U.S. Departure, Asians Rebuild Forces," *Wall Street Journal,* November 13, 1997.

56. See Alexander Chieh-cheng Huang, "The Chinese Navy's Offshore Active Defense Strategy," *Naval War College Review,* Summer 1994, pp. 7–32.

57. Quoted in ibid., p. 18.

58. For background, see John Dowling, "China's Evolving Maritime Strategy, Part 1," *Jane's Intelligence Review,* March 1996, pp. 129–33.

59. For details, see Richard Sharpe, ed., *Jane's Fighting Ships, 1997–98* (Coulsdon, Surrey: Jane's Information Group, 1997), pp. 118, 120.

60. Ibid., p. 117.

61. See John Downing, "China's Evolving Maritime Strategy, Part 2," *Jane's Intelligence Review,* April 1996, pp. 186–91; Nicholas D. Kristof, "China Builds Its Military Muscle, Making Some Neighbors Nervous," *New York Times,* January 11, 1993.

62. See Simon Saradzhyan, "China Explores Russian Aircraft Technology Option," *Defense News,* October 4, 1999, p. 34.

63. For discussion, see Buszynski, "ASEAN Security Dilemmas," pp. 90–101.

64. For discussion, see Joris Janssen Lok, "ASEAN Navies Extend Their Regional Reach," *Jane's Defence Weekly,* November 27, 1996, pp. 25–28; Peter Lewis Young, "Full Speed Ahead," *Armed Forces Journal,* December 1997, pp. 22–27.

65. Young, "Full Speed Ahead," pp. 22–23. For details of these vessels, see Sharpe, *Jane's Fighting Ships, 1997–98,* pp. 423–27.

66. Richard Scott, "Thailand Enters the Carrier Class," *Jane's International Defense Review,* April 1996, pp. 53–55.

67. For details, see Sharpe, *Jane's Fighting Ships, 1997–98,* pp. 702–03.

68. Young, "Full Speed Ahead," p. 26. For details, see Sharpe, *Jane's Fighting Ships, 1997–98,* pp. 302–09.

69. Lok, "ASEAN Navies Extend Their Regional Reach"; Young, "Full Speed Ahead." See also Yaacob Hussein, "Corvettes and Offshore Patrol Vessels in Asia," *Asia-Pacific Defence Review,* March 1994, pp. 6–13.

70. See Buszynski, "ASEAN Security Dilemmas"; Glain, "New Arms Race";

Hussein, "Corvettes and Offshore Patrol Vessels"; Lok, "ASEAN Navies Extend Their Regional Reach"; Young, "Full Speed Ahead."

71. For discussion, see "Japan's Constitution: The Call to Arms," *Economist,* February 27, 1999, pp. 23–25; Edward L. Martin, "The Evolving Missions and Forces of the JMSDF," *Naval War College Review,* vol. 48, no. 2 (Spring 1995), pp. 39–67; Stephanie Strom, "Japan Beginning to Flex Its Military Muscles," *New York Times,* April 8, 1999; Valencia, *China and the South China Sea Disputes,* pp. 27–28.

72. "National Defense Program Outline in and After Fiscal Year 1996," electronic document obtained from the Japanese Ministry of Foreign Affairs at http:// www2.nttca.com:8010/infomafa/ju on August 7, 1997.

73. See Sharpe, *Jane's Fighting Ships, 1996–97,* p. xii.

74. See Strom, "Japan Beginning to Flex Its Military Muscles."

75. For background on U.S. interests in the South China Sea, see Kenny, "The South China Sea," pp. 102–06; Valencia, *China and the South China Sea Disputes,* pp. 25–30.

76. On the initial U.S. reaction to the Mischief Reef incident, see Nigel Holloway, "Jolt from the Blue," *Far Eastern Economic Review,* August 3, 1995, pp. 22–23.

77. U.S. Department of State, "Spratlys and the South China Sea," statement by Christine Shelly, Acting Spokesman, May 10, 1995 (xerox copy).

78. Quoted in Michael Richardson, "U.S. Bolsters Japan Security Ties," *International Herald Tribune,* June 23, 1995. Nye's remarks were made in a June 16, 1995, video interview with a group of Japanese journalists in Tokyo. For further discussion, see "Jolt from the Blue."

79. See Patrick E. Tyler, "China Pledges Safe Passage Around Isles," *New York Times,* May 19, 1995.

80. See, for example, the statement by Assistant Secretary of State Winston Lord before the Asia and Pacific Subcommittee of the House International Relations Committee, May 30, 1996, published in *U.S. Department of State Dispatch,* May 27, 1996, pp. 267–71.

81. From interview in *Armed Forces Journal,* October 1999, p. 68.

82. U.S. Department of Defense, "DoD News Briefing, January 14, 1998," electronic document accessed at http://www.defenselink.mil/news on May 15, 1998.

83. See "Reef-Stricken."

84. The first outcome of this effort was the signing of a "Joint Declaration on Security" by President Clinton and Japanese Prime Minister Ryutaro Hashimoto in April 1996. While noting that the end of the Cold War has reduced the risk of global war, the declaration stated that "instability and uncertainty persist in the region." Among the causes of such instability, it observed, are "unresolved territorial disputes"—a clear reference to the South China Sea. To address these and other regional threats, Clinton and Hashimoto called for the adoption of new forms

of military cooperation. See Government of Japan, Ministry of Foreign Affairs, "Japan-U.S. Joint Declaration on Security," April 17, 1996, electronic communication accessed at http://www2.nttca.com:8010/infomofa/ju/security on August 7, 1997. See also Teresa Watanabe, "Security Pact Expected to Alter Way Japan Sees Its Military Role," *Los Angeles Times,* April 18, 1996.

85. See Steven Lee Myers, "Risking China's Wrath, U.S. and Japan Bolster Military Ties," *New York Times,* September 24, 1997.

86. "Joint Statement of U.S.-Japan Security Consultative Committee on Completion of the Review of the Guidelines for U.S.-Japan Defense Cooperation," U.S. Department of Defense News Release, September 23, 1997, electronic communication accessed at http://www.defenselink.mil/news/Sep1997 on September 23, 1997.

87. See Myers, "Risking China's Wrath."

88. See "Japan's Constitution: The Call to Arms."

89. For background, see Nicholas D. Kristof, "Asian Tensions Rise over Sea's Wealth," *New York Times,* May 19, 1996; Kristof, "Would *You* Fight for These Islands?" *New York Times,* October 8, 1996; Clive Schofield, "Island Disputes in East Asia Escalate," *Jane's Intelligence Review,* November 1996, pp. 517–21; Valencia, "Energy and Insecurity in Asia," pp. 97–98.

90. For background, see U.S. Department of Energy, Energy Information Administration, "Indonesia," Country Analysis Brief, February 10, 1997, electronic document accessed at http://www.eia.doe.gov/emeu/cabs/indonesia.html on March 17, 1997.

6: WATER CONFLICT IN THE NILE BASIN

1. For general discussion on water as a source of conflict, see Natasha Beschorner, *Water and Instability in the Middle East,* Adelphi Paper no. 273 (London: Brassey's and the International Institute for Strategic Studies, 1992); Kent Hughes Butts, "The Strategic Importance of Water," *Parameters,* Spring 1997, pp. 65–83; Peter H. Gleick, "Water and Conflict," *International Security,* vol. 18, no. 1 (Summer 1993), pp. 79–112; Gleick, *The World's Water, 1998–1999* (Washington, D.C., and Covelo, Calif.: Island Press, 1998), pp. 107–35; Jacques Leslie, "Running Dry," *Harper's,* July 2000, pp. 37–52; Sandra Postel, "The Politics of Water," *World Watch,* July-August 1993, pp. 10–18; Joyce R. Starr, "Water Wars," *Foreign Policy,* no. 82 (Spring 1991), pp. 17–36; Marq de Villiers, *Water* (Boston: Houghton Mifflin, 2000), pp. 185–230.

2. Quoted in M. S. Drower, "Water-Supply, Irrigation, and Agriculture," in Charles Singer, E. J. Holmyard, and A. R. Hall, eds., *A History of Technology* (Oxford: Clarendon Press, 1954), p. 554.

3. For background on this episode, see Robert O. Collins, *The Waters of the Nile* (Princeton: Marcus Wiener, 1996), pp. 49–63.

4. For a roster of such conflicts, see Gleick, *The World's Water, 1998–1999,* pp. 127–31.

5. For discussion, see sources cited in note 1 above. See also Miriam R. Lowi, "Rivers of Conflict, Rivers of Peace," *Journal of International Affairs,* vol. 49, no. 1 (Summer 1995), pp. 123–44; Al J. Ventnor, "The Oldest Threat: Water in the Middle East," *Jane's Intelligence Review,* February 1998, pp. 21–26.

6. For a discussion of what is known and suspected about the impact of climate change on water availability, see Gleick, *The World's Water, 1998–1999,* pp. 137–53.

7. For discussion, see Beschorner, *Water and Instability in the Middle East;* Leslie "Running Dry"; Lowi, "Rivers of Conflict, Rivers of Peace"; Postel, "The Politics of Water."

8. Quoted in Michael Brecher, *Decisions in Israel's Foreign Policy* (New Haven: Yale University Press, 1975), p. 184, from *Divrei Ha-Knesset,* vol. 15 (November 30, 1953), pp. 270–71.

9. For discussion, see Butts, "The Strategic Importance of Water."

10. For discussion, see Dower, "Water Supply, Irrigation, and Agriculture," pp. 535–55; Daniel Hillel, *Rivers of Eden: The Struggle for Water and the Quest for Peace in the Middle East* (New York and Oxford: Oxford University Press, 1994), pp. 41–73; de Villiers, *Water,* pp. 46–64.

11. See Greg Shapland, *Rivers of Discord* (New York: St. Martin's Press, 1997), pp. 62–63.

12. From an interview in the January 1, 1999, edition of *Environmental Science and Technology,* as cited in "Water Wars Forecast If Solutions Not Found," Environmental News Service, January 1, 1999, electronic document accessed at http://ens.lycos.com/ens/archives/Jan99/1999L-01-01-02.html on August 9, 2000.

13. Quoted in Scott Peterson, "What Could Float—or Sink—Peacemaking," *Christian Science Monitor,* July 14, 1999.

14. The World Bank, *A Strategy for Managing Water in the Middle East and North Africa* (Washington, D.C.: World Bank, 1994), p. 11.

15. Peter H. Gleick, "Water and Conflict," *International Security,* vol. 18, no. 1 (Summer 1993), pp. 90, 100–01. Gleick derives this figure from Malin Falkenmark, "Fresh Water—Time for a Modified Approach," *Ambio,* vol. 15, no. 4 (1986), pp. 194–200.

16. Sandra Postel, *Last Oasis* (New York: W. W. Norton, 1997), pp. 19–20, 48–59.

17. For discussion, see ibid., pp. 48–59. See also Lester R. Brown, *Tough Choices: Facing the Challenge of Food Scarcity* (New York: W. W. Norton, 1996); Peter H. Gleick, *The World's Water, 2000–2001* (Washington, D.C.: Island Press, 2000), pp. 63–92.

18. United Nations, Commission on Sustainable Development (UNCSD), *Comprehensive Assessment of the Freshwater Resources of the World,* Report of the Secretary General, U.N. doc. E/CN.17/1997/9, February 4, 1997, pp. 8–9. See also Gleick, *The World's Water, 2000–2001,* pp. 19–38; W. Maurits la Rivière, "Threats to the World's Water," *Scientific American,* September 1989, pp. 80–94; Igor A.

Shiklomanov, "World Fresh Water Resources," in Peter H. Gleick, ed., *Water in Crisis* (New York and Oxford: Oxford University Press, 1993), pp. 13–24.

19. See la Rivière, "Threats to the World's Water"; Sandra Postel, "Dividing the Waters," *Technology Review,* April 1997, pp. 54–62.

20. Postel, "Dividing the Waters," pp. 56–57; la Rivière, "Threats to the World's Water"; UNCSD, *Comprehensive Assessment of the Freshwater Resources of the World,* pp. 8–9. See also Shiklomanov, "World Fresh Water Resources."

21. For background, see Sandra Postel, "When the World's Wells Run Dry," *World Watch,* September-October 1999, pp. 30–38; de Villiers, *Water,* pp. 146–65.

22. Postel, *Last Oasis,* pp. 27–37; UNCSD, *Comprehensive Assessment of Freshwater Resources,* p. 9. On desalination, see Gleick, *The World's Water, 2000–2001,* pp. 93–111.

23. UNCSD, *Comprehensive Assessment of Freshwater Resources,* p. 8.

24. World Bank, *From Scarcity to Security: Averting a Water Crisis in the Middle East and North Africa* (Washington, D.C.: World Bank, 1995), pp. 6–7.

25. A. T. Wolf, J. A. Natharius, J. J. Danielson, B. S. Ward, J. Pender, "International River Basins of the World," *International Journal of Water Resources Development,* vol. 15, no. 4 (1999), as summarized in Gleick, *The World's Water, 2000–2001,* pp. 27–35.

26. See Leslie, "Running Dry," pp. 49–50; de Villiers, *Water,* pp. 190–91, 200–01.

27. For background and discussion, see Beschorner, *Water and Instability in the Middle East;* Gleick, *The World's Water, 1998–1999,* pp. 107–13; Hillel, *Rivers of Eden;* Lowi, "Rivers of Conflict, Rivers of Peace"; Shapland, *Rivers of Discord.*

28. For background on this episode, see Marc Reisner, *Cadillac Desert: The American West and Its Disappearing Water* (New York: Penguin, 1986).

29. See Gleick, "Water and Conflict," p. 93.

30. "Bolivia Calls an Emergency After Protest over Water," *New York Times,* April 9, 2000.

31. For discussion of the merits of privatization and the creation of markets in the distribution of water, see "Nor Any Drop to Drink," *Economist,* March 25, 2000, pp. 69–70; Postel, *Last Oasis,* pp. 165–82; de Villiers, *Water,* pp. 293–306.

32. For a chronology of these conflicts, see Gleick, *The World's Water, 1998–1999,* pp. 125–27.

33. See Collins, *The Waters of the Nile,* pp. 26–65; "Sudan," *The New Encyclopaedia Britannica,* 15th ed., vol. 28, 1997, pp. 256–70.

34. For background on the Nile's geography and hydrology, see Collins, *The Waters of the Nile,* pp. 26–65; Hillel, *Rivers of Eden,* pp. 111–20; John Waterbury, *Hydropolitics of the Nile Valley* (Syracuse: Syracuse University Press, 1979), pp. 12–42.

35. On the relative contribution of the Blue Nile and the White Nile, see Hillel, *Rivers of Eden,* pp. 118–19.

36. For background on these plans, see Collins, *The Waters of the Nile,* pp. 103–44.

37. For background, see ibid., pp. 145–97.

38. For background, see ibid., pp. 247–300. See also Shapland, *Rivers of Discord,* pp. 68–72, 77–78.

39. For discussion, see Waterbury, *Hydropolitics of the Nile Valley,* pp. 77–86.

40. Gleick, *The World's Water, 1998–1999,* p. 129. This was the Halayeb Triangle on the Red Sea coast, a potential source of minerals and oil.

41. For background and discussion, see Collins, *The Waters of the Nile,* pp. 247–77; Shapland, *Rivers of Discord,* pp. 72–74; Waterbury, *Hydropolitics of the Nile Valley,* pp. 67–74, 98–109.

42. Quoted in Starr, "Water Wars," p. 19.

43. See Beschorner, *Water and Instability in the Middle East,* p. 60; Shapland, *Rivers of Discord,* pp. 78–80.

44. Quoted in Gleick, "Water and Conflict," p. 86.

45. See Beschorner, *Water and Instability in the Middle East,* pp. 58–60.

46. See Amy Dockser Marcus, "Egypt Faces a Problem It Has Long Dreaded: Less Control of the Nile," *Wall Street Journal,* August 22, 1997.

47. Ibid. See also "Africa Worried About Egypt's Nile Mega-Project," *New African,* April 1997, p. 34.

48. See Human Rights Watch, *Sudan: Global Trade, Local Impact* (New York and Washington, D.C.: Human Rights Watch, August 1998), pp. 12–14.

49. Shapland, *Rivers of Discord,* pp. 89–90. See also Arif Gamal, "Deconstructing Nubia: Kajabar Damns Entire Ancient Culture," *World Rivers Review,* October 1998, pp. 6–7, 11.

50. Population projections are from World Resources Institute, *World Resources 1998–99,* p. 244.

51. See "Egypt: Back from the Desert," *Economist,* April 12, 1997, pp. 36–38; Mark Huhand, "Egypt a Step Nearer to Taming the Nile," *Financial Times,* February 20, 1998; Marcus, "Egypt Faces a Problem It Has Long Dreaded."

52. See Marcus, "Egypt Faces a Problem It Has Long Dreaded"; Shapland, *Rivers of Discord,* pp. 63–65, 94–96.

53. World Resources Institute, *World Resources 1998–99,* p. 244.

54. See Marcus, "Egypt Faces a Problem It Has Long Dreaded"; Shapland, *Rivers of Discord,* pp. 82–90.

55. For discussion of these predictions, see Declan Conway et al., "Future Availability of Water in Egypt," *Ambio,* vol. 25, no. 5 (August 1996), pp. 336–42.

56. Quoted in "War of Words and Water," *Al-Ahram Weekly,* July 6–12, 1995, as cited in Shapland, *Rivers of Discord,* p. 101.

57. See Beschorner, *Water and Instability in the Middle East,* p. 60.

58. For the air combat inventories of Egypt and these other states, see IISS, *The Military Balance 1999–2000.*

59. In one such episode, occurring in January 1994, Egyptian troops opened

fire on Sudanese police forces guarding the area. The Egyptian forces had been sent into the area after Sudan awarded a contract to a Canadian company to drill for oil in waters adjacent to the district. See "Oil Potential Sparks Sudan-Egypt Conflict," *New African,* January 1994, p. 25.

60. For details on Egyptian and Sudanese military capabilities, see IISS, *The Military Balance 1999–2000,* pp. 130, 275.

61. For discussion of such schemes, see Hillel, *Rivers of Eden,* pp. 130–42. See also Collins, *The Waters of the Nile,* pp. 247–386; Yahia Abdel Mageed, "The Nile Basin: Lessons from the Past," in Asit K. Biswas, ed., *International Waters of the Middle East* (Bombay: Oxford University Press, 1994), pp. 156–84.

7: WATER CONFLICT IN THE JORDAN, TIGRIS-EUPHRATES, AND INDUS RIVER BASINS

1. Estimate covers Iran, Iraq, Israel, Jordan, Lebanon, Pakistan, Syria, Turkey, and one-fifth of the population of India. Projections from World Resources Institute, *World Resources 1998–1999,* p. 244.

2. For discussion of this point, see Hillel, *Rivers of Eden,* pp. 148–50; Lowi, *Water and Power,* pp. 40–41, 51–52.

3. For background on these efforts, see Hillel, *Rivers of Eden,* pp. 158–162; Lowi, *Water and Power,* pp. 54–105.

4. World Bank, *A Strategy for Managing Water,* p. 68.

5. Postel, *Last Oasis,* p. 28.

6. For background on the Jordan River dispute, see Beschorner, *Water and Instability in the Middle East,* pp. 8–26; Hillel, *Rivers of Eden,* pp. 143–76; Miriam Lowi, *Water and Power* (Cambridge and New York: Cambridge University Press, 1995), pp. 19–53, 79–182; and Naff and Matson, *Water in the Middle East,* pp. 17–61.

7. On the hydrology of the Jordan River, see Hillel, *Rivers of Eden,* pp. 152–56; 143–76; Lowi, *Water and Power,* pp. 23–28; and Naff and Matson, *Water in the Middle East,* pp. 17–21.

8. For background on the Ionides and Lowdermilk plans, see Lowi, *Water and Power,* pp. 43–45; Naff and Matson, *Water in the Middle East,* pp. 30–32.

9. For background, see Lowi, *Water and Power,* pp. 79–81; Naff and Matson, *Water in the Middle East,* pp. 35–39.

10. For background on the Johnston effort, see Lowi, *Water and Power,* pp. 79–114; Naff and Matson, *Water in the Middle East,* pp. 34–35.

11. For background on these efforts, see Hillel, *Rivers of Eden,* pp. 162–68; Naff and Matson, *Water in the Middle East,* pp. 43–44.

12. For background, see Lowi, *Water and Power,* pp. 118–27; Naff and Matson, *Water in the Middle East,* pp. 43–44.

13. Quoted in Lowi, *Water and Power,* p. 119.

14. Quoted in ibid., p. 125.

15. For background, see Lowi, *Water and Power,* pp. 124–25, 131.

16. For a list of water-related clashes in the Israel-Syria border area in 1966–67, see Naff and Matson, *Water in the Middle East,* p. 37.

17. On Jordan's hydrological dilemma, see Hillel, *Rivers of Eden,* pp. 169–75; Naff and Matson, *Water in the Middle East,* pp. 50–53. On the situation in the West Bank, see Sharif S. Elmusa, *Water Conflict* (Washington, D.C.: Institute for Palestine Studies, 1997), pp. 77–133.

18. See Naff and Matson, *Water in the Middle East,* p. 45.

19. See Beschorner, *Water and Instability in the Middle East,* p. 21; Lowi, *Water and Power,* pp. 171–81.

20. The 5:1 ratio comes from Shapland, *Rivers of Discord,* p. 24; the 8:1 ratio is from the BBC, "West Bank Water Row," August 26, 1998, electronic document accessed at http://news.bbc.co.uk/hi/english/world/middleeast on July 2, 1999. For background and discussion, see Beschorner, *Water and Instability in the Middle East,* pp. 22–24; Allan Cowell, "Hurdle to Peace: Parting the Mideast's Water," *New York Times,* October 10, 1993; Lowi, "Bridging the Divide," pp. 120–33; Peterson, "What Could Float—Or Sink—Peacemaking."

21. For text of Article 6, see Gleick, *The World's Water, 1998–1999,* p. 116. For discussion, see Shapland, *Rivers of Discord,* pp. 29–31. On the lack of cooperation, see Christine Chesnot, "Water Disputes Undermine Peace Talks," *Le Monde Diplomatique,* February 2000, English-language edition, electronic document accessed at http://ensubscribers@london.monde-diplomatique.fr on February 21, 2000.

22. See William A. Orme Jr., "In West Bank, Water Is As Touchy as Land," *New York Times,* July 15, 2000.

23. See Shapland, *Rivers of Discord,* pp. 31–38.

24. For background and discussion, see Alain Gresh, "Middle East Holds Its Breath: Israel and Syria on the Brink of Peace," *Le Monde Diplomatique,* January 2000, from English-language edition, electronic document accessed at http//ensubscribers@london.monde-diplomatique.fr on January 12, 2000. See also Chesnot, "Water Disputes Undermine Peace Talks."

25. For background on the geography and hydrology of the two rivers, see: Hillel, *Rivers of Eden,* pp. 92–99; John Kolars, "Problems of International River Management: The Case of the Euphrates," in Biswas, *International Waters of the Middle East,* pp. 51–54; Naff and Matson, *Water in the Middle East,* pp. 83–87; and Shapland, *Rivers of Discord,* pp. 103–06.

26. For background and discussion, see Hillel, *Rivers of Eden,* pp. 93–102.

27. See Shapland, *Rivers of Discord,* pp. 107–08.

28. For background and discussion, see Beschorner, *Water and Instability in the Middle East,* pp. 29–36; Hillel, *Rivers of Eden,* pp. 107–09.

29. For background and discussion, see Beschorner, *Water and Instability in the Middle East,* pp. 29–44; Hillel, *Rivers of Eden,* pp. 102–10; Shapland, *Rivers of Discord,* pp. 115–24.

30. For background on the Tabqa Dam and the 1975 crisis, see Eberhard Kienle, *Ba'th v. Ba'th: The Conflict Between Syria and Iraq, 1968–1989* (London and New York: I. B. Tauris, 1990), pp. 97–109. See also Beschorner, *Water and Instability in the Middle East,* pp. 39–40; Naff and Matson, *Water in the Middle East,* pp. 90–91, 93–95.

31. Kienle, *Ba'th v. Ba'th,* pp. 100, 107–9. See also coverage of these events in *The New York Times,* May 2, 4, and 19, June 4 and 29, and July 9, 1975.

32. Kienle, *Ba'th v. Ba'th,* p. 107. See also coverage in *The New York Times,* July 9 and August 3, 1975.

33. See coverage of these events in *The New York Times,* August 15, 1975.

34. See Beschorner, *Water and Instability in the Middle East,* pp. 41–42; Shapland, *Rivers of Discord,* pp. 121–22.

35. See Alan Cowell, "Now a Little Stream. Later, Maybe, a Water War," *New York Times,* February 7, 1990; Thomas Goltz, "Turkey Dams the Euphrates, but Distrust Trickles Through," *Washington Post National Weekly Edition,* January 22–28, 1990; George D. Moffett III, "Downstream Fears Feed Tensions," *Christian Science Monitor,* March 13, 1990.

36. For background on GAP, see Beschorner, *Water and Instability in the Middle East,* pp. 30–32; Hillel, *Rivers of Eden,* pp. 104–07; Kolars, "Problems of International Water Management," pp. 66–77; Shapland, *Rivers of Discord,* pp. 119–25. For a Turkish government perspective on the role of GAP, see Government of Turkey, Ministry of Foreign Affairs, "Water: A Source of Conflict or Cooperation in the Middle East," electronic document accessed at http://www.mfa/gov.tr/srupf/water/facts.htm on July 2, 1998.

37. See Beschorner, *Water and Instability in the Middle East,* p. 37; Cowell, "Now, a Little Stream."

38. See Beschorner, *Water and Instability in the Middle East,* pp. 41–42.

39. Quoted in International Institute of Strategic Studies (IISS), *Strategic Survey 1991–92* (London: IISS, 1992), p. 229.

40. For background, see "A New and Bitter Brew in the Middle East," *Economist,* October 10, 1998, pp. 43–44; Stephen Kinzer, "Where Kurds Seek a Land, Turks Want the Water," *New York Times,* February 28, 1999.

41. For background, see Celestine Bohlen, "War on Rebel Kurds Puts Turkey's Ideals to Test," *New York Times,* July 16, 1995; Alan Cowell, "Turks' War with Kurds Reaches a New Ferocity," *New York Times,* October 18, 1993; Cowell, "War on Kurds Hurts Turks in U.S. Eyes," *New York Times,* November 17, 1994.

42. See Stephen Kinzer, "A Corner of the World That Peace Forgot," *New York Times,* July 4, 1999; Kinzer, "Where Kurds Seek a Land."

43. Douglas Jehl, "Mubarak Visits Syria in Effort to Defuse Crisis with Turkey," *New York Times,* October 5, 1998.

44. See "A New and Bitter Brew"; Daniel Pipes, "Turkey and Syria Gird for War," *Wall Street Journal,* October 9, 1998.

45. Pipes, "Turkey and Syria Gird for War."

46. See Jehl, "Mubarak Visits Syria"; "More Nations Try to End Turkey-Syria Dispute," *International Herald Tribune,* October 10–11, 1998.

47. See Stephen Kinzer, "Accord Set for Syria and Turkey," *New York Times,* October 22, 1998.

48. See "Sharing Mesopotamia's Water," *Economist,* November 13, 1999, pp. 43–44.

49. See Shapland, *Rivers of Discord,* p. 124. See also "Sharing Mesopotamia's Water"; Kolars, "Problems of International Water Management," p. 77; Moffett, "Downstream Fears Feed Tensions."

50. See Beschorner, *Water and Instability in the Middle East,* p. 31; Hillel, *Rivers of Eden,* p. 106.

51. See Peter Bosshard, "Turkish Dam Will Fuel Regional Tensions," *World Rivers Review,* February 1999, pp. 6–7.

52. World Resources Institute, *World Resources 1998–99,* p. 244.

53. For discussion of such options, see Özden Bilen, "Prospects for Technical Cooperation in the Euphrates-Tigris Basin," in Biswas, *International Waters of the Middle East,* pp. 95–116.

54. Turkey, which would have to curb its plans for the GAP in order to satisfy the needs of its downstream neighbors, has shown no inclination to agree to any water-sharing plan in the region. "We oppose the concept of sharing the Euphrates and Tigris rivers, which are the Turkish people's resources," Turkey's minister of public works, Cengiz Altinkaya, declared in 1990. This demand is as objectionable, he added, as "Turkey asking the Arab countries for the right to share their oil." Quoted in Sam Cohen, "Iraq, Syria Challenge Turkey on Water Use," *Christian Science Monitor,* July 2, 1990.

55. For a full description of the Indus River's course, see John Fairly, *The Lion River* (New York: John Day, 1975). See also Niranjan D. Gulhati, *Indus Waters Treaty: An Exercise in International Mediation* (Bombay: Allied Publishers, 1973), pp. 18–30; Aloys Arthur Michel, *The Indus Rivers* (New Haven: Yale University Press, 1967).

56. See Fairley, *The Lion River,* pp. 204–15; Gulhati, *Indus Waters Treaty,* pp. 6–47; Michel, *The Indus Rivers,* pp. 51–98.

57. Gulhati, *Indus Waters Treaty,* pp. 56–59.

58. Ibid., pp. 63–71. See also Fairley, *The Lion River,* p. 212; Lowi, *Water and Power,* p. 64; Michel, *The Indus Rivers,* pp. 195–204.

59. For a thorough account of these negotiations, see Gulhati, *Indus Waters Treaty,* pp. 91–309. See also Michel, *The Indus Rivers,* pp. 219–53.

60. For the text of the treaty and an assessment of its provisions, see Gulhati, *Indus Waters Treaty,* pp. 339–411.

61. For discussion, see Lowi, *Water and Power,* pp. 65–67.

62. For discussion, see Gulhati, *Indus Waters Treaty,* pp. 348–70; Lowi, *Water and Power,* pp. 65–66; Michel, *The Indus Rivers,* pp. 254–340.

63. For background, see Seymour M. Hersh, "On the Nuclear Edge," *New Yorker,* March 29, 1993, pp. 56–73.

64. See Barry Bearak, "Frozen in Fury on the Roof of the World," *New York Times,* May 23, 1999; Celia W. Dugger and Barry Bearak, "Kashmir Thwarts India-Pakistan Attempt at Trust," *New York Times,* July 4, 1999; "Kashmir's Violent Spring," *Economist,* May 29, 1999, pp. 35–36.

65. See "Who Really Runs Pakistan," *Economist,* June 26, 1999, pp. 41–42; "Pakistan's New Old Rulers," *Economist,* October 16, 1999, pp. 39–40.

66. For discussion, see John Kifner, "On Pakistan's Side, Hopes of Ending 'a Perpetual State of Confrontation,' " *New York Times,* June 14, 1998; Kifner, "Pakistan Wants India Pressed on Kashmir," *New York Times,* June 3, 1998; Amin War, "Kashmir Is Bleeding," *Bulletin of the Atomic Scientists,* March-April 1997, pp. 24–32.

67. World Resources Institute, *World Resources 1998–99,* p. 244.

68. See Postel, *Last Oasis,* pp. 36–37, 53–56.

69. See Lester R. Brown, *Tough Choices: Facing the Challenge of Food Scarcity* (New York: W. W. Norton, 1996), pp. 85–96.

70. For discussion of the impact of global warming on global water supplies and the production of food, see Postel, *Last Oasis,* pp. 87–95; Gleick, *The World's Water,* pp. 138–43.

8: FIGHTING FOR THE RICHES OF THE EARTH: INTERNAL WARS OVER MINERALS AND TIMBER

1. For discussion of this point, see Collier and Hoeffler, "Justice-Seeking and Loot-Seeking in Civil War."

2. For background on the diversion of oil revenues to the MPLA's senior leadership, see Global Witness, *A Crude Awakening: The Role of the Oil and Banking Industries in Angola's Civil War and the Plunder of State Assets* (London: Global Witness, 1999). See also Jon Lee Anderson, "Oil and Blood," *New Yorker,* August 14, 2000, pp. 46–59. For evidence of the diversion of diamonds to the personal coffers of Jonas Savimbi, the leader of UNITA, see U.N. Security Council, *Report of the Panel of Experts on Violations of Security Council Sanctions Against UNITA,* U.N. doc. S/200/203, March 10, 2000.

3. See "Sierra Leone: Diamond King," *Economist,* January 29, 2000, pp. 51–52. For background on the conflict in Sierra Leone, see David J. Francis, "Mercenary Intervention in Sierra Leone: Providing National Security or International Exploitation?" *Third World Quarterly,* vol. 20, no. 2 (1999), pp. 319–38; William Reno, *Warlord Politics and African States* (Boulder: Lynne Rienner, 1998), pp. 113–45; Alfred B. Zack-Williams, "Sierra Leone: The Political Economy of Civil War, 1991–98," *Third World Quarterly,* vol. 20, no. 1 (1999), pp. 143–62.

4. See Global Witness, *A Rough Trade* (London: Global Witness, 1998); Blaine Harden, "U.N. Sees Violation of a Diamond Ban by Angola Rebels," *New York Times,* March 11, 2000.

5. Douglas Farah, "Diamonds Are a Rebel's Best Friend: Mining of Gems Helps Sierra Leone Militia Stall Peace Process," *Washington Post,* April 17, 2000.

6. See William Reno, "Reinvention of an African Patrimonial State," *Third World Quarterly,* vol. 16, no. 1 (1995), pp. 109–20.

7. For discussion of this point, see David Keen, *The Economic Functions of Violence in Civil Wars,* International Institute of Strategic Studies (IISS), Adelphi Paper no. 320 (Oxford: Oxford University Press and IISS, 1998).

8. On Angola, see Global Witness, *A Rough Trade;* on Sierra Leone, see Farah, "Diamonds Are a Rebel's Best Friend."

9. See Reno, *Warlord Politics and African States,* pp. 147–81.

10. See Stephen Erlanger, "Burmese Teak Forest Falls to Finance a War," *New York Times,* December 9, 1990.

11. For an excellent case study of this phenomenon, covering Charles Taylor's Liberia, see Reno, "Reinvention of an African Patrimonial State." For further discussion of warlordism, see Reno, *Warlord Politics and African States.*

12. For an excellent analysis of this phenomenon in Indonesia, see Charles Victor Barber, *The Case of Indonesia,* Project on Environmental Scarcities, State Capacity, and Civil Violence (Cambridge: American Academy of Arts and Sciences, 1997).

13. For background on these events, see Joel Krieger, ed., *The Oxford Companion to the Politics of the World* (New York and Oxford: Oxford University Press, 1993), pp. 279, 825–26.

14. World Resources Institute, *World Resources 1994–95* (Oxford and New York: Oxford University Press, 1994), pp. 340–41.

15. For an extraordinary picture of how Jonas Savimbi worked with private firms to transport diamonds to the outside world and acquire fuel and other vital commodities for his troops, see U.N. Security Council, *Report of the Panel of Experts on Violations of Security Council Sanctions Against UNITA.*

16. For background on these companies, see Thomas K. Adams, "The New Mercenaries and the Privatization of Conflict," *Parameters,* vol. 24, no. 2 (Summer 1999), pp. 103–16; Elizabeth Rubin, "An Army of One's Own," *Harper's,* February 1997, pp. 44–55; David Shearer, *Private Armies and Military Intervention,* Adelphi Paper no. 316 (Oxford: Oxford University Press and IISS, 1998); Shearer, "Outsourcing War," *Foreign Policy,* Fall 1998, pp. 68–80.

17. See Reno, *Warlord Politics and African States,* pp. 60–65; Shearer, *Private Armies and Military Intervention,* pp. 46–48.

18. For background, see Bob Drogin, " 'Mine of Tears' Conflict Imperils Papua New Guinea," *Los Angeles Times,* December 17, 1989; David Hyndman, "Digging the Mines in Melanesia," *Cultural Survival Quarterly,* vol. 15, no. 2 (1991), pp. 32–39; David Minkow and Colleen Murphy-Dunning, "Pillage in the Pacific," *Multinational Monitor,* June 1992, pp. 7–11; James P. Sterba, "Mine Games: Papua New Guinea Bumbles Ever Closer to Ending Civil War," *Wall Street Journal,* March 18, 1998.

19. According to James P. Sterba of *The Wall Street Journal,* the Bougainvilleans "got peanuts" from the Panguna mine. Sterba, "Mine Games."

20. See Drogin, "Mine of Tears"; Hyndman, "Digging the Mines."

21. For background, see Hyndman, "Digging the Mines"; Sterba, "Mine Games"; Peter Lewis Young, "Bougainville—the Seven Year War," *Jane's Intelligence Review,* August 1995, pp. 375–79.

22. Young, "Bougainville—the Seven Year War."

23. See Lawrence Whelan, "Foreigners Causing Controversy in PNG," *Jane's Intelligence Review,* May 1997, p. 8.

24. See "Executive Incomers," *Economist,* March 1, 1997, pp. 39–40; Peter Lewis Young, "Bougainville Conflict Enters Its Ninth Year," *Jane's Intelligence Review,* June 1997, pp. 282–85. For background on E.O., see Shearer, *Private Armies and Military Intervention,* pp. 39–45.

25. See "Australian Jets Intercept Plane Carrying Mercenaries' Weapons," Associated Press dispatch accessed at http://www.boston.com/dailynews/wire on March 28, 1997; Young, "Bougainville Conflict Enters Its Ninth Year."

26. See Sterba, "Mine Games"; Whelan, "Foreigners Causing Controversy"; Whelan, "PNG Government's Fight to Survive," *Jane's Intelligence Review,* July 1997, p. 10; Young, "Bougainville Conflict Enters Its Ninth Year."

27. See Kevin Pamba, "Papua New Guinea: With Truce, Rebellion Inches Toward Peace," InterPress Service dispatch, February 4, 1998; Sterba, "Mine Games."

28. See Peter Waldman, "Hand in Glove: How Suharto's Circle and a Mining Firm Did So Well Together," *Wall Street Journal,* September 29, 1998.

29. For background and discussion, see Reno, *Warlord Politics,* pp. 115–28.

30. For background, see ibid.; "Sierra Leone,"*Europa World Year Book 1995,* pp. 2676–78.

31. For background, see William O'Neill, "Liberia: An Avoidable Tragedy," *Current History,* May 1993, pp. 213–17.

32. For discussion, see Reno, *Warlord Politics,* pp. 91–102; Reno, "The Business of War in Liberia," *Current History,* May 1996, pp. 211–15.

33. See Norimitsu Onishi, "U.N.'s Unlikely Ally for Sierra Leone," *New York Times,* May 16, 2000.

34. For background, see Reno, *Warlord Politics,* pp. 123–27; Amadu Ssay and Abiodun Alao, "Sierra Leone's Forgotten War," *Jane's Intelligence Review,* May 1995, pp. 234–35.

35. See Francis, "Mercenary Intervention in Sierra Leone"; Jim Hooper, "Sierra Leone—the War Continues," *Jane's Intelligence Review,* January 1996, pp. 41–43; Shearer, *Private Armies and Military Intervention,* pp. 49–51; A. L. Venter, "Sierra Leone's Mercenary War," *International Defense Review,* November 1995, pp. 65–67.

36. See Reno, *Warlord Politics,* pp. 130–39. See also Khareen Pech, "Too Late for Mercenaries," *Electronic Mail and Guardian,* May 30, 1997, electronic document accessed at http://www.web.co.za/mg/news/97 on August 27, 1997.

37. See Fran Abrams and Andrew Buncombe, "Secret Plans Reveal Plot Behind Coup," *Independent* (London), May 7, 1998, electronic document accessed at http://www.independent.co.uk on May 7, 1998; Raymond Bonner, "U.S. Reportedly Backed British Mercenary Group in Africa," *New York Times,* May 13, 1998.

38. See Caroline Hawley, "A Country Torn by Conflict," BBC News, January 12, 1999, electronic document accessed at http://news.bbc.co.uk/hi/english on February 11, 2000; Norimitsu Onishi, "Sierra Leone Measures Terror in Severed Limbs," *New York Times,* August 22, 1999.

39. See Elizabeth Blunt, "Eight Years of Civil War: Fragile Peace for Sierra Leone," *Le Monde Diplomatique,* December 1999, English-language edition, electronic document accessed at http://dispatch@Monde-diplomatique.fr on December 16, 1999.

40. See Norimitsu Onishi, "Sierra Leone Awaits Return of Rebel Leader," *New York Times,* August 18, 1999.

41. See Farah, "Diamonds Are a Rebel's Best Friend"; "Sierra Leone's Agony," *Economist,* May 13, 2000, pp. 45–46.

42. Barbara Crossette, "Sierra Leone Rebel Leader Reportedly Smuggled Gems," *New York Times,* May 14, 2000.

43. Philip Hurst, *Rainforest Politics: Ecological Destruction in Southeast Asia* (London: Zed Books, 1990), p. 84.

44. Barber, *The Case Study of Indonesia,* p. 55.

45. U.N. Food and Agricultural Organization (FAO), *State of the World's Forests 1997* (Rome: FAO, 1997), p. 128.

46. For background and discussion, see Peter Dauvergne, *Shadows in the Forest: Japan and the Politics of Timber in Southeast Asia* (Cambridge: MIT Press, 1997); Michael Leigh, "Political Economy of Logging in Sarawak, Malaysia," in Philip Hirsch and Carol Warren, eds., *The Politics of Environment in Southeast Asia* (London and New York: Routledge, 1998), pp. 93–106.

47. Wade Davis, "Death of a People: Logging in the Penan Homeland," in Marc S. Miller and the Staff of Cultural Survival, *State of the Peoples: A Global Human Rights Report on Societies in Danger* (Boston: Beacon Press, 1993), p. 23.

48. Barber, *The Case Study of Indonesia,* pp. 36, 42–45, 60, 63.

49. For background and discussion, see Marcus Colchester, "The Struggle for Land," *The Ecologist,* vol. 16, no. 2–3 (1986), pp. 99–110; Davis, "Death of a People," pp. 23–32; Wade Davis, Ian Mackenzie, and Shane Kennedy, *Nomads of the Dawn: The Penan of the Borneo Rainforest* (San Francisco: Pomegranate Artbooks, 1995).

50. For background, see Hurst, *Rainforest Politics,* pp. 88–95.

51. Quoted in Davis, "Death of a People," p. 28.

52. Hurst, *Rainforest Politics,* pp. 119–20.

53. See Davis, "Death of a People," pp. 28–30; Davis, Mackenzie, and Kennedy, *Nomads of the Dawn.*

54. See "Global Rights Summary" in Cultural Survival, *State of the Peoples,* pp. 142–43; Mizan Khan and Deepla Khosla, "Dayaks in Malaysia: Major Developments Since 1990," Minorities at Risk Project, University of Maryland, March 22, 1996, electronic document accessed at http://www.bsos.umd.edu/cidcm/mar/maldayak.htm on November 30, 1998.

55. Amnesty International, *Annual Report 1998,* electronic version, accessed at http://www.amnesty.org/ailib/aireport/ar98/asa28.htm on November 30, 1998.

56. See Colchester, "The Struggle for Land"; Dini S. Djalal, "Marginalized Dayaks Violently Assert Their Rights," *Jakarta Post,* March 2, 1997.

57. "Indonesia's Latest Uprising," *Economist,* February 15, 1997, pp. 34–35.

58. See Janet N. Abramovitz, *Taking a Stand: Cultivating a New Relationship with the World's Forests,* Worldwatch Paper 140 (Washington, D.C.: Worldwatch Institute, 1998), pp. 42–43; Seth Mydans, "Southeast Asia Chokes as Indonesian Fires Burn," *New York Times,* September 25, 1997; Peter Waldman, "Southeast Asian Smog Is Tied to Politics," *Wall Street Journal,* September 30, 1997; "Haze—Who Starts the Fires?" BBC World Service, February 25, 1998, electronic document accessed at http://news2.thls.bbc.co.uk on February 16, 2000.

59. "Descent into Darkest Borneo," *Economist,* March 27, 1999, p. 42; "Borneo Engulfed by Terror," BBC World Service, March 21, 1999, electronic document accessed at http://news2.thls.bbc.co.uk on February 16, 2000.

60. "More Troops Arrive to Stem Borneo Violence," CNN News, March 23, 1999, electronic document accessed at http://cnn.com on March 23, 1999.

61. On Indonesia, see Barber, *The Case of Indonesia.* On Brazil, see Alexander López, "Environmental Change, Security, and Social Conflicts in the Brazilian Amazon," *Environmental Change and Security Project Report,* Woodrow Wilson Center, no. 5, Summer 1999, pp. 26–33.

62. See Robert Bryce, "Spinning Gold," *Mother Jones,* September-October 1996, pp. 66–69; Curtis Runyan, "Indonesia's Discontent," *World Watch,* May-June 1998, pp. 15–20; Waldman, "Hand in Glove."

63. On the pro-independence movement in West Papua, see "Another Separatist Group in Indonesia Asserts Independence," *New York Times,* June 5, 2000; Jeremy Wagstaff, "Indonesia Faces Another Secession Threat," *Wall Street Journal,* June 6, 2000.

64. For an extraordinary account of Belgian colonialism in Congo, see Adam Hochschild, *King Leopold's Ghost* (Boston: Houghton Mifflin, 1998).

65. For background, see Reno, *Warlord Politics and African States,* pp. 147–72.

66. See Robert Block, "Congo Revolt Erupts into Regional War," *Wall Street Journal,* August 24, 1998; Ian Fisher and Norimitsu Onishi, "Many Armies Ravage Rich Land in the 'First World War' in Africa," *New York Times,* February 13, 2000; David Shearer, "Africa's Great War," *Survival,* vol. 41, no. 2 (Summer 1999), pp. 89–106; "Congo: War Turns Commercial," *Economist,* October 24, 1999, pp. 42–43.

67. See Robert Block, "General Partners: Zimbabwe's Elite Turn Strife in Nearby Congo into a Quest for Riches," *Wall Street Journal,* October 9, 1998.

68. *Report of the Panel of Experts on Violations of Security Council Sanctions Against UNITA* (see note 2).

69. Quoted in Raymond Bonner, "U.S. May Try to Curb Diamond Trade That Fuels African Wars," *New York Times,* August 8, 1999.

70. Paul Collier, "Economic Causes of Civil Conflict and Their Implications for Policy," unpublished paper, World Bank, Washington, D.C., June 15, 2000. See also G. Pascal Zachary, "Market Forces Add Ammunition to Civil Wars," *Wall Street Journal,* June 12, 2000.

71. "Angola, Belgium Cooperate on Diamond Trade Curbs," Reuters dispatch, March 31, 2000, electronic document accessed at http://www.cnn.com on March 31, 2000.

72. Barbara Crossette, "U.N. Warns It Will Enforce Angola Trade Ban," *New York Times,* April 19, 2000.

73. "Security Council Bars Gem Purchases from Sierra Leone," *Washington Post,* July 6, 2000.

74. "BP Defends Big Angola Payment, Denies Fuelling War," Reuters dispatch, June 1, 2000, electronic document accessed at http://www.cnn.com on June 5, 2000.

9: THE NEW GEOGRAPHY OF CONFLICT

1. For discussion, See "Chávez's Muddled New World," *Economist,* November 20, 1999; Jennifer L. McCoy, "Demystifying Venezuela's Hugo Chávez," *Current History,* February 2000, pp. 66–71; Larry Rohter, "Venezuela Leader Pushes for New Charter, But Is It Reformist Tool or a Power Grab," *New York Times,* July 25, 1999. For background on Venezuela's oil potential, see U.S. Department of Energy, Energy Information Administration, "Venezuela," Country Analysis Brief, January 2000, electronic document accessed at http://www.eia.doe.gov/emeu/cabs/venez.html on February 9, 2000.

2. See Tim Golden and Steven Lee Myers, "U.S. Plans Big Aid Package for a Reeling Colombia," *New York Times,* September 15, 1999; Eric Schmitt, "Senate Approves $1 Billion to Aid Colombia Military," *New York Times,* June 22, 2000. For background on Colombia's oil potential, see U.S. Department of Energy, Energy Information Administration, "Colombia," Country Analysis Brief, June 1999, electronic document accessed at http://www.eia.doe.gov/emeu/cabs/colombia.html on June 21, 1999.

3. For discussion, see Michael T. Klare, "Quest for Oil Drives Aid to Colombia," AlterNet dispatch, May 4, 2000, electronic document accessed at http://www.alternet.org on May 8, 2000; Diana Jean Schemo and Tim Golden, "Bogotá Aid: To Fight Drugs or Rebels?" *New York Times,* June 2, 1998.

4. See Diana Jean Schemo, "Haunted Treasure: In Brazil, Indians Call on

Spirits to Save Land," *New York Times,* July 21, 1996; Schemo, "Data Show Recent Burning of Amazon Is Worst Ever," *New York Times,* January 27, 1998.

5. For details and discussion, see U.S. Geological Survey (USGS), *Minerals Yearbook 1996,* vol. 3 (Washington, D.C.: USGS, 1997).

6. Worldwatch Institute, *Vital Signs 1998,* p. 148.

7. See Virginia Luling and Damien Lewis, "The Scramble for African Timber," *Multinational Monitor,* September 1992.

8. FAO, *State of the World's Forests 1997,* pp. 36–37.

9. BP Amoco, *Statistical Review of World Energy 1999,* pp. 4, 20.

10. DoE/EIA, *IEO 1999,* Table D1, p. 201.

11. Quoted in Margaret Ross, "Africa's Elephants of the Deep," *Lamp,* Winter 1998–99, p. 4. *The Lamp* is an official publication of the Exxon Corporation.

12. See Alexei Barrionuevo, "Texaco Says Oil Find May Hold a Billion Barrels," *Wall Street Journal,* January 7, 2000; U.S. Department of Energy, Energy Information Administration, "Nigeria," Country Analysis Brief, August 1999, electronic document accessed at http://www.eia.doe.gov/emeu/cabs/nigeria.html on August 23, 1999.

13. Quoted in Barrionuevo, "Texaco Says Oil Find May Hold a Billion Barrels."

14. For details, see U.S. Department of Energy, Energy Information Administration, "Chad," Country Analysis Brief, February 2000, electronic document accessed at http://www.eia.doe.gov/emeu/cabs/chad.html on February 2, 2000. See also "Punting on a Pipeline," *Economist,* June 10, 2000, p. 82.

15. See Peter Rosenblum, "Pipeline Politics in Chad," *Current History,* May 2000, pp. 195–99.

16. "The U.S. Stake in a Secure, Prosperous Africa," address by Susan E. Rice at Howard University, Washington, D.C., November 3, 1999, electronic document accessed at http://www.state.gov/www/policy_remarks/1999 on February 28, 2000.

17. "U.S. and Africa in the 21st Century," address by Susan E. Rice to the World Affairs Council of Seattle, Seattle, Wash., November 9, 1999, electronic document accessed at http://www.state.gov/www/policy_remarks/1999 on February 28, 2000.

18. For background and discussion, see Steven Metz, *Refining American Strategy in Africa* (Carlisle, Pa.: Strategic Studies Institute, U.S. Army War College, February 2000).

19. Includes arms sales through the Pentagon's Foreign Military Sales (FMS) program, commercial military sales, military training under the Pentagon's International Military Education and Training (IMET) program, and deliveries of surplus arms under the Excess Defense Articles (EDA) program. Data from the Section 655 Report for Fiscal Year 1998, as summarized by the Council for a Livable World (CLW) in "Arms Trade Insider," no. 28, February 22, 2000, electronic document accessed at http://www.clw.org/cat/inside28.html on March 8, 2000.

20. Douglas C. Lovelace Jr. in the foreword to Metz, *Refining American Strategy in Africa,* p. iii.

21. See U.S. Department of Defense, "Background Briefing: SecDef Trip to Africa," the Pentagon, February 8, 2000, electronic document accessed at http://www.defenselink.mil/news/Feb2000 on February 29, 2000.

22. See Metz, *Refining American Strategy in Africa,* pp. 33–34.

23. This effort is highly controversial, both because Sudan is viewed as a "rogue" state by the United States for its support of extremist Islamic movements, and also because the oil fields themselves are located in or near areas that are the site of recurring battle between government forces and the SPLA. For details, see U.S. Department of Energy, Energy Information Administration, "Sudan," Country Analysis Brief, November 1999, electronic document accessed at http://www.eia.doe.gov/emeu/cabs/sudan.html on November 17, 1999.

24. See Raymond Bonner, "New Weapons Sales to Africa Trouble Arms-Control Experts," *New York Times,* December 6, 1998. For data on actual deliveries, see the *SIPRI Yearbook,* published annually by the Stockholm International Peace Research Institute and Oxford University Press.

25. See Section 655 data as recorded in CLW, "Arms Trade Insider," no. 28 (see note 18).

26. See Youssef M. Ibrahim, "Saudi Rebels Are Main Suspects in June Bombing of a U.S. Base," *New York Times,* August 15, 1996; Douglas Jehl, "Saudis' Heartland Is Seething with Rage at Rulers and U.S.," *New York Times,* November 5, 1996.

27. For discussion, see Michael Renner, "Assessing the Military's War on the Environment," in Brown, et al., *State of the World 1991,* pp. 133–52.

28. U.S. Department of Defense (DoD), *Conduct of the Persian Gulf War* (Washington, D.C.: DoD, April 1992), p. 394.

29. Campbell and Laherrère, "The End of Cheap Oil," p. 79.

30. For background on the origins of the International Energy Agency, see Yergin, *The Prize,* pp. 630, 643, 653–54, 689, 691, 711–13.

31. James Brooke, "Canada Tries to Make Clear Its Diamonds Are Different," *New York Times,* August 12, 2000.

32. See Blaine Harden, "De Beers Halts Its Hoarding of Diamonds," *New York Times,* July 13, 2000; "Washed Out of Africa," *Economist,* June 3, 2000, pp. 69–70.

33. See Abramovitz, *Taking a Stand,* pp. 50–56.

ACKNOWLEDGMENTS

I began work on *Resource Wars* in the spring of 1997, and spent much of the next three and a half years on research, writing, revising, and editing the book. During this period, I received support, encouragement, and assistance of various kinds from a great many people. Without their help, I never could have finished a project this time-consuming and demanding. I am deeply grateful to all of you.

My greatest debt of gratitude is due to my partner, Andrea Ayvazian, and my son, Sasha Klare-Ayvazian. At every step of the way, they reinforced my interest in this project and encouraged me to see it through to its conclusion. Even when it seemed as if the writing would go on forever, they greeted my nightly and weekend work sessions with patience and forbearance. I am immensely thankful for their support. Many thanks are also due to Dr. L. Fred Ayvazian for reading the manuscript (twice!) with great care and alerting me to previously undetected errors.

I also owe enormous gratitude to my editors, Sara Bershtel and Stephen Hubbell of Metropolitan Books. Sara was enthusiastic about the project from the very beginning, and provided essential support at every stage of production. Steve helped me to conceptualize the book and then did a fabulous job of editing the manuscript; he continually encouraged me to deepen and sharpen my analysis, and the book is substantially better for his guidance. Many thanks to both of you for helping me to complete this demanding project!

At various stages of this project I discussed aspects of the book with many friends and colleagues. I cannot always recall the details of these conversations, but I know that I benefited immensely from such intellectual interaction. Particular thanks are due in this regard to: Jeffrey Boutwell of the American Academy of Arts and Sciences; James Boyce, James Der Derian, Gerald Epstein, and Peter Haas of the University of Massachusetts; Mary Geske and Gregory White of Smith College; Lee Feinstein of the U.S. Department of State; Vincent Ferraro and Kavita Khory of Mount Holyoke College; Elizabeth Hartmann, Frank Holmquist, and Ali Mirsepassi of Hampshire College; Katrina vanden Heuvel of *The Nation* magazine; Thomas Homer-Dixon of the University of Toronto; Mary Kalder of the London School of Economics; Lora Lumpe of the Federation of American Scientists; Andrew Mack of the United Nations staff; Robert Pastor of Emory University; Stephen del Rosso of the Carnegie Corporation of New York; Sandra Postel of the Global Water Policy Project; Daniel Volman of the Africa Research Project; Cora Weiss of the Samuel Rubin Foundation; and Chris Wing of the Ford Foundation.

During the period I was working on this book, I served as director of the Five College Program in Peace and World Security Studies (PAWSS), based at Hampshire College in Amherst, Massachusetts. In this capacity, I worked closely with Yogesh Chandrani, the assistant director of PAWSS. Yogesh assisted me in innumerable ways, and provided an invaluable source of intellectual stimulation. I remain enormously grateful for his help and support over the past seven years.

Many thanks are also due to the staff and faculty of Hampshire College, to its president, Gregory Prince, and to the dean of faculty, Aaron Berman. Hampshire has provided a wonderfully stimulating and hospitable environment in which to work, and I am very grateful for all of the ways in which the people there have supported my endeavors. A similar debt of gratitude is owed to the staff of the Five Colleges Incorporated (the parent organization of PAWSS), and especially to its coordinator, Lorna Peterson.

—Michael Klare
Northampton, Massachusetts
October 2000

INDEX

ABOUT THE AUTHOR

Michael T. Klare is director of the Five College Program in Peace and World Security Studies based at Hampshire College in Amherst, Massachusetts, and author of numerous books on the changing nature of warfare, including *Low Intensity Warfare, World Security,* and *Rogue States and Nuclear Outlaws.* He lives in Northampton, Massachusetts.